SAHIR L

Akshay Manwani turned to freelance writing after a brief career in the corporate world that gave him little personal satisfaction. He has since written on Indian cinema and popular culture for a variety of publications such as *The Caravan, Business Standard, Man's World* and *Mumbai Mirror*.

His attempt to profile the life and work of Sahir Ludhianvi through this book stems from the belief that much needs to be done to preserve the legacy of unsung legends. It is also his way of saying thank you to the poet-lyricist who has given him immeasurable joy through his songs.

Akshay lives in Mumbai with his wife and daughter.

SAHIR LUDHIANVI

THE PEOPLE'S POET

Akshay Manwani

HarperCollins *Publishers* India

First published in India in 2013 by
HarperCollins *Publishers* India

Copyright © Akshay Manwani 2013

ISBN: 978-93-5029-733-9

2 4 6 8 10 9 7 5 3 1

HarperCollins *Publishers*
A-53, Sector 57, Noida 201301, India
77-85 Fulham Palace Road, London W6 8JB, United Kingdom
Hazelton Lanes, 55 Avenue Road, Suite 2900, Toronto, Ontario M5R 3L2
and 1995 Markham Road, Scarborough, Ontario M1B 5M8, Canada
25 Ryde Road, Pymble, Sydney, NSW 2073, Australia
31 View Road, Glenfield, Auckland 10, New Zealand
10 East 53rd Street, New York NY 10022, USA

Typeset in 12/15 Linden Hill Regular at
SÜRYA

Printed and bound at
Thomson Press (India) Ltd.

To
Mom, Dad, Amma, Achchan,
Naina and Vidya

Main har ek pal ka shaayar hoon, har ek pal meri kahaani hai
Har ek pal meri hasti hai, har ek pal meri jawaani hai

(I am the eternal poet, my story has no end
I am in every moment, my youth never spent)

Contents

Introduction

In his insightful account of the genesis of cricket in India, the historian Ramachandra Guha writes, 'The social history of Indian cricket suffers from one enormous disadvantage: that we, as a people, have a criminal indifference to the written record.'[1]

Guha might well have been speaking for Hindi cinema, for we, as a nation, have mostly ignored documenting the history of perhaps the only obsession other than cricket that cuts across the cultural milieu of India. There is scant literature available on the Hindi film industry, as indeed of the many people who shaped it into its current form. The few biographies that hit bookshelves each year have either the usual suspects, Guru Dutt, Lata Mangeshkar, Amitabh Bachchan, Shah Rukh Khan, as their subjects or are bereft of any substance.

What about the likes of Khwaja Ahmad Abbas, Akhtar Ul Imaan, Renu Saluja, V.K. Murthy and scores of other technicians who helped in the evolution of popular Hindi cinema without ever stepping into the limelight? Bunny Reuben's *...and Pran*[2] and Jerry Pinto's *Helen*,[3] the latter written without any input from the lady in question, are exceptions, and efforts that must be fêted.

---

1. Ramachandra Guha, *A Corner of a Foreign Field*, 'Claiming the Heartland', Picador, 2002, p. 46.
2. Bunny Reuben, *...and Pran: A Biography*, HarperCollins Publishers India, 2005.
3. Jerry Pinto, *Helen: The Life and Times of an H-Bomb*, Penguin Books India, 2006.

Ganesh Anantharaman's *Bollywood Melodies*, an outstanding piece of work on the Hindi film song, is another such exception.[4] In many ways, *Bollywood Melodies* is a catalyst for this book, for it was while reading Anantharaman's work that a fundamental truth about the plight of lyricists dawned on me. That of the many times we find ourselves enjoying a melody, there is little or no cognizance of the songwriter. How we never tire of praising Talat Mahmood's or Kishore Kumar's vocals. How very frequently we dole out compliments appreciating the genius of Naushad or S.D. Burman. Yet, there is no recollection of the men who penned the words, the men who gave soul to the melody.

Ganesh even offers a plausible explanation for this stepmotherly treatment handed out to lyricists: 'They [the lyricists] haven't usually generated that degree of awe and adulation from film music lovers. Possibly because we are a country with a much stronger oral tradition than a written one, compounded by our higher levels of illiteracy.'[5]

Also, a melody isn't constrained by geographical boundaries or distances. Which is why, in a culturally dissimilar nation like ours, where language changes every 500 miles, it was possible for 'Bombay' Ravi[6] to gain popularity in the Kerala film industry, but impossible for Kaifi Azmi to captivate the state's Malayalam-speaking population with his Urdu lyrics. A corollary to this characteristic of a melody works to the advantage of composers in another way as well. There are innumerable instances of film compositions being inspired by folk music or having strong regional

---

4. Ganesh Anantharaman, *Bollywood Melodies: A History of the Hindi Film Song*, Penguin Books India, 2008.
5. Ibid., 'The Songwriters', p. 99.
6. Moniker used for music director Ravi Sharma in Kerala. Ravi (1926–2012) was the immensely successful composer of films like *Chaudhvin Ka Chand*, *Gumraah*, *Hamraaz*, *Waqt* and *Nikaah*.

or Western influences. Yet, it is the craft of the songwriter that gives the song an identity of its own.

Take, for example, the evergreen '*Ae dil hai mushkil, jeena yahaan*' from *C.I.D.* (1956). The tune for this is directly inspired from an American folk ballad '*Oh my darling, Clementine*'. The words in the original are those of a bereaved lover who loses his beloved in a drowning accident. In contrast, the song in C.I.D. has an element of joy to it. It is bereft of the lament that characterizes the original and is, instead, a vivid, lyrical description of Bombay. If the song has become Bombay's unofficial anthem over the years, it is Majrooh Sultanpuri's wonderful play with words, rather than O.P. Nayyar's score, that is responsible. It is Majrooh's '*Yeh hai Bombay meri jaan*' that makes this song 'ours'.

This awareness of the plight of songwriters set me on the idea of doing something that would put in perspective their invaluable contribution to Hindi cinema. It was then that I started thinking of doing a biography of one of the lyricists from the golden era of the Hindi film song, viz., the 1950s and the 1960s, all of whom were stalwarts in their own right. I actively sought reading material on each one of them towards this end. I then followed a process of elimination to narrow down on the choice of subject.

Majrooh Sultanpuri and Kaifi Azmi were amongst the first to be struck off the list. This is not because their work lacked in quality, but because I firmly believed that any attempt on my part to outline their legacy would pale in front of the efforts of their immediate families to do the same. Hasrat Jaipuri, too, from what I have read of him, is survived by family members, but his work did not have quite the same timbre that Majrooh's or Kaifi's lyrics possessed. A closer examination of his work also reveals that, working with the same music director duo of Shankar–Jaikishan for Raj Kapoor, Shailendra was able to create a far bigger impact than Hasrat. In fact, poet–lyricist–film-maker Gulzar rates Shailendra as probably the finest of film lyricists.[7]

Jan Nisar Akhtar's contributions were few and far between. If anything, the quality of the man is better gauged by his standing as an Urdu poet espousing the cause of the Progressive Writers' Movement. And I must confess that during this exercise in elimination, I did not know much about Rajinder Krishan. This is a comment on my ignorance than on Rajinder's quality as a songwriter. Over the course of my research for this book, I have learnt to appreciate Rajinder's legacy, which now leads me to say that he remains perhaps the most unsung songwriter of his time.

Shakeel Badayuni was a difficult option to eliminate. The romantic essence of his songs was unmatched. But compared to the two lyricists left on my list, his work never quite touched me in the same way. Even so, it has to be admitted that Shakeel, like Majrooh and Kaifi, was one of the more difficult names to drop while selecting the subject for this book.

I was then left with Shailendra and Sahir Ludhianvi. It was now a question of selecting one who appealed to me the most.

Admittedly, Shailendra fascinated me more initially. He died really young, at the age of forty-three, in 1966. In this time, in a career spanning a little over fifteen years (the least in comparison to the aforementioned songwriters), Shailendra left an indelible imprint on our cinema through films like *Shri 420* (1955), *Madhumati* (1958), *Anari* (1959) and *Guide* (1965). However, one catch remained: Shailendra's family members have also planned a book on him, which influenced me in my decision to plump for Sahir.

But what clinched it for me in Sahir's favour was his personal life. He drew from his experiences to express himself through the medium of the film song. The memories of his childhood, his brush

---

7. In Ganesh Anantharaman, *Bollywood Melodies: A History of the Hindi Film Song*.

with the Progressive Writers' Movement, his relationship with his mother and the other women in his life, were all channelized to his songwriting. This was in contrast to his peers who wrote, largely, as per the demands of the script. In a couplet, Sahir even admitted to being inspired from personal incidents in his poetry and, by extension, in his songwriting:

Duniya ne tajurbaat-o-havaadis ki shakl mein
Jo kuch mujhe diya hai, lauta raha hoon main

(Whatever the world by way of experience and accident
Has given me, I return it now)

Above all, Sahir was not without fault. His human side was never too far behind his brilliance as a songwriter. In the words of Pramila Le Hunte, one-time British politician and Indian national who in 2009 directed and presented the play *Sahir: His Life and Loves* in New Delhi, 'He had the gift of genius and the weakness of genius.' Also, because he died a bachelor and did not leave behind any family to remind coming generations of his legacy, I felt compelled to repay my debts to a man who, through his songs in *Pyaasa* (1957), *Hum Dono* (1961), *Waqt* (1965) and *Kabhi Kabhie* (1976), has given me innumerable moments of joy.

His was simply too strong a case to be ignored.

There are a few other things I would like to point out regarding this book.

This book is not meant to be a one-dimensional account of Sahir the lyricist. For, it is impossible to reach out to Sahir the lyricist without approaching Sahir the person. Unlike the literature available on Sahir in Urdu, which focuses either on his personal life or his non-film poetry, this book attempts to bring together the three main facets of Sahir: his personal life, his non-film poetry and his career as a lyricist. At the same time, it in no way attempts to provide a scholarly opinion of Sahir's non-film poetry, for my own understanding of Urdu poetry, as indeed its many stalwarts, can at best be termed 'basic'. If anything, the book details Sahir's personal life and provides an overview of his role as an Urdu poet to set the stage for an understanding of Sahir's work as a lyricist.

In order to provide this 360-degree view of Sahir's life and his work, this book makes use of two main sources of information.

For Sahir's early years, I have relied primarily on *Fann Aur Shaksiyat*, Sahir Ludhianvi Number and Prof. Dr Syed Zeyaur Rahman's *Sahir Ludhianvi: Hayaat Aur Shaayari*. *Fann Aur Shaksiyat* is a compilation of writings on Sahir by his friends and family, people who knew him intimately, including a couple of interviews of the poet. These were put together by Saabir Dutt, a man who, allegedly, lived at Sahir's house for many years even after Sahir died. Unfortunately, the verdict is still out on whether Saabir was a friend or just someone who benefitted from Sahir's largesse. Saabir died sometime in the late 1990s. *Sahir Ludhianvi: Hayaat Aur Shaayari* is a broad biographical account of Sahir's life, where the author has also made a concerted effort to analyse Sahir's poetic contributions in the context of the Progressive Writers' Movement.

A few other books that proved handy in reconstructing Sahir's early life were Azhar Javed's *Nakaamey Mohabbat*, Ajaib Chitrakar's *Sahir: Khaaban Da Shaizada* (Punjabi translation of Krishan Adeeb's *Sahir: Yaadon Ke Aayney Mein*) and Hameed Akhtar's *Ashnaiyaan Kya Kya*.

For tracing Sahir's career in the Hindi film industry, the information produced is basically a result of interviews with several people who worked with Sahir or who knew him personally in some capacity.

As a result, the account of Sahir's early years tends to be sketchier than the latter half of his career because of fewer first-hand accounts in the former. Also, since there is a heavy dependence on Urdu literature to reconstruct Sahir's early years, there is a chance that the translations might appear too literal. This is because I didn't want to get too ahead of myself with a figurative translation and preferred, instead, to err on the side of caution. Also, as someone correctly pointed out to me, when one attempts to translate a language into another, the endeavour is actually towards interpreting a culture, an exercise that proves futile without a suitable exposure to both cultures.

Therefore, in some places, as also with some of the face-to-face interviews, I have produced the original text (with their English translations alongside) because these were simply too invaluable to exclude.

The effort has been alternately painstaking (working on translations, sitting through some seriously banal films), adventurous (living in seedy accommodations in Ludhiana, enjoying an evening's cuppa with the legendary Salim Khan, hitching two-wheeler rides in the bylanes of Laxmi Nagar, Delhi, striking random but genuine acquaintances with bookshop owners in Jama Masjid, Delhi), frustrating (serving as a typing minion for a veteran film journalist as a quid pro quo to get an audience with some film luminaries) and full of quirks (praying for the good health of all the octogenarians before my meeting with them). I hope that I have met with a modicum of success in what I started out to do: produce a wholesome portrait of one of the giants of Hindustani songwriting.

In this regard, I hope to have done justice to Ajaib Chitrakar's (one of Sahir's few friends from his childhood years whom I met in Ludhiana) only request when I briefed him on the purpose of my meeting with him: *'Beta, jo bhi karna, mehnat aur imaandari se karna.'* (Son, whatever you do, do it with utmost hard work and honesty.)

Prologue

The late Urdu poet from Punjab, Naresh Kumar Shaad, once had the opportunity to interview Sahir Ludhianvi.

'When and where were you born?' asked Shaad, to start the interview.

Sahir's reply, a potent mix of wit, sarcasm and a hint of tragedy went thus: '*Aye jidat pasand naujawaan, yeh toh bada rawaayti sawaal hai. Is rawaayat ko aagey badhaatey huey is mein itna izaafa aur kar lo — kyun paida hua?*' (Young man, this is a routine question. Instead, when you ask me that question, add 'why were you born?').

— in Saabir Dutt, *Fann Aur Shaksiyat*, Sahir Ludhianvi Number, 'Sahir Ke Saath Ek Shaam', Naresh Kumar Shaad, p. 52.

1

A Bittersweet Inheritance

Mere maazi ko andhere mein daba rehne do
Mera maazi meri zillat ke siva kuch bhi nahin[1]

(Let my past remain cloaked in darkness
My past brings me nothing but disgrace)

There is little to celebrate about the city of Ludhiana. It does not have the cultural or historical legacy of Santiago, or the idyllic charm of Stratford-upon-Avon, or the royal patronage that Delhi had under the Mughals, which may have driven the likes of Pablo Neruda, the Bard and Mirza Asadullah Ghalib, respectively, to their poetic pursuits. Yet, the city has thrown up a number of poets. The Punjabi writer Nirupama Dutt sums it up best:

> Punjab's Manchester is known for its hosiery industry, its cycle factories, its business money, the agricultural university, migrant labourers, who come by the thousands on trains nicknamed Bhaiyya Express, the filthy sewer that runs through the old town, and rampant pollution. Yet this familiar picture of

---

1. From the poem 'Farar' (Escape), published in the anthology *Talkhiyaan*.

Ludhiana misses one important aspect – the city has been home to a large number of poets in modern times, with Sahir Ludhianvi, famed Hindi film lyricist who bore the city's name, topping the list.[2]

Sahir Ludhianvi was born Abdul Hayee on 8 March 1921 in Ludhiana, situated in the heart of Punjab. It is said that Abdul's parents gave him the name – which means 'the servant of' in Arabic – after referring to the Quran-e-Sharif.

According to Prof. Dr Syed Zeyaur Rahman, former head of department of Urdu at L.N. Mithila University, Darbhanga, Bihar, who authored the book *Sahir Ludhianvi: Hayaat Aur Shaayari*, Abdul's paternal grandfather Fateh Mohammed was a wealthy landlord who belonged to the Gujjar community and owned vast tracts of land around Seekhowal, situated on the outskirts of Ludhiana. Abdul's father, Chaudhri Fazl Mohammed, inherited this wealth. Abdul's mother, Sardar Begum, was a Kashmiri and the daughter of a wealthy thekedaar, Abdul Azeez, and the youngest of her siblings.

Thanks to Fazl Mohammed's decadent lifestyle, not entirely uncommon amongst zamindars of the era, Abdul's parents seldom found marital bliss. Among the more famous personalities of Ludhiana at that time, Fazl Mohammed was an arrogant man whose character brings to mind the wealthy debauched landlords often depicted in yesteryear Hindi cinema, for example, the ruthless Ugranarayan played by Pran in *Madhumati* (1958), or the depraved 'Chhote Sarkar' enacted by Rehman in *Sahib Bibi Aur Ghulam* (1962).

Fazl Mohammed married as many as twelve times but did not have any children from any of his first ten wives. Sardar Begum was Fazl Mohammed's eleventh wife. However, even the birth of a

---

2. *The Caravan*, 'Love and Longing in Ludhiana: Poetry from Sahir's city', 1 May 2010.

much-awaited son, Abdul, did not bring any change in Fazl Mohammed's dissolute ways. He continued to lead a life characterized by womanizing and an utter disregard towards the plight of others less fortunate than him. Abrasive by nature, he never lost an opportunity to put one over his opponent, even if it involved denigration of filial ties.

A particularly disturbing incident, which highlighted the trauma the young Abdul was subjected to, courtesy his father's petty ways, involved Fazl Mohammed's immediate neighbour, one Mian Abdul Hayee.

In order to finance his decadent lifestyle and his many marriages, Fazl Mohammed often resorted to selling his land. Litigation was a natural fallout. One such bout of litigation concerned Fazl Mohammed and Mian Abdul Hayee. In an obvious attempt to humiliate his adversary, Fazl Mohammed sat every evening in his courtyard, in the presence of his servants, and hurled the choicest invective at Mian Abdul Hayee. When Mian Abdul Hayee would seek an explanation for such behaviour, Fazl Mohammed would reply, nonchalantly, that he was merely berating his son.

Fazl Mohammed's errant ways eventually forced Sardar Begum to leave him. She knew of the Chaudhri's habit of selling land to raise money to finance his depraved lifestyle. She tried to correct him, but to no avail. A hapless Sardar Begum took the six-month-old Abdul and left for her brother's house. Within a few days of Sardar Begum leaving, Fazl Mohammed married again. This, in Zeyaur Rahman's words, 'proved his lust for the fairer sex, than marrying solely for the purpose of an heir'.[3]

Zeyaur Rahman also hints at Fazl Mohammed's reluctance to give Sardar Begum her due as his spouse. Fazl Mohammed never considered Sardar Begum an equal in terms of their family

---

3. Prof. Dr Syed Zeyaur Rahman, *Sahir Ludhianvi: Hayaat Aur Shaayari*, p. 11.

backgrounds. That is why he shied away from openly declaring their relationship. She, on the other hand, wanted him to acknowledge his relationship with her and give them their rightful place in the household.

A somewhat different version surrounding Sardar Begum's separation from her husband was given to me by Hameed Akhtar. Hameed, who was then in his late eighties and who died in October 2011, had lived in Lahore, Pakistan, since a few years before partition. He got to know Abdul during their college years in Ludhiana, a little after Abdul had adopted the name Sahir Ludhianvi. Frail of health but firm of mind, Hameed Akhtar was one of the few surviving repositories of information on Sahir's formative years when I spoke to him a couple of times over the phone from Mumbai in early 2010. Even then, a conversation concerning the life and times of one of his dearest friends made Hameed Akhtar nostalgic about their times together.

According to Hameed, Fazl Mohammed and Sardar Begum separated when Abdul was about three or four years old. Until this time, Sardar Begum had no option but to bear the ill-treatment that came her way at the hands of her husband. Hameed made no mention, either directly or in his writings on Sahir, of the Chaudhri failing to recognize his relationship with Abdul's mother. However, even he confirmed that it was Fazl Mohammed's wanton ways that compelled Sardar Begum to leave her husband.

Sardar Begum moved with Abdul to her brother's house, in the area adjacent to Jagraon Pul, near the railway line. She and her son were looked after by Abdul's chhotey maamu, Abdul Rasheed, a fruit merchant. Realizing the need to provide her child with a good education, Sardar Begum enrolled Abdul in Malwa Khalsa High School, Ludhiana. Hameed makes a keen observation of the young Abdul at this juncture:

> When Abdul started going to Khalsa School, he was not aware
> that he was a Muslim and was consequently unaware of its

religious tenets. He would gain familiarity with Islam eventually, but initially he was familiar only with the Sikh religion. Even in later life, during his college days, he was friendlier with students from the Sikh and Hindu communities. He was always more comfortable when someone greeted him with an aadab or a namaste, instead of salaam alaikum.[4]

Chaudhri Fazl Mohammed, meanwhile, continued with his hedonistic ways. He kept selling land to finance his life of vice, even when he did not have the lawful right to do so. Sardar Begum was forced to go to court to put an end to her husband's excesses. She asked the law to intervene, to stop her husband from selling the land and to have the land illegally sold to be returned. The litigation between the two continued for close to eighteen years. Since these cases were largely decided in favour of Sardar Begum, the many people who had bought land from the Chaudhri, at throwaway prices, became enemies of Sardar Begum.

To stop Sardar Begum from taking recourse to legal action, Fazl Mohammed even threatened to snatch Abdul from her. Sardar Begum reacted to her husband's threat by surrounding Abdul with guards. Abdul was made to travel even the relatively small distance between home and school in their company. And when he was not at school, Sardar Begum confined Abdul within the four walls of their house. At no point, did she leave Abdul alone.

In the face of a determined Sardar Begum, Fazl Mohammed finally requested the court for Abdul's custody. Concurrently, Sardar Begum, too, initiated divorce proceedings against her husband and sought the legal right to keep Abdul with her. Abdul was studying in standard five at the time. The court turned to Fazl Mohammed one last time.

'Are you Abdul Hayee's father? Do you undertake to educate and take care of him?' asked the judge adjudicating the case.

---

4. Hameed Akhtar, *Ashnaiyaan Kya Kya*, pp. 90–91.

True to his nature, Fazl Mohammed, already irked that the son of a zamindar was engaged in the plebeian pursuits of a school, replied, 'Why does the son of a zamindar like me need to be educated? Education is the recourse of those who need to seek employment as a way of earning their living.'

A baffled judge then turned to Abdul and asked him the question that left him with the responsibility of determining his own fate, 'Son, whom do you wish to stay with?'

'With my mother,' answered Abdul.

The learned judge concluded in his judgment, 'If a father wants to deprive his child of an education on account of his wealth as a zamindar, it is better that the child stays with his mother who wishes to educate and bring him up to be a responsible citizen.'[5]

In all this, Abdul was deprived of his childhood. Fear and anxiety marked what should have been years of carefree existence. The negative experiences of his childhood scarred him for life. His father's immoral ways, the ill-treatment of his mother and the uncertainty of those years remained bitter memories Sahir carried within himself all his life.

Suraj Sanim, Hindi film scriptwriter from the 1980s and 1990s, reveals the effects that Fazl Mohammed's behaviour had on Sahir:

> Differences between Abdul's mother and father culminated in a court battle. Abdul who was only a child took the side of his mother. His father couldn't bear this and threatened to either have him kidnapped or killed. His mother had to, therefore, employ security guards to protect him. This caused him to lead a rather sheltered, protected life. He grew up to be suspicious of everyone. Highly insecure, he could never travel alone, not even short distances. He could never trust anyone.[6]

---

5. Prof. Dr Syed Zeyaur Rahman, *Sahir Ludhianvi, Hayaat Aur Shaayari*, p. 20.
6. *Filmfare*, 16–31 August 1985, p. 77.

The lasting impact the Chaudhri had on Abdul is visible in the poem 'Jaageer' (Inheritance), written sometime in the early 1940s. Here, Abdul revealed his contempt for the cavalier and morally corrupt behaviour of zamindars. The mocking tone of its verses is a commentary on the perverse legacy of Abdul's forefathers:

> Phir usi waadi-e-shadaab mein laut aaya hoon
> Jisme pinhaan mere khwaabon ki tarabgaahein hain
> Mere ahbab ke saamaan-e-taayyush ke liye
> Shokh seeney hain, jawaan jism, haseen baahein hain
>
> Sabz kheton mein yeh dubki hui doshizaayein
> Inki shiryanon mein kis-kiska lahoo jaari hai?
> Kis mein jurrat hai ki is raaz ko tash-heer karey?
> Sabke lab par meri haibat ka phoosoon taari hai . . .
>
> Yeh lahaktey hue paudhey, yeh damaktey huey khet
> Pehley ajdaad ki jaageer thay, ab mere hain
> Yeh chaargaah, yeh revad, yeh maveshi, yeh kisaan
> Sabke sab mere hain, sab mere hain, sab mere hain
>
> Inki mehnat bhi meri, haasil-e-mehnat bhi mera
> Inke baazoo bhi mere, kuvat-e-baazoo bhi meri
> Main khudavand hoon is wusat-e-bepaayaan ka
> Mauj-e-aariz bhi meri, nakhat-e-gesoon bhi meri

> (I return again to that verdant valley
> Where lie veiled my fulfilled desires
> My friends, for satisfying their carnal pleasures, have before them
> Heaving bosoms, nubile bodies, beautiful arms
>
> The coy beauties who roam these green fields
> Whose blood runs through their veins?
> Who has the courage to reveal these secrets?
> Everyone's lips quiver with tales of my debauchery . . .
>
> These plants that glitter, these fields that shine
> Earlier they were the inheritance of my forefathers, now they
>   are mine

These grasslands, the flock of sheep, the cattle, these farmers
All of them belong to me, all to me, all to me

Their labour belongs to me, the fruit of their labour also to me
Their arms belong to me, the strength in their arms also to me
I am the lord of this vast expanse
Their beautiful cheeks belong to me, the perfume of their tresses
        also to me)

But as much as he loathed his father, Abdul was influenced in subtle
ways by Fazl Mohammed's persona. In her recollections about her
brother's life, Sarwar Shafi, Abdul's cousin from his mother's side,
recalls an incident where Abdul's behaviour carried distinct shades
of Chaudhri Fazl Mohammed.

Sarwar's father, Abdul's uncle, fell ill in 1954 and eventually
succumbed in 1955 despite Abdul's best efforts to have him treated
in Bombay. On his uncle's demise, Abdul promised to look after
the two sisters, Sarwar and Anwar Sultana (Sarwar's younger
sister), which he did dutifully, till the end of his own days.

After her father's death, Sarwar continued to live in Allahabad,
with Abdul providing for her from Bombay. Anwar had already
moved to Bombay in 1950, as an eight-year-old. Sarwar would
visit Bombay frequently during her college vacations. But when the
time to take leave of her brother's hospitality would near, Abdul
would get very upset. As Sarwar sought to explain that she had
overstayed and was missing out on college, Sahir would ask his
mother, who lived with him in Bombay at that time, 'Kya karegi
zyaada padhkar? Kya isko mulaazimat karni hai? Main kis ke liye kamaata
hoon? Inhi logon ke liye. Apni shaayri ko bazaar mein bitha diya hai, kis cheez
ki kami hai?'[7] (What will she do by studying so much? Does she
want to work as an employee? Whom do I earn for? For their sake

---

7. Saabir Dutt, *Fann Aur Shaksiyat*, Sahir Ludhianvi Number, Sarwar Shafi,
'Ammee Kehtee Thee', pp. 68–69.

only. I have put my poetry for sale, what is it that we cannot afford?)

Equally significant was the impact of Sardar Begum on Abdul's life. Aware that her son had been denied the luxuries that would have automatically come his way as Chaudhri Fazl Mohammed's heir, she made every possible effort to provide for him. She brought him up like a prince, like he was royalty. She sold her jewellery to fund his upbringing. When there was no jewellery left to sell, she turned to her siblings, which included another brother, a stationmaster who lived in Allahabad. Needless to say, the pampering he received at the hands of his mother and the trauma of his childhood made Abdul a difficult child. Sarwar recalls vividly:

> Bhai jaan was a very stubborn child. He would make ridiculous demands. While taking a bath, he would soap himself, but have the towel wrapped around. He would tell his mother, my aunt, to go away, that he would take a bath himself. While drinking milk also he could be very difficult. He would ask for water to be added to the milk. When water would be added, he would want it removed so that he could drink the milk. My aunt, troubled by bhai jaan's behaviour, would break into tears. On seeing her plight, my father would ask bhai jaan to come to him so that he could remove the water. He would ask bhai jaan to close his eyes. My father would then take two glasses, fill one with water and the other with milk. He would then ask bhai jaan to open his eyes. Bhai jaan, on seeing the water separated from the milk, would then settle down to have his milk.[8]

The hardships of those days aside, mother and son developed a bond that cannot be described in words alone. As Abdul grew older, and their house was besieged by a regular influx of his friends, Sardar Begum found new joy in hosting her son's friends. She would feed them continuously, serve tea a dozen times a day

8. Ibid., p. 66.

and fulfil every whim of her son and his friends. At no point did she complain about the increased expenditure or workload that hosting Abdul's friends involved. Seeing Abdul with his friends gave her immense satisfaction that her son would never be alone. In the absence of anything else to look forward to, Sardar Begum put Abdul at the centre of her life.

Indeed, in the aftermath of his parents' separation Abdul immersed himself in the company of friends. In the years to come, he would regard them as his life's treasures, forgetting everything when he was with them. He was willing to give everything up for his friends. They were the balm that healed his wounds. He would constantly be on the lookout for his friends and greatly relished the idea of entertaining them at his home in Ludhiana.

Ajaib Chitrakar, one of Abdul's childhood friends, whom I was fortunate to meet in the city of Ludhiana in May 2009, spoke fondly of Abdul's inclination to host his friends at the slightest opportunity. Old and barely able to speak, Chitrakar managed to recall Abdul's magnanimity despite the penurious circumstances he had found himself in following his mother's separation from his father. 'He [Abdul] would spend on us lavishly, feeding us pakodas and tikkis every evening at the redi waala,' said Chitrakar.

Even later, much after he had made the transition from Abdul to Sahir Ludhianvi, his enthusiasm to host his friends remained undiminished. They were the only constant in Abdul's life as circumstances forced him to move from Ludhiana to Lahore to Delhi before he finally settled in Bombay where he spent the last thirty years of his life.

Abdul's longing for company may have been a subconscious reaction to his father's threats. By surrounding himself with people, he probably sought to protect himself from harm. At the same time, it could also have been a reflection of his father's character traits, for Fazl Mohammed, too, spent a lot of time in the company of friends. He would constantly invite people over and have a handful of people around him at any given point. Sardar Begum often lost her patience with Fazl Mohammed and even picked fights with him in this regard. Yet, the Chaudhri never changed his ways. After Abdul was born, Sardar Begum worried that he too would eventually take to his father's habits.

The other concern that dogged Sardar Begum as Abdul grew older was the course the latter's career would take. As Sarwar writes:

> When bhai jaan was born, a sagacious man recited the azaan in his ear. The learned man also said that bhai jaan would grow up to be a very good and able individual. On hearing this, a fair degree of expectation arose within my aunt. She could often be heard saying that she would make her son a judge or a civil surgeon . . . Instead, when bhai jaan began his poetic pursuits, my aunt would get troubled that examinations were round the corner and bhai jaan was not studying. She would then wonder, 'How would he be successful?'[9]

It is possible that Abdul gravitated towards poetry to give expression to the circumstances of his childhood. There is nothing to suggest that any of his immediate relatives, particularly if one uncle was a fruit merchant and the other a stationmaster, had any influence on him on this front. Abdul's was possibly a natural disposition towards writing in verse, a salve that soothed all that had happened in so little a lifetime.

Hameed Akhtar, nonetheless, points to a possible source of influence:

> As a child, Abdul had only one hobby. Whenever there would be a festive occasion in Ludhiana, be it Dussehra or a mela, the theatre would come to town and he would go to watch it. At

9. Ibid., pp. 65, 67.

times, he would go daily. He would bully his mother into giving him money, even save his pocket money. These dramas were generally written by the legendary playwright Agha Hashr Kashmiri and Abdul would remember them by heart. Around this time, he also got hold of Master Rehmat's collection of poems . . . When I look back now, I think he learnt the language from Master Rehmat, while he learnt the key to good writing from Agha Hashr Kashmiri. He was not familiar with the traditions of poetry. Yet, poetry was in his genes.[10]

Sarwar, too, corroborates her brother's fascination with poetry from a very young age:

Bhai jaan was very interested in reading and writing. Whenever he would go to the market, he would buy books of every kind. My aunt would tell him to buy these books when he grew up and could read properly. He would reply saying, 'I will have uncle read them out to me.' He would collect these books and derive immense happiness in this. Once, when he was in the fourth standard, he went with his uncle to the market. They reached a bookshop where he saw Muhammad Iqbal's *Bal-e-Jibril* (Wings of Gabriel). He immediately asked for this book. His uncle assured him that he would buy it for Abdul when he reached a higher class. Bhai jaan started crying and insisted on the book being bought. His solution to his uncle's objection was that his uncle would read it out to him and he would find the meaning on his own. His uncle had no other option but to buy the book. Abdul would ask his uncle to read from the book every night, so that he could memorize what was being read. He would sit with a pencil and paper and write. My mother would tell me that bhai jaan had written very well, he would try and write in the manner in which the book was written. Then, when he reached matriculation, he started reciting poetry himself. He would sit on the terrace and let his thoughts take

10. Hameed Akhtar, *Ashnaiyaan Kya Kya*, p. 92.

shape in the darkness of the night. Food and water would cease to matter for him at this point.[11]

His own inclination aside, the one person responsible for Abdul's development as a poet was his teacher at Malwa Khalsa High School, Faiyaaz Haryanvi. The Maulana taught Abdul Urdu and Persian and fostered in his young ward a taste for poetry and literature. Abdul acknowledged Faiyaaz's influence by saying, 'I did send my first nazm through a friend to my teacher Faiyaaz Haryanvi for his opinion. Faiyaaz's feedback was that the couplets were proper, as per the grammar of poetry, but that the entire poem in itself was quite ordinary. For me, the fact that the couplets were good was enough.'[12]

The other influences Abdul admitted to were of the Urdu poets of the early to mid-twentieth century – Muhammad Iqbal, Faiz Ahmed Faiz, Majaz Lucknawi and Josh Malihabadi. And there is no bigger proof of Iqbal's influence on Abdul than in the matter concerning his 'takhallus'. As per the traditions of Urdu poetry, most poets adopt a pen-name called the takhallus to establish an identity. For example, Shabbir Hasan Khan came to be known as Josh Malihabadi with 'Josh' as his takhallus. Ali Sikandar courted fame as Jigar Moradabadi with the takhallus 'Jigar'. Abdul's search for a takhallus was therefore very much in keeping with Urdu poetic tradition.

It was in 1937, a little after Abdul had appeared for his matriculation examinations but before the results had been declared, that he chanced upon what would be his pen-name. While perusing the pages of his course books, Abdul found the following lines written by Iqbal in his poem 'Daagh', which eulogized the great Urdu poet of the late nineteenth century, Daagh Dehlvi:

11. Saabir Dutt, *Fann Aur Shaksiyat*, Sahir Ludhianvi Number, Sarwar Shafi, 'Ammee Kehtee Thee', pp. 66–67.
12. Ibid., Naresh Kumar Shaad, 'Sahir Ke Saath Ek Shaam', p. 53.

Chal basa Daagh, aah! Mayyat uski zeb-e-dosh hai
Aakhiri shaayar Jahanabad ka khaamosh hai . . .

Is chaman mein hongey paida bulbul-e-shiraaz bhi
Saikdon sahir bhi hongey, sahib-e-ijaaz bhi . . .

Hoo bahoo kheinchega lekin, ishq ki tasveer kaun?
Uth gaya nawak fagan, marega dil par teer kaun?

(Alas! Daagh is no more! His bier on our shoulders
The last poet of Delhi departs in abject silence . . .

There will be many nightingales born in this garden
Countless magicians, men who work miracles as well . . .

But who will sketch such a vivid portrait of love?
Who will enchant the heart, now that the marksman is gone?)

The poem is Iqbal's tribute to the genius of Daagh's poetry. Lamenting Daagh's demise, Iqbal rates him ahead of other notable Urdu poets like Mirza Ghalib, Mehdi Majrooh and Amir Khusro. The words '*bulbul-e-shiraaz*' in the second couplet refer to Hafez Shirazi, Persian poet of the fourteenth century. In the second line of the same couplet, the word '*sahir*', which literally translates to 'magician', establishes the point that while there could be several poets like Hafez Shirazi and other men who could work magic with words, there would never again be one like Daagh.

Such fawning admiration by Iqbal for Daagh's poetic legacy proved to be Abdul's cue in the search for his takhallus. As Sahir himself said, 'Since I never had much of an opinion about my poetry and always considered myself as one amongst several poets, the word "sahir" and its use in the poem, immediately caught my eye and I chose it as my takhallus.'[13]

Also in keeping with the tradition of Urdu poets adding the city of their birth to their pen-name – Majrooh 'Sultanpuri' (from

13. Ibid.

Sultanpur), Josh 'Malihabadi' (from Malihabad), Jigar 'Moradabadi' (from Moradabad), Daagh 'Dehlvi' (from Delhi) – Abdul added 'Ludhianvi' to reflect his relationship with his birthplace.

The genesis of 'Sahir Ludhianvi' is of far greater relevance than serving as mere trivia. Viewed strictly within the tradition of poets of that time foregoing their birth name for a takhallus, the transition of Abdul to Sahir is probably insignificant. But it is in the understanding of his traumatic childhood that the true significance of Abdul's need to take on a takhallus reveals itself. For 'takhallus', other than 'pen-name', also literally translates to 'an escape' or 'to get rid of'. In Abdul's case, the need to escape a dysfunctional childhood, best epitomized by the incident of his father hurling invectives at his neighbour, Mian Abdul Hayee, with young Abdul as the convenient alibi, was enough for him to seek redemption by way of his takhallus.

With the takhallus serving as his new identity, Sahir set about venting his emotions. Poetry became a matter of cathartic release for him. A way in which he gave expression to the contrasting influences his parents had on him. 'I had seen and read a lot but I did not start writing because of this. It would often happen that whenever an important incident took place in my life, I wrote under the influence of that particular episode,' he said.[14]

The shadow his father's behaviour cast on him magnified into Sahir's disillusionment with capitalism, a hatred for the zamindari set-up and sympathy towards the abject conditions of the poor and helpless. All these subjects found a way into his poetry. Ironically, the man who was at the core of some of Sahir's most scathing criticisms in his poetry, eventually sought reconciliation when his son's fame as a poet began to grow in the city of Ludhiana. Sahir, however, spurned Fazl Mohammed's overtures. As far as he was concerned, he wanted no part of the wealth that had been earned by

---

14. Ibid., Balwant Singh, 'Hum Ke Thehere Ajnabee', p. 48.

sucking the life out of hapless workers and farmers and which had given his mother immense grief and ruined her youth.

Yet, if Sahir reserved a perpetual barbed tone for one parent, he placed his mother on a high pedestal. Seeing her fend for him, Sahir developed an overwhelming sense of gratitude for her. He realized that she had been wronged at the hands of his father. He felt her pain and was aware of the injustice she had been subjected to.

If his poems and songs in later years eloquently expressed the plight of women in all spheres of society, this was largely due to Sahir's understanding of his mother's character, the tribulations and trials she had to go through. Perhaps as a way of acknowledging the sacrifices made by her in raising him, he consistently concerned himself with the atrocities heaped on women. He never considered them unequal to men, nor did he view them as objects whose only purpose was to serve the carnal needs of men. Scathing in its tone for the most part, ironical on the odd occasion, his poetry voiced the need for their emancipation.

The poetic influence aside, his mother became inseparable from him. As much as he was her raison d'être initially, she became the centre of his being when Sahir entered adulthood. Anwar Sultana provides a particularly poignant description of Sahir's anxiety towards his mother after he had established himself in Bombay:

> I cannot find words to describe how bhai jaan would react if maaji got upset. He would immediately get very tense. It was impossible for him to find a moment's rest at this time. He would continuously pace up and down and try his very best to appease her. We have seldom seen bhai jaan as stressed as when maaji would get upset with him. And when maaji would eventually forgive him, his joy would be unbridled. He would insist on taking all of us out, even if it were only for a round of juice. The only reason he did this was because he could not relax until he knew that all was well with maaji.[15]

---

15. Ibid., Mahmood Ayoobi, 'Anwar Bibi Ke Bhai Jaan', p. 41.

On 4 May 1978, *Trishul*, directed by Yash Chopra, released in cinema halls across India. The movie was the second in Amitabh Bachchan's 'angry young man' trilogy of films directed by Chopra, preceded by *Deewaar* (1975) and followed by *Kaala Patthar* (1979). The story of *Trishul* revolved around a young man, Vijay (Amitabh), seeking vengeance against his father, R.K. Gupta (Sanjeev Kumar), for having spurned his mother, Shanti (Waheeda Rehman), for a life of wealth and material success. The film's songs were written by Sahir.

The second song of this film involved Shanti telling Vijay of the troubles she had gone through in bringing him up after R.K. Gupta had left her. For the first part of this song, Sahir wrote:

> *Tu mere saath rahega, munney*
> *Taaki tu jaan sakey*
> *Tujhko parwaan chadhane ke liye*
> *Kitni sangeen marahil se teri maa guzri*
> *Tu mere saath rahega, munney*
>
> *Tu mere saath rahega, munney*
> *Taaki tu dekh sakey,*
> *Kitne paon mere mamta ke kalejey pe padey*
> *Kitne khanjar meri aankhon, mere kaanon mein gadey*
> *Tu mere saath rahega, munney*
>
> *Main tujhe raham ke saaye mein na palney doongi*
> *Zindagaani ki kadi dhoop mein jalney doongi*
> *Taaki tap-tap ke tu faulad baney*
> *Maa ki aulaad baney*
> *Tu mere saath rahega, munney*
>
> (You shall live with me, my son
> So that you know
> To raise you
> What ordeals your mother faced . . .
> You shall live with me, my son

You shall live with me, my son
So that you see
How many feet trampled on my motherly love
How many daggers were sunk into my eyes, my ears
You shall live with me, my son

I will not allow you to find succour in someone's largesse
Instead, I will put you through the rigours of life
So that your mettle turns to gold,
So that you are worthy of being my child
You shall live with me, my son)

We know where Sahir was coming from.

2

Alma Martyr

Lekin hum in fazaon ke paaley huey toh hain
Gar yahaan nahin toh yahaan se nikaale huey toh hain[1]

(But these environs nurtured me
So what if I no longer belong to this place,
I am still an exile from here)

Government College, Ludhiana, is situated right in the heart of the city, near the Civil Lines area. Its boundary walls, about six or seven feet high, do not allow the curious onlooker a peek into what lies beyond. Which is just as well. The college campus is in a state of disrepair, and the teaching standards are nothing to write home about. The walls are as much a veil on a once glorious past as a cloak to cover contemporary truths. For, as a journalist wrote in an article on the institution, 'Once known as the Oxford of north India – its science block is modelled after the English varsity – with an alumni list which sounds like the who's who of India, today it's just another teaching institution.'[2]

---

1. From the poem 'Nazrey-Kaalej' (A Tribute to College), published in *Talkhiyaan*.
2. Manraj Grewal, 'Bitter Lessons', 13 April 2003, http://www.indianexpress. com/oldStory/21885/

It was to this once hallowed institute that Sahir found admission in 1937, after his matriculation from Malwa Khalsa High School.

'Young people are in a condition like permanent intoxication, because youth is sweet and they are growing,' said the Greek philosopher Aristotle. And nothing seemed truer of Sahir during his college years. The two defining aspects of his character, his poetry and his romantic disposition, flourished within the four walls of his alma mater.

> Gaaye hain is fazaa mein wafaaon ke raag bhi
> Nagmaat-e-aatishi se bakheri hai aag bhi[3]

(I have sung songs of fidelity in these surroundings
As well as lit fires with songs of rebellion)

Ludhiana in 1937, much like the rest of undivided India, was simmering with discontent against the colonial rulers. The screams of those who had died in the Jallianwala Bagh massacre at the hands of the British in 1919 still reverberated loud and clear. Further, as Zeyaur Rahman says, the Indian economy was at the crossroads and the seeds of economic conflict had already been sown by the British:

> The rule of the zamindars was beginning to come to an end. Under English rule, the capitalist structure, with factories and mills, was beginning to come to the fore. As a result, a new class of workers was being created. The stage was set for conflict between the capitalists and the working class. Those who were landlords and zamindars till yesterday became moneylenders and capitalists. And the landless people working on the zamindars' lands became workers in their factories. Even then, after they had gone from being farmers to workers, they were still subject to the atrocities of the wealthy. The only thing that changed was their manner of dressing.[4]

---

3. From the poem 'Nazrey-Kaalej', published in *Talkhiyaan*.
4. Prof. Dr Syed Zeyaur Rahman, *Sahir Ludhianvi: Hayaat Aur Shaayari*, p. 8.

This conflict between the capitalists and the working class was at the heart of the growing fascination for communism in the Indian subcontinent. As Ajaib Chitrakar said, 'He [Sahir] was an avid reader of Karl Marx.' At the same time, war clouds were gathering, rather ominously, around the world. For someone as keenly aware of and sensitive to the social environment around him as Sahir was, there was far too much happening for him not to be influenced.

Then there were the Urdu poets like Faiz and Josh, who had strong communist leanings and who, as Sahir admitted, exercised a huge influence on him. At college, he opted to study philosophy and history but grew interested in economics and politics and started reading books on these subjects as well. With his political outlook taking shape from these encounters, he became a member of the Students' Federation at college and actively participated in political causes which also influenced his poetry.

The late Krishan Adeeb, himself an Urdu poet and a friend and admirer of Sahir from those years in Ludhiana, remembers that most of Sahir's poems were not accepted for publication. He was not yet a name to reckon with. However, poems like 'Jahaan Mazdoor Rehtey Hain' (Where Workers Reside) were published under the name of A.H. Sahir in an underground newspaper called *Kirti Lehar*. And these poems, as Krishan states, were brimming with ideas of revolution.[5]

Around this time, in 1937–38, Sahir met many workers of the All India Students Federation (AISF), which was affiliated to the Communist Party of India (CPI). The AISF, which was founded in the mid-1930s, was committed to working for the independence of India and opposed imperialism and colonialism in any form. The AISF's objectives aligned with Sahir's own personal and political

5. Saabir Dutt, *Fann Aur Shaksiyat*, Sahir Ludhianvi Number, Krishan Adeeb, 'Sahir: Yaadon Ke Aaynein Mein', p. 505.

leanings. Consequently, he began taking an active interest in the affairs of the organization. He gave speeches to students and workers at various forums and even recited poetry with weighty political connotations at these gatherings.

Azhar Javed, renowned Pakistani poet and writer, who authored a book on Sahir and who passed away at the age of seventy-four in February 2012, gives an example of Sahir's rebellious behaviour:

> There was yet another function being organized on the college premises. The British commissioner and deputy commissioner attended the celebrations. The students were also participating in the event and Sahir was to recite his poetry on stage. But when the moment to appear on stage presented itself, Sahir greeted the audience and spoke in his typical belligerent style saying, 'As long as this Union Jack is flying above our heads, neither my friends nor I will participate or recite our poetry.' Needless to say, Sahir's audacious act left those on stage and in the audience stunned.[6]

Sahir's political involvement meant long absences from home that left his mother fraught with anxiety. She worried about him being harmed by his enemies (this perhaps had more to do with his father's threats than anything else). However, when she got to know about the kind of work her son was involved in, she attended some of the functions without informing Sahir. When she saw that people heard her son speak at these gatherings with great attention, and on Sahir's cue indulged in sloganeering as well, she took comfort in the fact that nobody could harm her son.

This was also the time Sahir found himself drawn to the opposite sex. While these liaisons were fleeting most of the time, a couple of attachments were serious enough to alter the course of Sahir's life and inspire poetry tinged with romance. While the college romances

---

6. Azhar Javed, *Nakaamey Mohabbat*, Takhleeqkar Publishers, pp. 49–50.

did not lead to anything permanent, they give an insight to a character quite different from the average love-struck Romeo.

The first such girl to make her way into the young poet's heart was Mahinder Chaudhary. Mahinder was Sahir's classmate from college and the daughter of one of Ludhiana's prominent personalities, Ram Raj, a lawyer by profession and a respected member of the Congress party. The relationship between Sahir and Mahinder blossomed owing to their political leanings. Given her family's political background, Mahinder, too, was against the British establishment but could not come out against it openly. Knowing of Sahir's revulsion for the British, Mahinder was drawn to him. She idolized him and was influenced by his writings and poetry. She enjoyed Sahir's presence, for the budding poet gave expression to her thoughts which she could not bring herself to express. As time went by, Sahir's pen became a conduit for Mahinder's innermost feelings.

As another college classmate, Haafiz Ludhianvi, observes, Sahir was fascinated by the sheer beauty of Mahinder's eyes. They held him in thrall and he wanted to lose himself in their depths. All day, he longed to catch a glimpse of Mahinder. His feelings for her were so strong that every time he walked towards her house, he felt he had reached his 'destination'. On the one instance that Mahinder actually wandered out onto the terrace of her house, Sahir, inspired by her momentary glimpse, expressed his lovelorn state in verse:

Saamney ik makaan ki chhath par
Muntazir kisi ki ek ladki hai
Mujhko ussey nahin taaluk kuch
Phir bhi seeney mein aag bhadki hai

(Ahead, atop the terrace of a house
A young girl stands waiting
There is nothing that binds me to her
Yet an intense longing stirs within me)

However, the relationship was not destined to last. Mahinder died all too suddenly, of tuberculosis. Sahir was left distraught. While the onset of love had spurred Sahir to poetry, now pathos and sorrow entered his lexicon, inspiring him to new poetic heights. The irony is poignant. While Mahinder's death was a big personal loss for Sahir the young man in love, it helped Sahir the poet mature as a writer. Seeing Mahinder's body being consumed by the flames at the cremation ground, Sahir wrote the poem 'Marghat Ki Sarzameen' (The Cremation Ground), an intense outpouring of his love and grief for Mahinder. Through the poem, Sahir saw the place where Mahinder had been cremated as the custodian of his love:

> Mere tasavooratey kohan ki ami hai tu
> Marghat ki sar zameen mukaddas zameen hai tu
> Ek bevatan aseer-e-mehan ka salaam le
> Aazurda-e-bahaar-e-chaman ka salaam le
> Phitrat terey haram pe takaddus phishaar hai
> Tu mere dil ki khaak ki sarmaayadaar hai
>
> Viraaniyan teri mujhey jannat se kam nahin
> Yeh dhoop mujhko saaya rehmat se kam nahin
> Go terey raastey mein har ek sau babool hain
> Daaman mein tere iski jawaani ke phool hain
> Jo meri zindagi ki tamanna bani rahi
> Zaukey niyaaz-e-rooh ka kaba bani rahi . . .

(You are the guardian of my memories
Of all the cremation grounds, you are the most sacred
Accept the salutations of a grieving soul
Accept the salutations of the inconsolable environs
Nature stands witness to your purity
You are the custodian of my broken heart

I prefer the solitude here to the beauty of heaven
The sun that beats down here is no less than God's grace
Even if there are a hundred thorns leading to this place

You ultimately shelter the beauty of her youth
If I continue to wish to live
You will become the focal point of my love)

But as the poem progressed, Sahir's tone turned accusatory.

Tujhsey bhi intezaar ki zehmat na ho saki
Mahfooz do ghadi woh amaanat na ho saki
Ek bewatan ke dard ka chara na ho saka
Main dekh loon usey yeh gawaara na ho saka
Yeh dupahar, yeh dhoop, yeh veeraan aasmaan
Tu hi bata ki ab main pukaroon kisey yahaan

(You couldn't bear the trouble of waiting for some time
You did not wish to part with your possession a couple of
   minutes longer
She was the only happiness to a homeless person's woes
You couldn't bear that I saw her a few minutes longer
This afternoon, this sun, this vast, empty sky
You tell me, whom do I seek redressal from?)

Amidst the anguish, he sung high praises of Mahinder's beauty:

Kausar mein woh dhuli hui baahein bhi jal gayee
Jo dekhtee mujhey woh nigahein bhi jal gayee
Ambar sarisht gesu-e-shab goh bhi jal gaye
Woh deeda-e-mast purfuson bhi jal gaye
Masoom kehkahon ka tarannum bhi mit gaya
Jhipi hui nazar ka tabassum bhi mit gaya

(The arms that had been bathed in holy water have been burnt
The eyes that looked towards me have been burnt as well
The hair that was akin to the darkness of night has been burnt
Those eyes that brought excitement to my heart have been burnt
   as well
The innocent laughter that had a mellifluous ring to it is gone
The happiness caused by her coy gaze is also gone)

Finally, seeking an end to his misery, Sahir hoped that the sparks from the fire would consume him as well:

Us raakh mein falak ke sitaron ka noor hai
Is raakh mein zameen ki masoom hoor hai,
Sholay phir ek baar isi raakh se uthaa
Aur khatm kar de mere masaib ka silsila[7]

(That ash contains the brightest of the stars from the sky above
This ash consumes an innocent beauty of this earth
Embers, arise once again from this cinder
And end this relentless saga of my troubles)

Interestingly enough, despite this profound lament, Sahir's infatuation with Mahinder came to a rather abrupt end. Hurt as he was by Mahinder's death, Sahir begged Haafiz Ludhianvi to get him a photograph of Mahinder's so that he could have it framed. With her photograph in his keep, Sahir hoped to have Mahinder by his side forever. Yet, after Haafiz managed to get Mahinder's picture, Sahir eventually forgot about her in a few days and moved on.[8]

Just like spring follows winter, Sahir found himself smitten yet again soon after Mahinder's demise. This time it was a dainty, attractive young girl by the name Ishar Kaur who caught Sahir's attention. Ishar hardly ever spoke to anyone. She generally appeared a little lost and was different from the rest of the girls. Sahir would gaze at her for hours together, even as she tried to avoid eye contact with him. The girl, whose name was an anagram that emerged from his own (Ishar and Sahir), cast an irrepressible spell on his very existence. He was determined to win her over at any cost. Haafiz Ludhianvi outlines our protagonist's wily stratagems at wooing his lady love:

7. Ibid., pp. 54–56.
8. Saabir Dutt, *Fann Aur Shaksiyat*, Sahir Ludhianvi Number, Haafiz Ludhianvi, 'Rumaan Aur Inquilaab Ka Shaayar', pp. 129–31.

Since Sahir was the president of the college union, he asked Ishar to sing at one of the functions being organized by the union. He was already aware that Ishar was a very good singer. Ishar, though, was a little surprised by Sahir's request. Shy as she was, she turned down his invitation. Not perturbed by her outright refusal, Sahir continued to request Ishar to participate in the union's activities. She eventually relented.[9]

The gap between *inkaar* and *iqraar* bridged, Ishar started to reciprocate Sahir's feelings. The two grew close to each other. Soon, the whole college was abuzz with stories of the alleged affair. This unnerved Ishar. Not knowing where the relationship would lead and afraid of how it could harm her reputation, Ishar decided to end her association with Sahir. She told Sahir she would not meet him again and even started avoiding him.

Having cut Sahir out of her life, Ishar, who lived on the Government College premises, in the hostel, wept for hours together. Seeing her weep copiously and finding her void in his life too large to fill, Sahir produced yet another romantic gem: 'Kisi Ko Udaas Dekhkar' (On Seeing Someone Despondent). At the very outset, Sahir sought an explanation from Ishar for her troubled state of mind:

Tumhein udaas sa paata hoon main kayee din se
Na jaaney kaun se sadmey uthaa rahi ho tum?
Woh shokhiyaan, woh tabassum, woh kahkahe na rahein
Har ek cheez ko hasrat se dekhti ho tum
Chhupa chhupa ke khamoshi mein apni bechaynee
Khud apney raaz ki tash-heer bann gayee ho tum

(I find you in the throes of despondency for days now
Who knows what tragedy has befallen you?
That charm, that smile, that laughter all seem to have withered
    away

9. Ibid., p. 133.

There is a yearning that characterizes your every gaze
Hiding your anxieties in your own silence
You betray your own innermost secret)

He also hinted at the social pressures that could have led Ishar to abandon him:

Mujhe tumhaare tagaaful se kyun shikaayat ho?
Meri fanaa mere ehsaas ka takazaa hai
Main jaanta hoon ki duniya ka khauf hai tumko
Mujhe khabar hai, yeh duniya ajeeb duniya hai
Yahaan hayaat ke purdeh mein maut palti hai
Shikast-e-saaz ki aawaaz rooh-e-nagma hai

(Why should I complain of your neglect of me?
My ruin is reflective of the way I feel
I know that you are afraid of this world
I am aware that this world is a strange place
Here death lurks in the shadow of life
The soul cries out the song of defeat)

The poem, with its intense, melancholic tenor, only fuelled speculation about the relationship between Ishar and Sahir. Unable to bear being separated from her any more, Sahir decided to go to the college and meet Ishar. The college was closed for the vacations and there were very few girls staying in the hostel. Somehow, Sahir got Ishar to meet him. Yet, even though the college was empty, their secret rendezvous became public knowledge. It reached the ears of the college authorities, including the principal. Ishar was expelled from the college and, a few days later, Sahir also left Government College.

The popular version of the story has been that Sahir Ludhianvi, too, was expelled from Government College. While there were insinuations that Sahir was expelled 'for sitting in the principal's lawn with a female classmate', some accounts, like Azhar Javed's, exaggerate the episode:

The college was closed for vacations. Consequently, there was nobody staying in the hostel. Ishar Kaur had also gone home. Sahir was anxious to meet Ishar. He begged Ishar's friends to bring her to the hostel. Whatever the purpose of Sahir wanting to meet Ishar, the principal got to know of their meeting and reached the spot at the same time. He didn't like seeing them together and, therefore, expelled them both from the college.[10]

Another view holds that Ishar Kaur was just a pretext to expel Sahir and that the real reason lay elsewhere. Sahir's poems had long irked the college authorities because of their 'seditious' themes. In fact, some sources allude to Sahir having attended a political rally in a village called Sarabha, located close to Ludhiana, to commemorate the death of Kartar Singh Sarabha, a martyr who had died espousing the cause of the freedom struggle. It was alleged that the poem Sahir read at this function led to his expulsion.

It is entirely plausible that the college authorities used the Ishar Kaur incident to kill two birds with one stone. Tired of Sahir's political activities, they, perhaps, used his indiscretions with Ishar to prevail upon him to leave the college of his own will. And which is why, contrary to popular belief, there is no record of Sahir's expulsion from Government College.

Professor Bhupinder Parihar, former professor of English at the college and dean of cultural affairs, whom I met in June 2009, validates this theory: 'To the best of my knowledge there is no document in the college records that suggests that Sahir was expelled from here. What must have happened is that Principal Harvey convinced Sahir to leave the college on his own, for there is no written communication on the matter.'

Also, it is hard to imagine that a man like Principal Harvey would risk the future of a student by putting his expulsion on

10. Azhar Javed, *Nakaamey Mohabbat*, Takhleeqkar Publishers, p. 60.

record, for Hameed Akhtar recalls their principal as 'an extremely level-headed Englishman. He was very well educated, skilled in his field and dealt with everyone in a most courteous way. He loved his students like they were his own children.'[11] How could such a man, so fondly remembered by one of Sahir's best friends, have acted in a manner harmful to a student?

The final word on the matter though belongs to Dr Kewal Dheer who also lives in Ludhiana. An affable gentleman in his early seventies, Dr Dheer is a Punjabi writer and an avid fan of Sahir's poetry. Where there has been little or no attempt by the city of Ludhiana to nurture the memory of one of their best-known sons, Dr Dheer has single-handedly kept Sahir's flame burning all these years. As chairman of the Sahir Cultural Academy and general secretary of the Adeeb International, Dr Dheer has been organizing an annual mushaira called the 'Jashn-e-Sahir' since 1975 in memory of the poet. Sahir himself had been present at the very first Jashn-e-Sahir along with other leading luminaries from the world of Urdu poetry such as Kaifi Azmi, Ali Sardar Jafri and Jan Nisar Akhtar.

Sometimes, along with organizing the Jashn-e-Sahir mushaira, the Adeeb International, budget permitting, also brings out a souvenir to commemorate the event. The souvenir carries a brief write-up on Sahir Ludhianvi and photographs or other memorabilia linked with Sahir. The 1998 Jashn-e-Sahir souvenir, for example, carried a copy of Sahir's provisional character certificate from Malwa Khalsa High School and his Government College admission form.

Yet, despite his tireless efforts over all these years to collect material pertaining to the poet, Dr Dheer has not managed to lay his hands on the expulsion letter that is alleged to exist in the college records. Quite simply, as Dr Dheer puts it in his deep baritone,

---

11. Hameed Akhtar, *Ashnaiyaan Kya Kya*, p. 91.

'We never got the expulsion letter because there is no such document; in all probability Sahir was simply asked to leave the college.'

Irrespective of the many, sometimes bitter, experiences that Government College left him with, Sahir bore it no grudge. The sense of gratitude he had towards his alma mater is evident in these lines from his poem 'Nazrey-Kaalej' (A Tribute to College) written sometime around 1943:

Tu aaj bhi hai mere liye jannat-e-khayal
Hain tujh mein dafn meri javaani ke chaar saal . . .

Teri nawaazishon ko bhulaaya na jaayega
Maazi ka naqsh dil se mitaaya na jaayega

(You are still the heaven of my dreams
I have spent four years of my youth with you . . .

I will never forget your benevolence
The past lives forever etched in my heart)

The college too did its best to make amends. On 22 November 1970, when it celebrated its golden jubilee, Sahir, then at the pinnacle of his fame, was awarded a gold medal. Sahir used the opportunity to profess his appreciation for the institution in his poem 'Ae Nayee Nasl' (Oh New Generation), written specifically for the occasion:

Yaad aate hain in fazaaon mein
Kitne nazdeek aur door ke naam

Kitne khwaabon ke malgajey chehrey
Kitni yaadon ke marmari ajsaam . . .

Isi mitti ko haath mein lekar
Hum baney thay bagaawaton ke imaam . . .

Nazar karta hoon in fazaaon ko
Apna dil, apni rooh, apna kalaam

(I remember in these environs
Names familiar and distant

The blur of many a dream
The memory of many a beauty . . .

Carrying the dust of this very earth in our hands
We became the leaders of many a rebellion . . .

I dedicate to these environs
My heart, my soul, my poetry)

The ultimate recognition came when Government College dedicated its auditorium to Sahir, renaming it 'Sahir Auditorium'.[12]

So, what does one make of the years that Sahir spent at Government College? How did the two relationships, with Mahinder Chaudhary and Ishar Kaur, both of which ended suddenly, impact him? How did the prevailing circumstances of the nation state, the problems of the working class, influence his thought process? How did his poetry manifest in response to those situations?

From the various accounts of Sahir's life, there is evidence that Sahir was more disturbed by the sudden severance of his relationship with Ishar than he was with the abrupt end of the one with Mahinder. Perhaps this was also because there was very little Sahir could have done to avert Mahinder's death. But Ishar was a different matter. She had been separated from him under pressure from society, perhaps because she was a Sikh girl and he a Muslim. Determined to have her back in his life, following her expulsion from college, Sahir even brainwashed a friend, Faiz-ul-Hassan Chaudhary, into accompanying him to meet Ishar in her village, Rakba. They met Ishar but were forced to flee after she warned them of her father returning to the house.[13]

---

12. The exact year in which the rechristening took place could not be confirmed.
13. Hameed Akhtar, *Ashnaiyaan Kya Kya*, pp. 107–08.

In his poem 'Yaksui' (Stalemate), Sahir directed his ire at his beloved for being afraid of what the world thought of their relationship and her fear of social norms. In the context of events that transpired, it is perhaps safe to assume that Sahir wrote the poem based on his experiences with Ishar.

Main samajhta hoon takaddus ko tamaddun ka fareb
Tum rasoomaat ko imaan banaati kyun ho?
Jab tumhein mujhse zyaada hai zamaaney ka khyaal
Phir meri yaad mein yoon ashk bahaati kyun ho?
Tum mein himmat hai toh duniya se bagaavat kar lo
Warna maa baap jahaan kehtey hain shaadi kar lo

(I consider piousness to be a betrayal of culture
Why do you make customs a measure of your piety?
When you care more about society than about me
Why do you shed tears in my memory?
If you have the courage, rebel against the world
Otherwise marry wherever your parents want)

Yet, at other times, when his anger ebbed, Sahir nursed his wounded heart by seeking comfort in the problems confronting humanity:

Main apni rooh ki har ek khushi mita loonga
Magar tumhaari masarrat mita nahin sakta . . .

Tumhaare gham ke siva aur bhi toh gham hain mujhe
Nijaat jinse main ek lahza pa nahin sakta . . .

Gali gali mein yeh biktey huey jawaan chehre,
Haseen aankhon mein afsurdagi-si chaayee huyee . . .

Yeh gham bahut hain meri zindagi mitaaney ko,
Udaas rehke mere dil ko aur ranj na do[14]

---

14. From the poem 'Kisi Ko Udaas Dekhkar' (On Seeing Someone Despondent), published in *Talkhiyaan*.

(I will denounce everything that delights my soul
But I cannot take away your happiness . . .

I have other sorrows to tend besides yours,
Those from which I cannot free myself even for an instant . . .

These young faces being sold in every street
The despondency that fills their beautiful eyes . . .

All these troubles are enough to consume my life
By staying despondent do not burden my heart any more)

Indeed, this ability to find solace in the travails of mankind while regretting a failed romance was to become a recurrent theme in Sahir's poetry and, later, in his film songs as well. Take, for example, his song in *Waqt* (1965), which had Renu (Sharmila Tagore), a girl from a wealthy family, professing her love for Vijay (Shashi Kapoor), the youngest son of a family which had fallen on bad times. The opening lines of the song were an immediate throwback to Sahir's conflicting emotions vis-à-vis love and his sympathy for man's relentless saga coping with troubles.

Renu sings:

Din hai bahaar ke, tere mere iqraar ke
Dil ke sahaare aaja pyaar karey

(Spring is upon us, the time is nigh for you and me to confess our
     love
My beloved, let us partake in the joy of romance)

Vijay responds:

Dushmann hain pyaar ke jab laakhon gham sansaar ke
Dil ke sahaare kaise pyaar karey?

(It is difficult to love when several sorrows confront the world
My beloved, how are we to further our romance?)

It took a while for Sahir to get over the Ishar Kaur chapter. But eventually he did. Perhaps it was his age, his youth, that gave him the capacity to overcome. Only in his early twenties at the time, with an entire lifetime and its various exciting possibilities ahead of him, Sahir could not afford to wallow permanently in lost love. As Hameed Akhtar recalls:

> She [Ishar] eventually left for Bombay where she got married to a distant relative . . . Part of the reason for Sahir wanting to go to Bombay was because Ishar lived there. Yet, in the two years [1946 to 1947] that he lived in Bombay [initially], he never bothered to look for Ishar. But he would say, 'If I become famous; she will come looking for me herself.' We do not know whether this actually happened. When I met Sahir in 1979, the question of him having met Ishar seemed entirely irrelevant.[15]

Having parted ways with his college, Sahir left for Lahore in 1943. His decision to move to Lahore appeared to be a well-thought-out one, because as Hameed Akhtar writes of the city, 'While Lahore was not a very big city at that time, it was still the only city where intellectual, cultural and literary pursuits had reached a peak.'[16]

In Lahore, Sahir took admission at Dayal Singh College. It was his final year of BA and he became the president of the Lahore Students Federation. His political work became even more intense and here, too, he ran afoul of the college authorities because of this. He was not allowed to take his examinations. Once again, Sahir was forced to leave college and deprived of a full year's education. The next year he took admission at the Islamia College in Lahore. Disillusioned with the education system by now, he left Islamia College as well, without appearing for his BA examinations.

15. Hameed Akhtar, *Ashnaiyaan Kya Kya*, p, 108.
16. Saabir Dutt, *Fann Aur Shaksiyat*, Sahir Ludhianvi Number, Hameed Akhtar, 'Sahir: Mera Bachpan Ka Dost', p. 145.

However, disappointments on the academic front were more than offset by glad tidings when it came to his poetry. By this time, towards the end of 1943 and the beginning of 1944, his first anthology of poems, *Talkhiyaan* (Bitterness), was published. He was only twenty-three.

3

Of Poetry and Progressive Literature

Ek naya suraj chamka hai, ek anokhi jau-baari hai
Khatam huyee afraad ki shahi, ab jamhoor ki salaari hai[1]

(A new sun shines bright, a unique light falls upon us
The reign of a select few comes to an end, it is time for the masses to
stake claim)

In December 1932, *Angaare* (Embers), a collection of ten short stories was published in Lucknow. The stories, penned by Sajjad Zaheer, Rashid Jahan, Mahmuduzzafar and Ahmed Ali, 'dealt with prevailing familial and sexual mores, the decadence and hypocrisy of social and religious life in contemporary India, and took more than one pot-shot at religious orthodoxy, attacking it with what Ahmed Ali later referred to as "the absence of circumspection". Within months of its publication, the book generated an uproar within Muslim circles, and was condemned by a variety of organizations as being "obscene" and "blasphemous"

---

1. From the poem 'Tulu-e-Ishtrakiyat' (Dawn of Communism), published in *Talkhiyaan*.

. . . Undeterred by the widespread criticism, Sajjad Zaheer, the leader of the *Angaare* group, set about trying to use the field of literature as a battering ram to break down the orthodox and conservative fortifications of Indian society.'[2]

The Progressive Writers' Movement (PWM), born in 1936, was the fruit of Sajjad Zaheer's labour. The movement was directed at the masses — labourers, peasants and the middle class — and its literary endeavours opposed those who exploited and oppressed its target audience. It sought to combat all tendencies that gave rise to despair among the common man and at the same time build a sense of awareness and unity among them. Literature, as the founding fathers of the PWM realized, could no longer exist in isolation, as 'art for art's sake', but was to be used as an instrument to bring about social change. The movement did not ask writers to turn into political workers. Instead, it exhorted those who espoused the ideals of the movement not to ignore politics. A Progressive writer was expected to empathize with human suffering and advocate the values of freedom and democracy.

When the first all-India meeting of the PWM was held in Lucknow in 1936, Munshi Premchand, the doyen of Hindi literature, further elucidated the objectives of the movement for Progressive literature:

> A literature that does not produce in us the determination to overcome obstacles, is of no use for us today . . . If you cannot see beauty in a poor woman whose perspiration flows as, laying down her sleeping child on a mound along the field, she works in the field, it is your own vision which it to blame. For, behind those wilted lips and withered cheeks reside sacrifice, devotion and endurance. Youth is not the name for poetic ecstasy and sighing over the coyness, perverseness, and vanity of the fair sex, it is the name for idealism, courage, endurance and sacrifice.

---

2. Raza Mir and Ali Husain Mir, *Anthems of Resistance*, IndiaInk, 2006, pp. 2–4.

He ended his address with the following memorable sentence:

> On our touchstone, only that literature will be judged genuine, which embodies thought, the desire for freedom, the essence of beauty, the spirit of progress, the light of reality, the literature that will produce movement, restlessness and a tumult within us, that will not put us to sleep – because any more sleep can only be a precursor of death.[3]

While Premchand set the objectives for Progressive literature, the other famous litterateur of the era, Rabindranath Tagore, laid down the expectations of the writers participating in the movement. Tagore's message, which was read out at the second conference of the Urdu and Hindi Progressive writers in Allahabad in 1938, went thus:

> The love of solitude has become a second nature with me. But it is a fact that a writer who isolates himself from society cannot get to know humanity. An insulated writer deprives himself of the experience that comes from meeting many people. To understand society and discover its path of progress, it is unavoidable that we feel its pulse and listen to its heartbeats. And this is only possible if we are sympathetic to humanity, for then only can we understand the soul of man. Obviously, if we sequester ourselves from people, we can only become alien. Young writers must mingle with people. It will not do for them to become reclusive like me. I understand now the mistake I made by staying away from society, and that is why I am giving you this counsel. It is clear to me that one must love humanity and human society. Literature that is not in harmony with mankind is destined for failure. This truth is lit like a bright light within me, and no argument can put it out.

3. Sajjad Zaheer, *The Light: A History of the Movement for Progressive Literature in the Indo-Pak Subcontinent*, a translation of *Roshnai*, Oxford University Press, 2006, pp. 62–65.

Today our country is a desert where there is no trace of fertility and life. Every grain of our land is the reflection of pain. We must erase the unhappiness and depression, and bring life to this land once more. It should be the duty of a writer to breathe the spirit of new life into the country, sing of awakening and passion, give the message of hope and happiness to every individual, and not let anybody become hopeless and superfluous. To create among people of all ages the desire for the welfare of the nation, over one's own interests, should be the main duty of the writer.[4]

As a result of his childhood experiences, which nurtured a distaste for zamindars and capitalism, his interest in communism and his fervent involvement in student politics in college, Sahir was naturally drawn to the PWM. He realized that the ideals of the PWM complemented his poetry. An example of this manifested in his poem 'Mujhe Sochne De' (Let Me Reflect):

Jalsa-gaahon mein yeh dehshatzaada sahme amboh
Rahguzaaron pe falaakatzadaa logon ke giroh
Bhookh aur pyaas se pazmurda siyaahfaam zameen
Teer-o-taar makaan muflis-o-beemaar makeen
Nau-e-insaan mein yeh sarmaaya-o-mehnat ka tazdaad
Amno-tahzeeb ke parcham taley kaumon ka fasaad
Har taraf aatisho-aahan ka yeh sailaab-e-azeem
Nit naye tarz pe hotee hui duniya takseem
Lahlahaatey huey kheton pe javaani ka samaan
Aur deh-kaan ke chhappar mein na batti na dhuan
Yeh falak bos mill-ein dilkash-o-seemee bazaar
Yeh galaazat pe jhapatatey huey bhookhe nadaar
Door sahil pe woh shafaaf makaano ki kataar
Sarsaraatey huey purdoh mein simat-tey gulzaar
Daro-deewaar pe anvaar ka sailaab-e-ravaa
Jaisey ek shaayar-e-madhosh ke khwaabon ka jahaan
Yeh sabhi kyun hai? Yeh kya hai? Mujhe kuch sochne de
Kaun insaan ka khuda hai? Mujhe kuch sochne de

---

4. Ibid., p. 122.

(Amidst places of celebrations these crowds cowed down by fear
On the roads groups of impoverished people
Besieged by hunger and thirst this withered and blackened earth
The lonely and dark houses inhabited by the sick and poor
This conflict between labour and capital amongst humanity
Beyond the façade of peace and civility the clash between
    communities
From every direction the rising tide of fire and sword
Every day bringing with it a new kind of divide
The fields flourish ready for harvest
Yet there is no light or hearth that burns beneath the farmer's roof
These factories that grace the sky, these enchanting markets
The hungry poor who fight over grime
Far away, by the sea, the stretch of spotless houses standing in line
The floral decorations that adorn their rustling curtains
The light that illuminates the walls and the doors
Like a poet in a dream, in a state of thrall
Why is it like this? What is this? Let me reflect
Who does man worship? Let me reflect)

With such incisive verse of startling maturity, gravitas and anguish, Sahir articulated Premchand's and Tagore's expectations from the Progressive Writers' Movement perfectly. He saw, as Premchand had asked of the Progressive writers, the beauty in the poor woman who makes sacrifices to raise her child through his own mother's experiences. His literary output was directed towards humanity in keeping with Tagore's outlook for the movement.

Sajjad Zaheer corroborated Sahir's association with the PWM in the early 1940s:

> A few months after the start of the war [the Second World War], citizens' rights began to be impounded, and most of the Progressive writers, who were associated with the socialist movement, were arrested. As a result, the organization of the Association [of the Progressive writers] fell into a state of suspension. The rest of the members and workers of the

Association became nervous about holding meetings, because to do so was to risk arrest. During the period, from 1940 until the end of 1942, the organization of our Association remained suspended and its meetings and conferences stopped. The rulers and reactionaries were probably happy and satisfied that they had managed to crush the Movement.

But in that very period, Faiz's *Naqsh-e-Faryadi*, Krishan Chander's *Tilism-e-Khayal*, Bedi's *Dana-o-Daam*, Nadeem's and Ashk's collections of short stories were published by *Muktab-e-Urdu* in Lahore. In the same period, decent works of poetry, criticism, and short stories were brought out in *Adab-e-Lateef* and *Naya Adab*. Best of all, the new writers who were either students, or had not yet become professional writers, were influenced by the movement of Progressive literature and the Progressive point of view. All those whom we first heard of in 1943 and 1944 as Progressive writers were drawn to Progressive views during that period. Among them were Ahmed Nadeem Qasmi, Sahir Ludhianvi . . .[5]

However, Sahir's poems did not engage with the loftier motives of the Progressive agenda from the very beginning. Instead, his initial forays into poetry, perhaps as a consequence of his college romances, were directed at love and the emotions one experiences through it.

Chand kaliyaa nishaat ki chunkar
Muddaton maayoos rehta hoon
Tera milna khushi ki baat sahi
Tujhse milkar udaas rehta hoon[6]

(Having plucked a few buds of happiness
I wallow in despondency for hours together
Meeting you gives me great joy
But having met you, I turn despondent again)

In this, Sahir was not too different from many other individuals who in their youth experience that heady emotional roller coaster

---

5. Ibid., p. 171–72.
6. From the poem 'Radd-e-Amal' (A Reaction), published in *Talkhiyaan*.

called love. Except, however, that he articulated the frustration of unrequited love better than almost anyone else:

> *Mere khwaabon ke jharokon ko sajaane waali*
> *Tere khwaabon mein kaheen mera guzar hai ki nahin*
> *Pooch kar apni nigaahon se bata de mujhko*
> *Meri raaton ke muqaddar mein sehar hai ki nahin*[7]

(O woman who adorns the window of my dreams
Do I find mention in your dreams or not?
Let me know based on your perception
Is there a dawn at the end of my nights of darkness?)

In his love poetry, Sahir painted himself as a hapless victim who suffered terribly. Despair, despondency and defeat, consequently, were recurrent themes in his poems.

> *Apne seene se lagaaye huey umeed ki laash*
> *Muddaton zist ko nashaad kiya hai maine*
> *Tuney toh ek hi sadme se kiya thaa dochaar*
> *Dil ko har tarah se barbaad kiya hai maine*
> *Jab bhi raahon mein aayee hariri malboos*
> *Sard aahon mein tujhe yaad kiya hai maine*[8]

(Clinging to my chest are my dead hopes
I have made my life unhappy for a long time
You had only broken my heart once
But I have ruined my heart in every possible way
Whenever I see a woman approach me wearing silk
I remember you with many a cold sigh)

Eventually, he seemed to grow tired of love and the traditions it must respect and decided to give up on it:

7. From the poem 'Mataa-e-Gair' (Belonging to Someone Else), published in *Talkhiyaan*.
8. From the poem 'Shikast' (Defeat), published in *Talkhiyaan*.

Sochta hoon ki mohabbat pe kadi shartey hain
Is tamad-dun mein masarrat pe badi shartey hain . . .

Sochta hoon ki bashar aur mohabbat ka junoon
Aise boseeda tamad-dun mein hai ik kaar-e-jaboon
Sochta hoon ki mohabbat na bachegi zinda
Pesha-anzaam-waqt ki sadd jaaye yeh galti huyee laash
Yahi behtar hai ki begaana-e-ulfat hokar
Apne seeney mein karoon jazba-e-nafrat ki talaash[9]

(I think that love is hostage to many conditions
This world is too restrictive for such happiness . . .

I think the madness with which man falls in love
Has no place in this insular environment
I think that love will not survive for much longer
And before it withers completely, this dying emotion,
It is better that I divest myself of it completely
And cultivate within me feelings of hatred)

Having traversed the spectrum of romance, Sahir ultimately transformed into the people's poet. Moving away from love and its ecstasies, he began to address weightier matters. He developed a habit for deep thinking, which led him to raise crucial questions about the world around him. As he himself wrote in his poem 'Gurez' (To Avoid), romance only induced in him a temporary state of trance. It was not possible for him to seek eternal comfort in his lover's beauty while unpleasant, harsh realities of life confronted him daily:

Main zindagi ke hakayak se bhaag aaya thaa
Ki mujhko khud mein chhupa le teri phoosoon-e-zaayee . . .

Kahaan talak koi zinda haqeeqaton se bache
Kahaan talak kare chhup-chhup ke nagma-pairaayee . . .

---

9. From the poem 'Sochta Hoon' (I Think), published in *Talkhiyaan*.

Woh phir biki kisi mazdoor ki jawaan beti
Woh phir jhuka kisi dar pe guroor-e-barnaayee . . .

Nahin-nahin mujhe yoon multafit nazar se na dekh
Nahin-nahin mujhe ab taab-e-naghma-pairaayee
Mera junoon-e-vafaa hai zawaal-aamaada
Shikast ho gaya tera phooson-e-zebayee

(I had run away from the realities of life
To find shelter in the wonder of your beauty . . .

But for how long can one avoid the realities of life
For how long can one sing songs from the shadows? . . .

Yet again a labourer's young daughter finds a buyer
Yet again the pride of youth has been molested at someone's
       door . . .

No, do not look at me with compassion
No, I have not the strength to sing songs any more
I find my commitment to love on the decline
The charm of your beauty has failed)

Love for the beloved transformed into love for the entire world, establishing Sahir Ludhianvi's credentials as a Progressive poet. Having shed the romantic garb, Sahir's poems became synonymous with revolutionary poetry. They critiqued the nation state, gave hope of a better tomorrow to the citizens of the country and articulated communism as the only solution to the people's problems. In his characteristically blunt manner, he invited people to reflect on the various issues that confronted society:

Des ke adbaar ki baatein karey
Ajnabi sarkar ki baatein karey
Agli duniya ke fasaaney choddkar
Is jahannumzaar ki baatein karey[10]

---

10. From the poem 'Kuch Baatein' (Some Issues), published in *Talkhiyaan*.

(Let us talk about the travails of the nation
Talk about the foreign rule that is upon us
Instead of discussing the splendour of heaven
Let us talk about this hell that we inherit)

He declared his disillusionment with capitalism. It was, for him, an economic system that only led to the exploitation of the downtrodden and was the very antithesis of the utopian state he envisaged.

Kal bhi boondein barsee thi
Kal bhi baadal chhaaye thay
Aur kavi ne sochha tha . . .

Rut badlegi, phool khilengey, jhonkey madh barsaayengey
Ujley-ujley kheton mein rangeein aanchal lehraayengey . . .

Aaj bhi boondein barsengi
Aaj bhi baadal chhaaye hain
Aur kavi is soch mein hain . . .

Faslein kaat ke mehnatkash, gal-ley ke dher lagaayengey
Jaageeron ke maalik aakar, sab 'poonji' le jaayengey[11]

(It had rained yesterday
There were clouds on the horizon yesterday as well
And the poet had thought . . .

Things will change, spring will come, the breeze will bestow us
    with honey
Green and verdant fields will be garlanded with colourful
    scarves . . .

It will rain today too
There are clouds on the horizon
And the poet thinks . . .

---

11. From the poem 'Kal Aur Aaj' (Yesterday and Today), published in *Talkhiyaan*.

> After cutting the harvest, the hardworking farmers will stack
>   the grain
> Only for the owners of the fields to come and take all their
>   wealth away)

But perhaps, what epitomized Sahir's progressive credentials was 'Taj Mahal'.[12] Through this poem, Sahir used 'a powerful rhetorical device to turn our attention from our admiration of this edifice towards the blood, sweat and tears of the workers who slaved in order to construct it'.[13]

'Taj Mahal' reflected his growth as a poet, as a person who was not willing to forego his compassion for the struggles of millions of poor, hardworking labourers for the warmth of love in his beloved's arms. Moving away from the conventional approach of looking at the Taj Mahal as an ode to love, Sahir decries the vanity of an emperor in using the wealth at his disposal to create a structure that will forever mock the love of ordinary people.

> *Anginat logon ne duniya mein mohabbat ki hai*
> *Kaun kahta hai ki saadik na thay jazbey unkey?*
> *Lekin unke liye tash-heer ka saamaan nahin*
> *Kyunki woh log bhi apni hi tarah muflis thay . . .*
>
> *Yeh chamanzaar, yeh Jamuna ka kinaara, yeh mahal*
> *Yeh munak-kash daro-deewaar, yeh mehraab, yeh taak*
> *Ek shahenshah ne daulat ka sahaara lekar*
> *Hum gareebon ki mohabbat ka udaaya hai mazaak*
>
> (Countless individuals across humanity have been smitten by love
> Who is to say there was no sincerity in their feelings?
> But they had not the means to flaunt their love
> Because they were destitute like you and me . . .

---

12. Despite my best efforts, I have not been able to date this poem. My research tells me that it was most probably written a little before *Talkhiyaan* was published. That would be about 1943–44.

13. Raza Mir and Ali Husain Mir, *Anthems of Resistance*, IndiaInk, 2006, p. 155.

These gardens by the bank of the Yamuna, this dazzling abode
These ornate walls and domes, doors and awnings
An emperor has used his wealth
To mock the love of us impoverished souls)

'Taj Mahal', with its outright rebuttal of love being the sole prerogative of the rich and wealthy, captured popular imagination like never before. And the extent of its popularity can be gauged from the fact that years after the poem had been written, Hindi film heroes, comfortable in their indigent characters, have used '*Ek shahenshah ne daulat ka sahaara lekar, hum gareebon ki mohabbat ka udaaya hai mazaak*' as a punch line while romancing the daughters of aristocrats on screen. An example of this is *Dil Hi Toh Hai* (1963) where the protagonist, Yusuf (Raj Kapoor), responds to Khan Bahadur's (Nasir Hussain) threats to stay away from his daughter, Jamila Banu (Nutan), with this very line. Interestingly, in *Mahaan* (1983), Amitabh Bachchan, in the character of the comic actor Guru, even parodies this line in response to Zeenat Aman's (Rita) belittling process of choosing a husband by saying, '*Ek aurat ne daulat ka sahaara lekar, hum mardon ki izzat ka udaaya hai mazaak.*' (A woman has used her wealth to humiliate so many men.)

The 1964 movie *Ghazal*, starring Sunil Dutt and Meena Kumari, went one step further and wove the poem, as a song, into the film, though the film itself, a rather unremarkable love story, is bereft of any Progressive element and did not need the poem for its narrative purposes. It was possibly included only because the film's producers wanted to cash in on the poem's popularity – a good twenty-odd years after it had been written.

The poem's popularity, however, didn't stop it from creating an uproar in traditional literary circles. Right-wing Muslim newspapers led a wave of strident criticism against Sahir. They chastised him on the grounds that a man who did not adhere to religion, an atheist, had insulted the great emperor Shah Jahan for no reason. Sahir, though, as his friend Krishan Adeeb observes, 'was only too happy that his poem had been noticed even if the criticisms of "Taj Mahal" were at their acerbic best'.[14]

In an attempt to gain a more objective view of Sahir's 'Taj Mahal' vis-à-vis the great Mughal emperor's monument of love, I reached out to Gauhar Raza, eminent poet, scientist and social activist, who lives in Delhi. The moment Gauhar saab heard of my interest in Sahir, he invited me over to his house. Accordingly, one evening in August 2010, I met Gauhar saab in Dwarka. In between some fine whiskey and a meal I will cherish for years to come, Gauhar saab spoke of his views on Sahir's non-film poetry including 'Taj Mahal'.

According to him, the critics' assessment of Sahir's 'Taj Mahal' was absolutely uncalled for: 'How can anyone challenge the position of such a great monument which is a symbol of love and say that I don't want my love to have anything to do with it.' Sahir, as Raza pointed out, had taken the poem beyond the apparent magnificence of the Taj Mahal and raised class issues, reflected on social segregation and oppression. 'He (Sahir) did not say a word against its beauty. He only gave it a context. The ugly oppressive social order is the main focus and that makes the poem relevant even today,' said Raza to deflate the criticism that was directed towards this wonderful piece of poetry, which goes beyond classifications of just being Progressive.

Raza's support for Sahir's Progressive tenor aside, the most startling thing about 'Taj Mahal' is that Sahir Ludhianvi had never been to Agra, or seen the magnificent mausoleum Shah Jahan had built, before he wrote the poem.

'I wanted to write a poem on Noorjehan's grave, but I was not able to find the right inspiration for it and, instead, I wrote "Taj

---

14. Saabir Dutt, *Fann Aur Shaksiyat*, Sahir Ludhianvi Number, Krishan Adeeb, 'Sahir: Yaadon Ke Aaynein Mein', p. 506.

Mahal". Why does one need to go to Agra for this? I have read Marx's philosophy and I remember my geography as well. I know that the Taj Mahal was built by the side of the Yamuna by Shah Jahan for his wife Mumtaz Mahal,' Sahir is said to have told his friend Krishan Adeeb.[15]

It is not that Sahir deliberately wrote poems that had a bitter or critical tenor to them. He was overwhelmed by circumstances around him, which is why he explained his inability to write lullabies:

Mere sarkash taraano ki haqeeqat hai toh itni hai
Ki jab main dekhta hoon bhookh ke maarey kisaano ko
Gareebon, mufliso ko, bekaso ko, besahaaron ko
Sisakti nazneeno ko, tadaptey naujawaano ko
Huqumat ke tashad-dudd ko, amaarat ke taqabbur ko
Kisi ke cheethdon ko aur shahenshahi khazaano ko

Toh dil taab-e-nishaat-e-bazme-ishrat la nahin sakta
Main chaahoon bhi toh khwaab aawar taraaney ga nahin sakta[16]

(The only truth to my songs of revolution is this:
That when I see farmers starving of hunger
The poor, the needy, the impoverished, the deprived
Weeping beauties, desperate men in their youth
The atrocities of the government, hubris of the wealthy
Someone's poverty and the overflowing coffers of the aristocracy

My heart cannot accept the celebration of aristocratic gatherings
Even if I wish, I cannot compose songs of an ethereal nature)

It is this rare sensitivity towards the plight of the exploited sections of society that formed the cornerstone of his poetry. Consequently, he saw himself as a poet who would inspire the masses to rebel:

15. Ibid.
16. From the poem 'Mere Geet' (My Songs), published in Talkhiyaan.

Tumse kuvvat lekar ab main tumko raah dikhaaonga
Tum parcham lehraana saathi main barbat par gaaonga
Aaj se mere funn ka maqsad zanjeerey pighlaana hai
Aaj se main shabnam ke badle angaarey barsaaonga[17]

(Inspired by you, dear comrade, I will now be your guiding light
You hoist the flag, I will sing along
Beginning today, my art shall aim to melt the shackles
Beginning today, instead of dewdrops I will spew sparks of fire)

He remained true to the avowed agenda of the PWM: that literature should combat tendencies that give rise to despair. Accordingly, he urged the masses to bear the injustices a little longer, all the while giving them hope of the imminent arrival of a better tomorrow:

Aur kuch der bhatak le mere darmaada nadeem
Aur kuch din abhi zehraab ke saagar pee le
Noor-afshaan chali aati hai urus-e-farda
Haal, taareko-sam-afshaan sahi, lekin jee le[18]

(Wander on for only a few days more, o weary friend
Bear the humiliation just a little longer
A brighter future approaches
Your present, despicable it may be, but hold on just a little longer)

Sahir believed this better tomorrow would appear in the form of a communist state. For him, as for several other Progressive writers, communism alone was the solution to capitalism's many vices, the only real tonic for the proletariat's many woes:

Panaah leta hai jin mehbasaon ki teera nizaam
Wahin se subah ke lashkar nikalney waaley hain
Ubhar rahe hain fazaaon mein ahmari parcham
Kinaarey mashreeko-magrib ke milney waaley hain

---

17. From the poem 'Mere Geet Tumhaare Hain' (My Songs Are for You), published in *Talkhiyaan*.
18. From the poem 'Shuaa-e-Fardaa' (The Light of the Future), published in *Talkhiyaan*.

Hazaar barf girey laakh aandhiyaan uthey
Woh phool khil ke rahengey jo khilney waaley hain[19]

(Those factories in which this unjust government takes pride
From there shall arise the soldiers of tomorrow
Red flags sprout across the milieu
The corners of west and east are going to meet

No matter how many blizzards or storms obstruct the way
Those flowers will blossom whose time has come)

At the same time, while many of his poems – 'Ajnabi Muhafiz' (Unknown Travellers), 'Ehsaas-e-Kamraan' (A Feeling of Victory), among others – expressed his fascination and support for communism, Sahir did not believe that only a staunch communist could write Progressive literature.

'*Main nahin samajhta ke communist huey bina taraqqi pasand adab nahin paida kiya ja sakta. Koi bhi imaandaar shaayar aaj ki haalaton ka imaandaari se bayaan karey toh iska qalaam aagey badhne se ruk nahin sakta.*' (I do not believe that without being a communist it is not possible to produce Progressive literature. If any poet details today's circumstances with honesty, there is nothing that can stop him from writing Progressive literature.)[20]

If anything, he propagated that all writing must be an extension of the individual.

'While writing, the writer must remain true to his personality. Whatever he writes, his conscience must be a part of it . . . Literature, in reality, is the manner in which one expresses one's personality. It is a way of expressing one's self. If the writer writes contrary to his personality, his thought process, and writes bearing

---

19. From the poem 'Lahu Nazar De Rahi Hai Hayaat' (Mankind Offers Its Blood), published in *Talkhiyaan*.
20. Saabir Dutt, *Fann Aur Shaksiyat*, Sahir Ludhianvi Number, Balwant Singh, 'Hum Ke Thehere Ajnabee', p. 48.

in mind how he will be categorized, he will attain no satisfaction from his writing.'[21]

And so, if he was, through his poems in *Talkhiyaan*, 'A principled interlocutor, who insistently and powerfully critiques the structures of exploitation and their agents: the ruthless capitalist, the greedy usurer, the decadent priest, the bourgeois nationalist, the besotted lover, the rapacious colonialist and the self-absorbed poet',[22] this was primarily because of his personal experiences as a child leading into his youth.

In later years, Sahir would befriend one Prakash Pandit during his brief stay in Delhi after Partition. The two became extremely good friends and even worked together in a couple of literary publications in Delhi. Prakash Pandit spoke of Sahir's mother treating him like her own son in the introduction to his book on Sahir's poetry, *Sahir Ludhianvi (Life Sketch and Poetry)*. In that very introduction, Prakash Pandit also elaborates on Sahir's poetry being an outcome of his own experiences:

> Sahir came of age as a poet shortly after 'Iqbal' and 'Josh' [Malihabadi], when Firaq [Gorakhpuri], Faiz [Ahmed Faiz] and Majaz [Lucknawi] had not only become popular but were considered heavyweights in the field of poetry. It was obvious that in such an environment, any new poet would be influenced by men of such genius. Accordingly, Sahir, too, was heavily influenced by Majaz and Faiz. In fact, initially, when people sensed the delicate mood in Sahir's poetry, the beautiful interplay in his words and the lilting nature of his verse, they thought of it to be an absolute imitation of Faiz's poetry. But soon, his [Sahir's] own personal experiences came to the fore, his conscience tempered in the heat and fire of worldly sorrows showed him the way which led people to realize that instead of imitating

21. Prof. Dr Syed Zeyaur Rahman, *Sahir Ludhianvi: Hayaat Aur Shaayari*, p. 112.
22. Raza Mir and Ali Husain Mir, *Anthems of Resistance*, IndiaInk, 2006, p. 171.

Majaz and Faiz, Sahir's poetry bore its own distinctive stamp
. . . And I feel the reason Sahir earned a place much higher than
his contemporaries lay precisely in his unique personal
experiences which he presented without any hyperbole, except
the necessary creative embellishment. The venom and bitterness
he expressed towards society in his poetry were not borrowed,
but voiced the events of his own life.[23]

But perhaps the best compliment to *Talkhiyaan*'s quality, as indeed
to Sahir's attempt in bridging the gap between literary output and
the individual, was given by Sahir's peer and the late progressive
poet, Kaifi Azmi.

I often have to think whether I know Sahir through his poetry or
his poetry through him. However, I have to accept that I have
not reached any conclusion so far. It feels like Sahir has implanted
the subtle charms of his personality into his poetry and all the
magic of his poetry – he seems to have imbibed within his own
personality. 'Aayney se aayney gar ka ubharna' (From within the
mirror emerges its maker) might well be a metaphor, but on
reading *Talkhiyaan*, one will find the soul of the poet speaking
out loud and clear. And if you talk to the poet, you will know
that you are reading his poetry.[24]

Talkhiyaan did exceedingly well. In Sahir's own lifetime, twenty-
five editions of it had been published from Delhi, fourteen of which
were in Hindi. Countless other editions of the anthology have been
published in English, Russian and other languages. Legend has it
that in neighbouring Pakistan, where *Talkhiyaan* has been published
innumerable times, any individual looking to start a new publication
first publishes *Talkhiyaan*. Azhar Javed even goes to the extent of

23. Prakash Pandit, *Sahir Ludhianvi (Life Sketch and Poetry)*, Rajpal and Sons,
pp. 10–11.
24. Saabir Dutt, *Fann Aur Shaksiyat*, Sahir Ludhianvi Number, Kaifi Azmi, 'Mera
Hum Asra Mera Saathi', p. 302.

suggesting that *Talkhiyaan* is the most published work in Urdu literature after the *Diwan-e-Ghalib*.[25]

There is something hypnotic about Sahir's call for revolution in *Talkhiyaan*. No wonder, it had a Pied Piper effect on those who read it. His verses force an adrenaline rush when he writes:

Muskraa aye zameen-e-teer-o-taar
Sar uthaa aye dabee huyee makhlook . . .

Koi teri taraf nahin nigraan
Yeh giraan-baar, sard zanjeerey

Zang-khurda hain aahani hi sahi
Aaj mauka hai, toot sakti hain

Fursat-e-yak-nafas ghaneemat jaan
Sar uthaa aye dabee huyee makhlook[26]

(Smile, o inhabitants of this darkened earth
Raise your heads, o oppressed mankind . . .

No one looks at you
These heavy, callous chains

Made of iron, have rusted
Today there is an opportunity, they might break

Acknowledge the significance of this fleeting moment
Raise your heads, o oppressed mankind)

Despite the decades that have passed since these poems were first written, they continue to be relevant. There is remarkable prescience in the thoughts he articulated. While the benefits of globalization are being debated and the conflict between corporate and rural India plays itself out in the form of exploitation and land grabbing,

---

25. Azhar Javed, *Nakaamey Mohabbat*, Takhleeqkar Publishers, p. 12.
26. From the poem 'Lamha-e-Ghaneemat' (A Significant Moment), published in *Talkhiyaan*.

Sahir's 'Tarah-e-Nau' (A New Foundation), written around the time *Talkhiyaan* was published, warned of an impending uprising on these counts:

> *Fakakaashon ke khoon mein hai josh-e-inteqaam,*
> *Sarmaaya ke fareb-e-jahaan-parvaree ki khair*

(The hungry impoverished masses yearn for revenge
Let proponents of a treacherous capitalistic society beware)

Recognition for his rebellious brand of poetry came in the form of the title '*Inquilaabi Shaayar*' (The Revolutionary Poet). Then, when the All India Conference of Progressive Writers was convened in October 1945, in Hyderabad, Sahir was invited and he even presented 'a short but interesting paper on modern revolutionary poetry in Urdu'.[27]

More importantly, the success of his firebrand poetry spurred Sahir on to speak his mind when he established himself in the film industry. He regularly cried foul of the czars of capitalism as a lyricist, demanding an egalitarian society instead:

> *Takht na hoga, taaj na hoga, kal thaa lekin aaj na hoga*
> *Jisme sab adhikar na paaye, woh sachha swaraj na hoga*
>
> *Laakhon ki mehnat par kabza muthi bhar dhanwaano ka*
> *Deen dharam ke naam pe khooni batwaara insaano ka*
> *Jiska yeh itihaas raha hai ab woh andha raaj na hoga*
> *Jisme sab adhikar na paaye, woh sachha swaraj na hoga*
>
> *Janta ka farmaan chalega, janta ki sarkaar banegi*
> *Dharti ki behaq aabaadi, dharti ki haqdaar banegi*
> *Saamanti sarkar na hogi, poonjiwaad samaaj na hoga*
> *Jisme sab adhikar na paaye, woh sachha swaraj na hoga*[28]

---

27. Sajjad Zaheer, *The Light: A History of the Movement for Progressive Literature in the Indo-Pak Subcontinent*, a translation of *Roshnai*, Oxford University Press, 2006, p. 251.
28. The song '*Takht na hoga, taaj na hoga*' from the film *Aaj Aur Kal* (1963).

(There will be neither throne nor crown, it may have been there
      yesterday but today it shall not
Where everyone is not on an equal footing, that cannot be a real
      independence

Few wealthy lord over the hard work of millions
In the name of religion, macabre divisions take place between people
Those who have such a history, we cannot allow them to rule
Where everyone is not on an equal footing, that cannot be a real
      independence

The people shall rule, the people shall form the government
The fruit of the earth shall be for those who toil on it
There will be no feudalism, no place for capitalistic society
Where everyone is not on an equal footing, that cannot be a real
      independence)

The success of *Talkhiyaan* and his recognition as a young poet of
promise notwithstanding, Sahir had to grapple with the matter of
fending for himself and his mother (who at this time was in
Ludhiana). Commenting on his illustrious peer, Kaifi ponders upon
an inherent dilemma that faces most poets:

> How does one make a living is a thought that confronts every
> human being, but this issue is more complex in the context of
> our young poets and writers. Such people have to answer two
> questions simultaneously. How does one earn a living and how
> does one cultivate one's literary pursuits? It is difficult to live a
> life in unemployment.[29]

While in Lahore, Sahir worked as an editor at *Adab-e-Lateef*, a
popular literary publication which devoted itself to the objectives
of Progressive literature and furthering the cause of the Progressive
Writers' Movement. Such employment, though, did little to

---

29. Saabir Dutt, *Fann Aur Shaksiyat*, Sahir Ludhianvi Number, Kaifi Azmi, 'Mera
Hum Asra Mera Saathi', p. 291.

improve Sahir's economic condition. While his editorial column in *Adab-e-Lateef* became very popular, his indigent state can be best gauged by the fact that he earned a miserly wage of Rs 40 per month.

But the struggle to eke out an existence didn't entirely take away from the joy of living in Lahore and its literary ambience. Hameed Akhtar recalls:

> Both of us [Sahir and Hameed Akhtar] spent a lot of time in Lahore. We would walk around the entire city. From *Adab-e-Lateef's* office on Circle Road to Charing Cross, sometimes we would enjoy the tea at Crystal on Nisbat Road and on other occasions we would spend the evenings at Lorang's . . . At other times we would gather at Coffee House or at Nagina Bakery . . . We would discuss and debate everything under the sun – literature, politics, war, fascism – there was no topic outside our reach. Abdullah Butt, Gopal Matl, Ram Prakash Ashk, Dev Nadar Sitarthi and many other literary figures would grace these wonderful evenings. Every evening, people would gather, debate and disagree, but never get into a fight . . . [Saadat Hasan] Manto and [Ismat] Chughtai also happened to visit Lahore at this time from Bombay for some legal proceedings. Their presence further improved the literary quality of these gatherings.[30]

But Sahir yearned for more. By the end of 1945, the employment with *Adab-e-Lateef* had come to an end and Sahir was on the lookout for some other source of income. He had wanted to write songs for films for quite some time, and so, in late 1945, when he was asked to write a few songs for the film *Azaadi Ki Raah Par*, which starred Prithviraj Kapoor, Sahir decided to grab the opportunity.

However, not wanting to make the journey to Bombay alone,

---

30. Saabir Dutt, *Fann Aur Shaksiyat*, Sahir Ludhianvi Number, Hameed Akhtar, 'Sahir: Mera Bachpan Ka Dost', p. 145, and Hameed Akhtar, *Ashnaiyaan Kya Kya*, p. 102.

Sahir convinced Hameed Akhtar to come with him, but not before he had sought work for Hameed too with Hindustan Kalamandir, the production company making the film.

In January 1946, Sahir Ludhianvi made his way to the city of Bombay.

4

Partition Woes

Yeh jaltey huey ghar kiske hain, yeh kat-tey huey tann kiske hain
Takseem ke andhey toofaan mein, lut-tey huey gulshan kiske hain . . .
E-rehbar-mulk-o-kaum bata, yeh kiska lahu hai, kaun mara?[1]

(Whose houses are these that burn, these bodies that are being
butchered – to whom do they belong?
In this great mayhem caused by partition, these gardens that are being
desecrated to whom do they belong? . . .
O leaders of our nation and community, tell us, whose blood is this,
who died here?)

'Sajjad Zaheer's house, which the followers of the communist ideology used as a dharamshala, was on Walkeshwar Road. One night, we fell asleep after discussing the communal riots in the country. But one among us could not sleep. He remained anxious through the night. When we woke up in the morning, we found this man frantically combing the thick, black hair on his head. He was muttering under his breath, "*Mere Punjab mein aag lagi toh aasaani se nahin bujhegi, badi barbaadi hogi*" (If my

---

1. From the song '*Yeh kiska lahu hai, kaun mara?*' (Whose blood is this, who died here?) in *Dharamputra* (1961).

Punjab is consumed by these communal flames, it shall not be doused easily. There will be a great deal of bloodshed). It was Sahir Ludhianvi. His eyes were red. Sleep had deserted him and he was distraught at the prospect of violence in Punjab,' writes Dr Zoe Ansari, the eminent Urdu critic and a fellow Progressive writer, in a telling description of the effect of Partition on Sahir Ludhianvi.[2]

Towards the end of 1944, a large number of Progressive writers, most of whom had established links with the film industry or journalism, moved to Bombay. Krishan Chander, Saghar Nizami, Akhtarul Iman, Majaz (Lucknawi), (Moin Ahsan) Jazbi, Kaifi Azmi, Jan Nisar Akhtar, Hajra Masroor, Khadija Masroor and Majrooh Sultanpuri were some of the prominent names in this list. Even the legendary Indian writer Mulk Raj Anand, who wrote in English and had strong Progressive leanings, returned to India from England in 1945 and settled in Bombay. Sardar Jafri, Khwaja Ahmad Abbas and Sibte Hasan had already been in the city for some time. Some other Progressives, like Makhdoom Moheeuddin, also came unfailingly from other parts of the country to attend the activities of the association in Bombay.

Sahir Ludhianvi's journey to Bombay in early 1946 thus served a dual purpose. It introduced Sahir to the world of films and allowed him to befriend some of the finest luminaries of Urdu literature at that time.

This group of Urdu Progressive writers met every week to discuss various issues pertaining to Progressive literature. The meetings were held in the evenings and the attendance was anywhere between fifteen and fifty persons. Sahir's quick-wittedness manifested itself in no uncertain terms at such meetings.

The topic under discussion one week was literary stagnation.

---

2. Saabir Dutt, *Fann Aur Shaksiyat*, Sahir Ludhianvi Number, Dr Zoe Ansari, 'Sahir Ki Yaad Mein', p. 149.

The issues of sloganeering and jingoism in literature were also being discussed. Sahir, who had written a scathing critique of Kaifi Azmi's poetry using literary logic, pointed out that Kaifi was not a poet and if he was one, then of the most ordinary kind. This assessment was read out in the meeting, which was being chaired by Sardar Jafri. Sahir's point was generally well received and even though Sardar Jafri tried to soften Sahir's critique, the latter's point had struck home.

In the next meeting, held the following week, Sardar Jafri spoke on the subject of Sahir's poetry. He said that Sahir's poem 'Taj Mahal' had insulted an emblem that was part of the nation's rich heritage. In doing so, Sahir had revealed himself as parochial. He was a bad poet and his poetry bordered on the ridiculous.

Sahir heard Jafri's virulent outburst patiently. When Jafri finished, Sahir asked him, 'Is mazmoon se aap yeh saabit kar sakte hain ki Sahir Ludhianvi shaayar nahin hai, magar isse yeh kahaan saabit hota hai ke Kaifi Azmi achcha shaayar hai?' (Through this critique you may prove that Sahir Ludhianvi is no poet, but how does this establish that Kaifi is a good poet?)[3]

As part of the Bombay Association of Progressive Writers, Sahir, Sardar Jafri, Majrooh and Kaifi frequently travelled to Malegaon, Ahmedabad and Surat between early 1946 and mid-1947 to further the agenda of the Progressive Writers' Movement. They attended mushairas and often recited from their works on popular demand. Shaukat Kaifi, Kaifi Azmi's wife, and mother of film actor Shabana Azmi, recalls that it was mandatory for Sahir to recite 'Taj Mahal', while Kaifi would not be allowed to get off the stage without reciting his acclaimed poem 'Aurat'.

While both Progressive writers and other poets participated in mushairas, it was the former, 'who brought the house down, as

---

3. Prof. Dr Syed Zeyaur Rahman, Sahir Ludhianvi: Hayaat Aur Shaayari, p. 34.

cries of *vah vah* would resonate in the hall'.[4] This was because their poetry engaged the common man. It concerned itself with politics and the lives of ordinary people. Unlike traditional Urdu poetry, which focussed essentially on '*husn*' (beauty), '*saaki*' (lover), and '*ulfat*' (love), Progressive writing highlighted the hardships of the '*mazdoor*' (worker), the travails of the '*muflis*' (poor) and the unfortunate plight of the '*jamhoor*' (masses).

However, not everything about these mushairas was to Sahir's liking. The crowds may have wanted to hear his poems repeatedly, but facing a large gathering always unnerved Sahir, despite his past as a student leader. On approaching the microphone, he was almost always left tongue-tied. His problem would be compounded if one section of the audience asked him to recite 'Taj Mahal' while the other clamoured for 'Fankaar' (Artist). 'Torn between two different requests, the poem that Sahir had actually chosen to recite would disappear from his mind,' writes Kaifi in the context of Sahir's plight.[5]

This indecisiveness extended to the selection of attire, which was the cause of much splitting of hair. Sahir could never make up his mind on what to wear. The best of clothes would be bought and stitched for him, but he had to be helped, much like a child, in the selection of his outfit. Otherwise, he would just take everything out of the cupboard and create a mess, turning the whole room upside down. The smallest stain on his vest would anger him and he would ask if he was expected to wear such a vest.

If his cousins Anwar and Sarwar Shafi, accompanying him to the mushaira, were ready and his predicament had not yet been sorted, he would sulk, remarking, '*Dekhiye, yeh log taiyyaar ho gayee hain jaisey*

---

4. Shaukat Kaifi, *Kaifi & I: A Memoir*, edited and translated by Nasreen Rehman, Zubaan, 2010, p. 50.
5. Saabir Dutt, *Fann Aur Shaksiyat*, Sahir Ludhianvi Number, Kaifi Azmi, 'Mera Hum Asra Mera Saathi', p. 303.

inhey mushaira padhna hai aur jisey mushaira padhna hai, uskey kapdey tak durust nahin hai' (Look, they have got dressed as if they have to recite at the mushaira while the one who has to actually do so, his clothes are not yet ready).[6]

All this while, Sahir and Hameed Akhtar remained inseparable in Bombay. Sajjad Zaheer describes their friendship in glowing terms:

At first we knew Hameed Akhtar only as Sahir Ludhianvi's friend. Although there was a world of difference between their temperaments, their friendship had become proverbial. It was rare for anyone to meet them separately. Tall and slim, like parallel lines, the two of them were always seen together, whether it was at somebody's house, at a teahouse, in a meeting, or in their own homes.[7]

Hameed has his own vivid recollection of those days in Bombay:

Sahir had called for Ibrahim Jalees [another Urdu writer] from Hyderabad. The three of us lived together in the company [Hindustan Kalamandir] flat. Bombay, in those days, was a hub for Progressive writers – Sajjad Zaheer, Krishan Chander, Saadat Hasan Manto, Ali Sardar Jafri, Kaifi Azmi, Majrooh Sultanpuri – we were together in this vast, strange city. Most of them were related to films, but all of them were deeply involved with the changing situation in the country at that time . . . There would be meetings and conferences of the PWM every week. Everyone wanted the country to attain freedom. Materialism had still not come into vogue. There was more focus on the general emancipation of man. . . .

Sometime later, a fourth person by the name of Dirinder Devdas came to live with us in that flat . . . We lived together

6. Ibid., Mahmood Ayoobi, 'Anwar Bibi Ke Bhaijaan', p. 43.
7. Sajjad Zaheer, *The Light: A History of the Movement for Progressive Literature in the Indo-Pak Subcontinent*, a translation of *Roshnai*, Oxford University Press, 2006, p. 216.

for about a year and a half. All of us were very good friends and nothing remained hidden from anyone . . . These were not good days from the point of remuneration. Our salaries would vanish by the tenth of every month . . . and then the search for an advance would begin in right earnest . . . In those days, the storywriter Saeed Anwar, who was also an officer in the Indian Navy and was from Ludhiana, was based in Bombay. We became friendly with him. When we had no money, we would go to his house in Colaba, eat dinner and then request him for a loan of twenty-thirty rupees, which we always got but never returned. But the problem was that this loan was always given to us by cheque. Anwar never kept loose cash in the house. We would take the cheque and curse him through the entire journey back to our house, because someone would have to get up in the morning and go to Anwar's bank to collect the money. This continued for a long time.[8]

Gradually though, as the months passed and August of 1947 approached, the spectre of Partition threw its gory shadow over Bombay, as it did over the rest of the country. For Sahir, the calamitous event threw up challenges through his role in the Progressive Writers' Movement and on the personal front.

The Progressives played a stellar role in promoting harmony in the face of the rabid communalism of the time. They would urge the importance of unity through their literature and take part in processions to spread the message of peace. Khwaja Ahmed Abbas, fellow Progressive, film-maker and scriptwriter, writes of one such procession organized in Bombay on the eve of Independence:

> I remember that in all fifty-two associations [various progressive cultural associations] were mobilised to take out a unity procession that would parade from Bori Bunder to Bandra, passing through exclusively Hindu and Muslim areas, thus

---

8. Hameed Akhtar, *Ashnaiyaan Kya Kya*, pp. 93–94.

removing the unseen barriers that were dividing Bombay into little bits of 'Hindu Bombay' and 'Muslim Bombay'. The procession was a great success. We had different trucks – one with Prithviraj Kapoor, the doyen of film heroes, and his young teenaged sons – Raj Kapoor and Shammi Kapoor – beating the big drum. The IPTA [Indian People's Theatre Association] truck had Balraj Sahni and Prem Dhawan and Chetan Anand and Dev Anand. The Urdu Progressive writers were represented by Sajjad Zaheer, Ali Sardar Jafri, Kaifi Azmi, Sahir Ludhianvi and Majrooh Sultanpuri.[9]

Sahir would vent his disappointment at the turn of events through his poetry too. In his poem 'Mafaahmat' (A Compromise), written on Independence Day (15 August 1947), he issued an unequivocal warning that the freedom attained at the altar of communal hate had a hollow ring to it. He feared that Independence gained at such a cost would only snowball into a problem of far greater magnitude for the nation:

Yeh jashn, jash-e-masarrat nahin, tamaasha hai
Naye libaas mein nikla hain rahzani ka juloos
Hazaar shamaa-e-akhuvvat bujhakey chamkey hai
Yeh teergi ke ubhaarey huey haseen faanoos

Yeh shaak-e-noor jise zulmaton mein seencha hain
Agar fali toh sharaaron ke phool laayegi
Na phal saki toh nayee fasl-e-gul ke aaney tak
Zameer-e-arz mein ik zehar chhod jaayegi

(This celebration, is not one of joy, but a circus
In the guise of something new, the attempt to plunder is afoot
After putting out the lights on communal harmony, this radiance
Is of those lanterns that have been nurtured in the dark

---

9. Khwaja Ahmed Abbas, *I Am Not an Island: An Experiment in Autobiography*, Imprint One, 2010, pp. 194–95.

Such light that has been cultivated from the throes of darkness
If it spreads, shall only spark many a flame
And if it does not spread, until the break of a new dawn
Will poison this nation's soul)

While Sahir was in Bombay in the months leading up to Partition, his mother was still in Ludhiana where he had left her after quitting Government College and during his stay in Lahore. Since Ludhiana was not too far from the epicentre of the violence arising due to Partition, Sahir had to fetch her from there.

On his way, Sahir passed through Delhi, where he stayed with a couple of friends for a few weeks and experienced the rioting first-hand. It was during his stay in Delhi, on 11 September 1947, that Sahir recited the poem 'Aaj' (Today) on All India Radio. He appears to have been deeply traumatized by the violence and wrote the poem as a reaction to the carnage. The anguish in it is palpable. Through it, Sahir made an impassioned plea to the citizens of the nation to put a stop to the senseless bloodletting and make the most of the opportunity that awaited an independent India:

Saathiyon! maine barson tumhaare liye
Chaand, taaron, bahaaron ke sapne bunein . . .

Aaj lekin mere daaman-e-chaak mein
Gard-raahein-safar ke siva kuch nahin
Mere barbat ke seeney mein naghmon ka dum ghut gaya hai
Taaney cheekhon ke ambaar mein dab gayee hain
Aur geeton ke sur hichkiyaan bann gaye hain
Main tumhaara muganni hoon, naghma nahin hoon
Aur naghme hi takhleeq ka saaz-o-samaan
Saathiyon! Aaj tumney bhasm kar diya hai . . .

Aur main is tabaahi ke toofaan mein
Aag aur khoon ke haijaan mein
Sarningoon aur shikastaa makaano ke malbey se pur raaston par
Apney naghmon ki jholi pasaarey

Dar-ba-dar phir raha hoon
Mujhko aman aur tehzeeb ki bheek do
Mere geeton ki lai, mere sur, meri nai
Mere majrooh hoton ko phir saunp do . . .

Aaj zanjeer-e-mahakumiyat cut chuki hai
Aur is mulk ke bahr-o-bar, baam-o-dar
Ajnabi kaum ke zulmat-afsha pharere ki manhoos chhaon se aazaad hain
Khet sona ugalne ko bechain hain
Waadiyaan lehlahaane ko betaab hain
Kohsaaron ke seeney mein haijaan hain
Sang aur khisht bekhwaabon-bedaar hain
Unki aankhon mein taamir ke khwaab hain
Unkey khwaabon ko takmeel ka roop do . . .

Aaj saari fazaa hai bhikaari
Aur main is bhikaari fazaa mein apney naghmon ki jholi pasaarey
Dar-ba-dar phir raha hoon
Mujhko phir mera khoya hua saaz do
Main tumhaara muganni, tumhaare liye
Jab bhi aaya naye geet laata rahoonga

(Comrades, for years together
I dreamt of a heaven for you . . .

But today
I have nothing but the dust of the journey to offer
The melody has been stifled within my musical instruments
The chords have been drowned in the plethora of cries
And the notes of a song have been reduced to a few hiccups
I am your musician, not your composition
And the ambience in which a song is composed
Comrades! Today you have destroyed . . .

And in this typhoon of destruction
In this furiousness of fire and blood
On streets full of debris of broken and beaten houses
With my bag of compositions

I roam about, from pillar to post
Give me peace and compassion as alms
Give me back the mellifluousness of my songs, my melody, my
    flute,
Give them back to my wounded lips . . .

Today the chains of suppression have been removed
And the nation's oceans and lands, its roofs and doors,
Are freed of the shadow that the horrid darkness of foreign rule
    brings
The fields are anxious to produce gold
The valleys are eager to turn verdant
The mountains are brimming with fury
The stones and bricks are awake
Their eyes filled with dreams of new beginnings
Give shape and form to their dreams . . .

Today the entire ambience is reduced to begging
And in this desperate environment
I, with my bag of compositions,
Roam about from pillar to post
Give me back my lost melody
I, your musician
Whenever I come, shall continue to bring you new compositions)

Since Ludhiana also was besieged by communal forces at this time, Sahir was not able to go there. Meanwhile, he received information through some friends that his mother had found her way to Lahore as part of a 'muhajir' camp. Fluctuating between the twin emotions of hope and despair, Sahir reached Lahore from Delhi in September 1947, where he was relieved to learn that his mother was safe and living at his friend Sorish Kashmiri's house. Sahir reached Sorish's house where mother and son were finally reunited.

Hameed Akhtar too returned to Lahore from Bombay shortly thereafter, in November 1947. The three of them (including Sahir's mother) took up a rented accommodation on Abott Road, in front of Nishaad cinema. However, Hameed Akhtar's return did little to cheer up Sahir. He had been calmed by his friend's arrival but was a bundle of nerves nevertheless.

Lahore had been home to Sahir in the recent past. He had a lot of fond memories of the place. In a sense, Lahore too was part of his own country, yet Sahir found it difficult to adjust to the city in the changed environment after Partition. He was unwilling to live there and his mother shared his sentiment. Both were broad-minded individuals who had enjoyed living with people from all hues of life, irrespective of caste, creed and religious backgrounds.

Despite his misgivings about Lahore in this changed milieu, Sahir stayed on in the city for a while. He found work as the editor of a bimonthly magazine called *Savera* (The Dawn).

Around this time, some distinguished figures of the Muslim community, notable among them Saadat Hasan Manto, relocated to Pakistan to the dismay of their Indian brethren both within and outside their own community. K.A. Abbas writes of this development:

> I felt no hatred for Pakistan or Pakistanis. How could I when there were my relations, my friends whom I admired and loved? But [contradictory as it might seem] I was dismayed by the concept of 'one religion, one country' which was at the root of Pakistan. I felt instinctively antagonistic to this concept, and whatever the rationalizations of the fait accompli, I would never be able to make peace with this concept ... While I wished Pakistanis all luck in building up their country, it became a secret obsession of mine to try and bring back at least some intellectuals who belonged to Indian areas, but who had been persuaded by family considerations, or by political compulsions to migrate to Pakistan.
>
> In 1948, I wrote an 'Open Letter to Sahir Ludhianvi' in the now defunct *India Weekly* in which I appealed to this young Indian poet to return to India. I reminded him that so long as he

did not change his name, he would forever be regarded as an Indian poet, unless Pakistan invaded and conquered Ludhiana. To my surprise, some copies of the paper did find their way to Lahore where Sahir read it.[10]

Abbas's opinion of Pakistan's conception resonated with the restlessness Sahir felt in his own mind. He voiced his fears to Hameed Akhtar saying, '*Yahaan mullah, maulvi aur jageerdaar ki huqumat ho jaayegi.*' (Religious zealots and the affluent will rule over this nation in days to come.)

Meanwhile, the Pakistani authorities also started clamping down on the right to free speech and writing in a ruthless manner. As the editor of *Savera*, Sahir often wrote scathing critiques of the new nation state which had been carved out of undivided India. In his poem 'Aawaaz-e-Aadam' (The Voice of Adam), he condemned the Pakistani establishment for their insular approach towards the Progressive writers exercising their freedom of expression. He even warned them of an imminent reversal in fortunes coming at the hands of the masses:

> *Mukaafaat-e-amal, taareekh-e-insaan ki rivaayat hai*
> *Karoge kab talak naawak faraaham, hum bhi dekhenge*
> *Kahaan tak hain tumhaarey zulm mein dum hum bhi dekhengey*
>
> *Yeh hungaamey-vida-e-shab hai ae zulmat ke farzando,*
> *Sehar ke dosh par gulnaar parcham hum bhi dekhengey*
>
> (What one sows is what one reaps, this is the history of mankind
> For how much longer will you punish us, we shall also see
> How much more crippling can your injustices be, we shall also see
>
> The time for the darkness of the night to pass is nigh, o scions of
>   darkness,
> The red flag appearing at dawn shall be for everyone to see)

---

10. Ibid., pp. 202–03.

Needless to say, such inflammatory writings didn't go down particularly well with the authorities in Pakistan. The government issued an arrest warrant against Sahir and sometime in June 1948, he fled from Lahore to Delhi. Hameed Akhtar, who was away in Karachi at the time, was devastated by the sudden departure of his friend.

> When I came back from Karachi I found the house empty. After going to Delhi, Sahir had sent Prakash Pandit to bring his mother from Lahore. I felt very sad because the house that we had built, bit by bit – by borrowing a pillow from somewhere, a rug from someone else, a desk and a couple of chairs had been sent over by a kind friend – had been ransacked. I had once again been reduced to the level of a refugee. Once again, I had been robbed of a mother's affection. I could find shelter nowhere. I could not stay in this house or sleep in it and so I just left the house open and came away. The very next day the house was usurped by someone else. At this time I felt very angry with Sahir. I even remember complaining to some friends about him, but as time passed my wounds healed. I realized that the kind of opportunities Sahir would get in India, he would not find here.[11]

Sahir's arrival in India also marked a permanent, geographical separation from his father Chaudhri Fazl Mohammed, who migrated to Pakistan where he lived in Lyallpur (now Faisalabad) till the end of his days in 1964.

Prakash Pandit, whom Sahir had sent to Lahore to fetch his mother, was not surprised by the poet's decision to leave Lahore. According to him, 'Sahir could not have remained happy in Lahore. This is because he was surrounded by members of the same community over there . . . He was unable to bear the separation of friends who belonged to the Hindu and Sikh communities and

---

11. Hameed Akhtar, *Ashnaiyaan Kya Kya*, p. 97.

among whom he had spent all his life . . . That is why, when I met him in Delhi, I was not in the least bit surprised.'[12]

Delhi was merely a stopover for Sahir on the way to his final destination, Bombay, where, according to him, the film world was eagerly awaiting his arrival. Nonetheless, he stayed on in Delhi for a year.

While in Delhi, Sahir and his mother stayed with Prakash in the Pul Bangash locality of Delhi. Josh Malihabadi, another great Progressive poet, stayed in the same locality during this time. Sahir and Prakash worked together in the editorial department of a couple of Urdu publications called *Shah-raah* and *Preetladi*.

Much like his days at *Adab-e-Lateef* in Lahore, employment at the Delhi publications didn't exactly deliver Sahir into the lap of luxury. He struggled to make ends meet. While empathy towards the downtrodden remained an enduring hallmark of his poetry, he wanted a better life for himself and his mother.

With the ambition of joining the film industry, Sahir ultimately decided to bid adieu to independent India's capital city. Shortly after attending the fifth all-India conference of the Progressive Writers' Movement in Bombay, he returned to Delhi for a brief while. Thereafter, he went to Hyderabad, which had emerged as a major centre for the Progressive writers, from where he finally left for Bombay in May 1949 to fulfil his long-cherished desire of working as a lyricist in the Hindi film industry.

The sudden upheaval caused by Partition had left a profound psychological impact on Sahir. Having enjoyed the company of individuals from all communities since he was a child, he was appalled at the barbarism he had witnessed at such close quarters. Yet, there was an awareness, an intelligence within him that discerned and understood that sinister forces had engineered those

---

12. Prakash Pandit, *Sahir Ludhianvi (Life Sketch and Poetry)*, Rajpal and Sons, pp. 5–6.

gruesome course of events. He felt a lasting abhorrence towards all merchants of hate. But instead of letting it fester within and consume him, like it did so many others, he took the poetic discourse to remind human beings of the oneness of man.

The 1959 movie *Dhool Ka Phool* tells the story of an abandoned child, born out of wedlock to Mahesh (Rajendra Kumar) and Meena (Mala Sinha), the film's protagonists. Abdul Chacha (Manmohan Krishan), an elderly Muslim, finds the child and decides to take him home. But the members of the Hindu and Muslim communities in Abdul Chacha's neighbourhood question the antecedents of the child and object to his presence in the locality. Sahir responded to these divisive forces, in what has since become the definitive Hindi film song on Hindu–Muslim unity, with sarcasm and rage:

Tu Hindu banega na Musalmaan banega
Insaan ki aulaad hai insaan banega . . .

Maalik ne har insaan ko insaan banaaya
Humney usay Hindu ya Musalmaan banaya
Kudrat ne toh bakshi thi humein ek hi dharti
Humney kahin Bharat, kahin Iran banaaya

Jo tod de har bandh, woh toofan banega
Insaan ki aulaad hai insaan banega . . .

Yeh deen ke taajir, yeh watan bechney waaley
Insaanon ki laashon ke kafan bechne waaley
Yeh mehlon mein baithey huey kaatil, yeh lutere
Kaanton ke ewaz rooh-e-chaman bechney waaley

Tu inke liye maut ka elaan banega
Insaan ki aulaad hai insaan banega

(You will neither become a Hindu nor a Muslim
You are the child of man, you will become a human being . . .

The Almighty made everyone the same
It is we who branded him a Hindu or a Muslim

Nature bequeathed us one earth
It is we who carved an India or an Iran from it

He who clears every obstacle, you shall be that invincible force
You are the child of man, you will become a human being . . .

These merchants of faith, these traitors of the motherland
These traders who deal in dead bodies
These murderers, these thieves who rejoice in palaces
Those who trade these beautiful environs for hate

You shall come sounding their death knell
You are the child of man, you will become a human being)

5

'Bada Songwriter Banoonga'

Tadbeer se bigdi hui, taqdeer bana le
Apne pe bharosa hai toh ek daon laga le[1]

(Through action mend your rotten luck
If you believe in yourself, play the odds this once)

The Urdu word *takiyakalaam* literally translates to an 'oft-repeated word or phrase'. One that found its way into Sahir's vocabulary every time discussions between him and Hameed Akhtar veered towards Sahir's future was '*bada songwriter banoonga*' (I will become a prominent songwriter).

Sahir's fascination for the world of films was no sudden whim. Neither did he covet acceptability in cinema purely as a way to make a better living. Sahir's confidence in articulating '*bada songwriter banoonga*' was born out of a belief in his songwriting skills rather than dreams of future glory.

Having moved to Bombay in 1949, Sahir and his mother stayed at the legendary Urdu short-story writer Krishan Chander's house, Koover Lodge, in Versova. Since *Azaadi Ki Raah Par* (1948), the

---

1. From the song '*Tadbeer se bigdi hui, taqdeer bana le*' in *Baazi* (1951).

film for which Sahir had come from Lahore to Bombay in early 1946, had gone unnoticed, Sahir had to re-establish himself in the film world. Although he wrote four songs for *Azaadi Ki Raah Par*, none of them made any lasting impact. Its only significance in the rich oeuvre Sahir would eventually create for himself as a lyricist lies in one of the songs, 'Badal rahi hai zindagi'. Even if it was penned purely in response to the film's central motif, Independence, it echoed the hope characteristic of so many of Sahir's Progressive poems:

Yeh ujdi ujdi bastiyaan, yeh loot ki nishaaniyaan
Yeh ajnani pe ajnabi ke zulm ki nishaaniyaan
Ab in dukhon ke bhaar se nikal rahi hai zindagi
Badal rahi hai zindagi

(These ravaged hutments, these visuals of plunder
These atrocities inflicted by all kinds of strangers
Life finally appears to be freeing itself from such tyranny
Life is changing)

Despite the tepid response to *Azaadi Ki Raah Par*, it seemed only a matter of time before this gifted poet got a foothold in the film industry, given that his eminence as a Progressive poet was firmly established following the success of *Talkhiyaan*. But not everything went according to plan.

Sahir was a notoriously late riser. His mornings began closer to the time when people stopped for lunch. Yet, when he found his poetic credentials not opening any doors for him, this lad of leisure awoke as early as six in the morning. This, so that he could begin his rounds of the numerous film studios in the hope of finding work. If anything, his reputation as a poet only stymied his chances, for no producer was willing to risk a poet doing a lyricist's job. They were apprehensive about introducing the literary element in a medium that otherwise catered to the masses.

Krishan Adeeb explains the film-makers' dilemma in taking Sahir on board for a film:

> Sahir would go to the studios. Producers and directors would stand up in respect of his poetic stature. But the moment the topic of songwriting came to the fore, all of them would say, 'Sahir Saab! You are one of India's greatest poets. We have great regard for your poetry. But a film is made in eight lakh rupees and it is not necessary that a good literary poet can also become a good songwriter. And a film can also flop if its songs are poorly written.'[2]

If poetic pedigree proved to be an obstacle in Sahir's dream of becoming a lyricist, there was the additional hurt of dealing with tactless remarks:

> Shaheed Lateef, who was a successful producer/director, and had made hit films like *Ziddi* (1948) and *Arzoo* (1950), one day told Sahir, 'Sahir Saab! We do not deny that you are a poet of the highest quality. In the world of poetry, you enjoy an altogether different stature, which is why asking you to write songs for a film is inviting a great deal of trouble. If your financial circumstances are not good, you should not hesitate to eat at our house.' Sahir, who had fed people all his life, was naturally offended by this.[3]

Also, as Krishan Adeeb alleges, even when his songs were accepted by music directors, they would either not be filmed or would be credited to another lyricist.

There came a time when Sahir had to sell his mother's gold bangles to pay the electricity and water bills. He even rewrote and faired out Krishan Chander's unintelligible handwriting from the latter's scripts, for a measly sum of Rs 150, to make ends meet.

---

2. Saabir Dutt, *Fann Aur Shaksiyat*, Sahir Ludhianvi Number, Krishan Adeeb, 'Sahir: Yaadon Ke Aaynein Mein', pp. 508–09.
3. Ibid.

But Sahir didn't give up. He remained cheerful despite all his tribulations. His only explanation for his exacting circumstances was, 'Yaar yeh Bambai shehar hai, jo baahar se aaney waalon se kam-se-kam do saal tak jad-o-jehad maangta hai, aur iskey baad, bade pyaar se apne gale laga leta hai.' (My friend, this is Bombay. Here, every newcomer has to struggle for at least a couple of years before he finds acceptance.)[4]

Having spent a year in Bombay, following a protracted period of struggle, Sahir finally got the break that he had long waited for. Mohan Segal, a friend of Sahir's, told him that S.D. Burman, the music director, was on the lookout for a lyricist and that Burman appreciated new talent.

Acting on Segal's tip, Sahir went to meet Burman at the Green Hotel in Khar. As the story goes, there was a 'Please do not disturb' sign outside Burman's room, but Sahir took this to be of no more significance than the 'Please don't make noise' sign in a coffee house. He walked straight into Burman's room, introduced himself, and gave his reason for being there. Because Burman was Bengali, and essentially a composer, he was unaware of Sahir's stature in the world of Urdu literature. Yet, he greeted Sahir and gave him the film's tune and situation and asked Sahir to write some lyrics corresponding to the same.

While the task proposed by Burman appeared a fairly straightforward one for someone of Sahir's capability, there were a couple of complexities involved. Poetry is free of any predefined boundaries. The poet is not confined by a melody, a film's situation or the language of its protagonists. He is, therefore, solely responsible for his creative output in terms of theme, writing style and the language of the poem. Songwriting, on the other hand, is a diametrically opposite experience. Here, a lyricist has to write within the framework of the melody, bearing in mind the film's

---

4. Ibid.

situation while giving due recognition to the language of the movie and its characters.

It is in this context that Sahir's expertise over his craft shone through. Undaunted by the constraints of writing to a melody, Sahir requested Burman to play the tune once again. Burman obliged. As the notes wafted out of Burman's harmonium, an inspired Sahir wrote 'Thandi hawaein, lehra ke aayein, rut hai jawaan, tum ho yahaan, kaise bhulayein' (A pleasant breeze blows gently. The night is young, you are here, how does one feign ignorance?).

When Burman heard the lyrics, he was overjoyed. He immediately took Sahir to Kardar Studios so that he could present his new discovery to producer-director A.R. Kardar. It was a breakthrough moment for the young man, whose chequered journey from Ludhiana to Lahore to Delhi to Bombay had finally paid dividends.

'Thandi hawaein' was written and composed for the film Naujawan (1951). Its lilting melody formed the ideal backdrop for the heroine (Nalini Jaywant) to gush over her joy of being in love:

Dil ke fasaane, dil bhi na jaane
Tumko sajan, dil ki lagan, kaise bataaye?

(Matters of the heart, are oblivious to the heart as well
To you, o beloved, the heart's desires, how does one tell?)

The song, sung by Lata Mangeshkar, was an instant hit. It set the Burman–Sahir combine on its way to success for some years to come.[5]

Sahir's entry into the film industry in 1951 coincided with the arrival of a generation of songwriters who, through the genius of their work, would provide the Hindi film song its finest hour through the 1950s and early 1960s.

---

5. The mention of the circumstances leading to Sahir writing 'Thandi hawaein' is not to suggest that this was Sahir Ludhianvi's first song in Hindi cinema. That distinction goes to Azaadi Ki Raah Par, which released in 1948. The consistent

(Contd...)

Majrooh Sultanpuri was the first of the lot, having written the songs for *Shahjehan* which released in 1946. Shakeel Badayuni debuted in 1947 as the songwriter of *Dard*, while Rajinder Krishan too wrote his first lyrics for the film *Junta* that released in the same year. Shailendra became indispensable to Raj Kapoor's films beginning with *Barsaat* in 1949 and Kaifi Azmi joined these men in 1951 with the songs of *Buzdil*. Barring Shailendra and Rajinder Krishan, these lyricists (also Hasrat Jaipuri who debuted alongside Shailendra in *Barsaat*) predominantly fashioned the use of the Urdu language in their songs. Before them, lyricists like Kidar Sharma, D.N. Madhok and Kavi Pradeep largely used Hindi or local dialects thereof while writing lyrics for films in the 1930s and 1940s.

My quest for an authoritative view on the lyrics of that period led me to Manohar Iyer's doorstep in Mumbai. Manohar has a passion for the Hindi film song like few others. There is hardly a song, a music director, a playback singer or a lyricist from the 1930s to the 1970s that he cannot speak on convincingly. Having quit his job in the Industrial Development Bank of India (IDBI) in the early 1990s, Manohar founded Keep Alive, an organization through which he celebrates the legacy of the Hindi film song by commemorating its past masters. He has a terrific memory and an equally perceptive mind that helps separate the extraordinary from the banal. But beyond all his expertise, Manohar is a genuinely unselfish, helpful soul. I couldn't have hoped for a better voice on the matter.

'The films in those years [1930s and '40s] belonged to a broad spectrum. They ranged from socially relevant films [*Chandidas*, 1934;

(Contd...)

mention of this anecdote, of Sahir approaching S.D. Burman, in various accounts on Sahir, however, obviates the case of Sahir having written the songs of *Baazi* and *Sazaa*, the music for both of which was scored by S.D. Burman and both of which released in 1951, before he wrote *Naujawan* and to document the circumstances leading to the pairing between Sahir and S.D. Burman.

Achhut Kanya, 1936], to historical or period films [*Sikandar*, 1941; *Humayun*, 1945], or those that were mythological in nature [*Puran Bhakt*, 1933; *Ram Rajya*, 1943], to films that were works of fiction or based on love stories [*Kismet*, 1943; *Anmol Ghadi*, 1946]. These films, essentially, had a theatrical style of music and lyrics that complemented it. The lyrics were presented in pure or Sanskritized Hindi, had a nationalistic and socialistic flavour and were steeped in tradition and culture,' said Manohar on the kind of lyrics that were in vogue right after sound came to Hindi cinema.

Manohar then pointed to three songs to give an idea of the kind of language that was popularly used in film songs in those days:

From *Chandidas* (1934):

> *Prem nagar mein banaaungi ghar main taj ke ghar sansaar*
> *Prem ka aangan, prem ki chhat aur prem ke hongey dwaar . . .*
> *Prem ke sang bitaayengey jeevan, prem hi pran adhaar . . .*
> *Prem sudha se snaan karungi, prem se hoga singaar*
> *Prem hi dharm hai, prem hi karm hai, prem hi satya vichaar*

> (I will make my house in the city of love by spurning this material
>   world
> A house, whose courtyard, ceilings and walls are made of love
> We will live our lives in love, love will be the premise of our
>   lives
> I will bathe in the nectar of love, adorn myself in its beauty
> Love is religion, the only way of life, the only truth that matters)

From *President* (1937):

> *Ik bangla baney nyaara, rahe kunba jismein saara . . .*
> *Itna ooncha bangla ho ye maano gagan ka taara,*
> *Jis pe chadh ke indradhanush par jhoola jhoole chaand hamaara*
> *Bhandaar ho ye Lakshmi ke haanthon mein saara*
> *Paaye ab ji bhar ke sukh jisne vipat uthaayi*

(Let a beautiful bungalow be built, which houses the entire family
Let the bungalow touch such heights, that it appears a star in the sky
Climbing on top of which, the moon can swing perched on the
    rainbow
Let it be an abode of wealth in the hands of goddess Lakshmi
Here the inhabitants experience happiness for all their past
    travails)

From *Dharti Mata* (1938):

Duniya rang rangili . . .
Adbhut panchchi phool manohar, kali kali chatkili baba . . .
Kadam kadam par asha apna roop anoop dikhaati hai
Bigde kaaj banaati hai dheeraj ke geet sunaati hai
Iska sur misri se meetha, iski taan raseeli baba

(This world is a colourful place . . .
Of exquisite birds, beautiful flowers, radiant blossoms
Here at every step hope manifests itself in strange ways
It makes good what is lost while giving us lessons in fortitude
Its sound is sweeter than sugar, its tone extremely saccharine)

Words like 'taj', 'adhaar', 'vichaar', 'bhandaar', 'manohar', 'adbhut',
'raseeli' used in these songs, and words such as 'baalam' (beloved),
'paapan' (sinner), 'andhiyaari' (darkness) that were used in a few
others that Manohar referred to from that era, were far too prosaic
and thus hampered the melody. A plausible explanation for the use
of such vocabulary can be found in the words of M.K. Raghavendra,
film scholar and researcher, who, writing on the coming of sound
and music to popular Indian cinema, gives the specific example of
Amritmanthan (1934) to highlight how the earliest talkies were
often structured as verse plays and how songs were essentially a
continuation of speech in the film.

> The subject matter in *Amritmanthan* is violent but the speech is
> not tersely dramatic (as in later cinema) but rather singsong and
> conceived essentially as verse. The songs merely continued the

versified speech and since speech is 'already interpreted', each
song, usually occurring at the end of each tableau, only serves to
summarize its report.[6]

However, with India attaining Independence in 1947, and with
the onset of the 1950s, a nouveau modernity found its way into
Indian cinema, which brought the city into sharp focus.

We saw the intrusion of the city into key films of the post-
Independence era and the trend consolidates itself after 1950.
The fascination exhibited by popular cinema for the city was
with good reason. After 1947, Nehru's dominating nationalist
ambition in turn set out to recreate the city for its own purpose:
to make it not only the symbol of a new sovereignty but an
effective engine to drive India into the modern world. The city
was therefore a persuasive emblem for 'Nehruvian modernity'.[7]

As films broached more urban subjects and were based in urban
spaces, the arrival of the Urdu Progressive writers in Bombay
played a distinct part in adapting to this change in popular Indian
cinema towards the late 1940s. Their grounding in Urdu literature
resulted in film characters speaking a more urban language – Urdu
or Hindustani – that was in sync with the film's setting, since a lot
of the writers took to story, screenplay and dialogue writing.
Khwaja Ahmed Abbas (*Awaara*, 1951; *Shri 420*, 1955), Ismat
Chughtai (*Arzoo*, 1950; *Sone Ki Chidiya*, 1958), Krishan Chander
(*Andolan*, 1951; *Do Phool*, 1958) and Rajinder Singh Bedi (*Daag*,
1952) were some of the prominent Progressives who helped in the
advancement of a more urban expression in our films .

It was also natural that the songs sung by the protagonists in
'urban' films remained as close to the dialogue they spoke over the

---

6. M.K. Raghavendra, *Seduced by the Familiar: Narration and Meaning in Indian Popular Cinema*, 'Indian Cinema before 1947', p. 82, Oxford University Press, 2008.
7. Ibid., pp. 132–33.

course of the film. Having any one of Dev Anand's urban characters from *Taxi Driver* (1954), *Milaap* (1955) or *C.I.D.* (1956) mouthing something similar to K.L. Saigal's *'Do naina matwaare'* from *Meri Bahen* (1944) would have sounded absurd. This led to the arrival of the second generation of lyricists such as Majrooh, Kaifi, Hasrat, Shakeel and Sahir, all Urdu poets.

In order to get another expert opinion on Sahir, his life and times, I reached out to prominent film writer and poet-lyricist, Javed Akhtar.[8] Javed's father, Jan Nisar Akhtar, was a very close friend of Sahir's and a fellow Progressive writer. Because of the friendship between Sahir and Jan Nisar Akhtar, Javed saab had the good fortune of knowing Sahir intimately. I finally met Javed saab one late afternoon in March 2010 in his plush Juhu apartment in Mumbai's western suburbs. When I was ushered into what I presume is his study-cum-drawing room, Javed saab was seated behind a desk, wearing an immaculately starched white kurta. He appeared to be in the midst of writing a song whose melody had been recorded on an old two-in-one tape recorder kept on his left.

Besides the changing themes, which dictated a more urban expression in dialogue and lyrics, Javed Akhtar also pointed out a fundamental aspect of Urdu poetry that played a part in the emergence of the Urdu poets in the late 1940s:

Urdu has a rich legacy of poetry. There has been a lot of emphasis in Urdu on phonetics, which has been polished over the decades. Accordingly, poets in the Urdu language have a very sharp ear for phonetics; they know what does not sound good. Further, Urdu poetry has very strict and stringent laws of craft. The poet knows what is wrong metering, what makes for good rhyming. Therefore, a competent Urdu poet is highly trained; trained as far as the metering is concerned and trained in judging the

---

8. Sahir also wrote the songs for a few films that Javed scripted with Salim Khan, all directed by Yash Chopra: *Deewaar*, *Trishul* and *Kaala Patthar*.

phonetic effect of a particular line. Besides that, he has a rich heritage; his repertoire is very big – very polished, very sophisticated; what more could one want?

Sahir's entry into the world of songwriting happened in this cinematic milieu.

Sahir and S.D. Burman partnered together in more than fifteen films over the course of their seven-year working relationship between 1951 and 1957. Barring the odd film with music director N. Dutta – *Marine Drive* (1955) and *Milaap* (1955) – Sahir, largely, gave himself to Burman-da in this period. Their success rivalled those of two other prominent music director–lyricist combinations of the era: Shankar–Jaikishan with Shailendra and Naushad with Shakeel Badayuni. And though SJ–Shailendra and Naushad–Shakeel partnerships survived for long after Sahir and Burman split, the result of their brief association has an eternal quality to it.

Their next big hit, which coincided with the release of *Naujawan*, was *Baazi* (1951), best remembered as Guru Dutt's directorial debut. For *Baazi*, Sahir wrote '*Tadbeer se bigdi hui, taqdeer bana le*', but whose success, as Ganesh Anantharaman says, could mostly be credited to Burman-da: 'Sahir was aghast when S.D. Burman turned his ghazal into a club song in *Baazi* for Geeta Dutt to waft through. His protests went unheeded by Burman who never brooked any interference, and it was Sahir who repented when the song became a rage.'[9]

I met Dev Anand, whose Navketan produced *Baazi*, one evening in May 2010 as part of my research. Operating out of a makeshift office in Mumbai's Khar area, Dev saab, despite his age, was as sharp as ever during our half-hour chat. With his trademark muffler draped around his neck, he broke into an impromptu soliloquy on

---

9. Ganesh Anantharaman, *Bollywood Melodies: A History of the Hindi Film Song*, 'The Songwriters', Penguin Books India, 2008, p. 113.

Sahir as soon as I was seated. When I finally managed to get an opportunity to speak, I asked him to reflect on the popularity of 'Tadbeer se bigdi hui'. In response to my question, he turned nostalgic. 'I was in Jodhpur at the release of Baazi. There is an air force station there. I was told by the distributors that at a certain time in the film, when this song plays, all the pilots would come to the theatre, buy their tickets and see the song. They would come only for the song – yeh popularity hoti hai.'

Partnering with Burman through Jaal (1952), Taxi Driver (1954), Munimji (1955), Devdas (1955) and a few other Navketan films – House No. 44 (1955) and Funtoosh (1956) – Sahir wrote songs for a variety of themes: romance, despair, cabaret and freewheeling ditties. One prominent aspect of his writing for Burman's ballads is that the songs have a strong visual aspect to them. Beginning with 'Thandi hawaaein, lehra ke aayein', there is an immediate recourse to nature's beauty every time a romantic theme unfolds.

Nikhra nikhra sa hai chaand ka joban
Bikhra bikhra sa hai noor ka daaman
Aaja mere tanhayee ke sahaare

Chup hai dharti, chup hain chaand sitaare
Mere dil ki dhadkan tujhko pukaare[10]

(The moon's youth is in full splendour
Its light is scattered
Come, companion of my solitude

The earth is silent, as are the moon, the stars
My heart calls out to you)

A similar motif can be seen in 'Phaili huyee hain sapnon ki bahein':

Jhulaa dhanak ka dheere dheere hum jhule
Ambar toh kya hain taaron ke bhi labh choo le

---

10. From the song 'Chup hai dharti, chup hain chaand sitaare' in House No. 44 (1955).

Masti mein jhume aur sabhi gham bhoole
Dekhe na peeche mudke nigahe, aaja chalde kahi duur[11]

(Let us swing gently perched on the rainbow
Not just the sky, but the stars are within our reach
We dance with abandon, forgetting all our worries
Let us not look back, but go far, far away)

Javed Akhtar agrees. 'Sahir would synthesize nature with the love between a man and a woman. It was a fusion between the two. Song after song, he would have lines which first describe nature and then go on to address the romance. He would turn the romance between the couple into some kind of universal dance. Because of nature's participation, the affair would become ethereal and larger than life.' He also cites the example of '*Yeh raat, yeh chandni phir kahaan?*' (Where will one find this night, such moonlight again?) from *Jaal* (1952):

Pedon ke shaakhon pe soyee soyee chandni
Tere khyaalon mein khoyi khoyi chandni
Aur thodi der mein thak ke laut jaayegi
Raat yeh bahaar ki phir kabhi na aayegi
Do ek pal aur hai yeh samaa
Sun ja dil ki dastaan

(The moonlight rests on the branches of the trees
It is lost in your thought
It shall go away in some time, tired of waiting for you
And this night of romance shall never return again
This ambience is of a few moments,
Come, listen to the tale of the heart)

'Constantly he would make things soft-focused through the haze of nature. Ultimately, what is he saying? He is saying come and meet me. But it is getting dimensions and vista because of nature,' says Javed.

---

11. From *House No. 44* (1955).

There were songs of profound agony too. Take the lines of 'Dukhi mann mere' (My despondent heart) from *Funtoosh* (1956):

> Apne liye kab hain yeh mele
> Hum hain har ek mele mein akele
> Kya paayega usmein rehkar
> Jo duniya jeevan se khele

(When have these carnivals ever been for us?
We are always alone in any gathering of people
What will you gain by living there?
In a world that toys with human life)

In fact, whenever the mood was downcast, Sahir regularly sought death as the only solution to life's woes:

> Teri duniya mein jeene se toh behtar hai ki mar jaayein
> Wohi aasoon, wohi aahein, wohi gham hain jidhar jaayein[12]

(From living in your world, it is better that we die
The same tears, the same laments, the same sorrows greet us
        wherever we go)

or

> Maayusiyon ka majmaa hain jee mein
> Kya reh gaya hai is zindagi mein[13]

(An abundance of despondency plagues the heart
What is there to look forward to in this life?)

But remarkably, when the screenplay changed to reflect a lighter moment, Sahir didn't go all out with the inane stuff – a la 'Mere piya gaye rangoon, kiya hai wahaan se telephone' (*Patanga*, 1949) or 'C-A-T

---

12. From the song 'Teri duniya mein jeene se', *House No. 44* (1955).
13. From the song 'Jaayein toh jaayein kahaan?' (Where, if at all, do I go from here?), *Taxi Driver* (1954). S.D. Burman won a Filmfare Award for this song. In the first
(Contd...)

cat, cat maaney billi' (*Dilli Ka Thug*, 1958). Instead, he used humour to make veiled attacks at the hollow ways of this world:

> *Duniya ki gaadiyan chalti hain jhoot par*
> *Duniya ko maar de Baate ke boot par*[14]

> (The wheels of humanity are greased by deceit
> Shun this world by the tip of your Bata boot)

He even scoffed at the Creator:

> *Waah re upar waaley, tere khel niraaley*
> *Gadhon ko halwa baatein, bhaison ko shaal dushaale*
> *Buro ke moonh mein shakkar aur bhalo ke moonh sarkaale*[15]

> (Oh great Almighty, bizarre are your ways
> You give freely to the undeserving,
> The bad are blessed with more while the needy are kept deprived)

Another film of the era for which he penned songs was *Devdas* (1955). Writing for a film with a triad of doomed protagonists, Sahir was able to succinctly capture the essence of its characters. For Devdas, he wrote:

> *Kisko khabar thi, kisko yakeen tha*
> *Aise bhi din aayengein*
> *Jeena bhi mushkil hoga*
> *Marne bhi na payengey*

(*Contd...*)

two years since the inception of the category (1954), the Filmfare Award to a music director was handed out for a particular song in the film. It was only from 1956 onwards that the music director started receiving the Filmfare Award for the entire soundtrack of the film. The Filmfare Award for Best Lyricist was handed out from 1959 onwards.

14. From the song '*Oonche sur mein gaaye ja*' (Continue singing aloud) in *House No. 44* (1955).

15. From the song '*Denewaala jab bhi deta*' (Whenever the Almighty gives), *Funtoosh* (1956).

(Who was to know, who would believe
That such days would lie in wait
Where it would be difficult to live
And impossible to die as well)

On the other hand, for Chandramukhi, he wrote:

Tujhe aur ki tamanna, mujhe teri aarzoo hai
Tere dil mein gham hi gham hai, mere dil mein tu hi tu hai[16]

(You desire someone else, I yearn for you
Your heart is plagued by sorrow, my heart brims over with you)

There were some duds along the way – *Lal Kunwar* (1952), *Jeevan Jyoti* (1953), *Armaan* (1953) – but with the music of films like *House No. 44*, *Taxi Driver*, *Devdas* and *Funtoosh* doing so well, the Burman–Sahir duo became one of the most successful music director–lyricist pairings in the industry in the mid 1950s.

Thus, it isn't surprising that Guru Dutt, who had already created a reputation for himself as a master of song picturization in films like *Baazi*, *Aar Paar* and *Mr and Mrs 55*, and whose films had come to stand for great music, would enlist the services of the Burman–Sahir combine for his dream project, *Pyaasa* (1957).

---

16. From the song *'Jise tu qubool kar le'* (That what is acceptable to you) in *Devdas* (1955).

6

Pyaasa: The Lyrical Platinum Standard

Thukra raha tha mujhko badi der se jahaan
Main aaj sab jahaan ko thukra ke pee gaya[1]

(The world has ignored me far too long
Today, having spurned the world, I drown myself in liquor)

Pyaasa, arguably, remains Guru Dutt's finest cinematic creation. In 2005, *Time Magazine* ranked it as one of the 100 best films of all time. The film's music earned similar plaudits, with French film director Olivier Assayas even saying that *Pyaasa* was his second favourite film soundtrack of all time when, in 2004, *Sight and Sound*, the British Film Institute magazine, invited film-makers and musicians from across the world to reflect upon 'The Best Music in Film'.[2]

However, the tragedy of *Pyaasa's* success is that it marked the end of the working relationship between Sahir and S.D. Burman.

---

1. From the song '*Gham iss qadar badhe*' (My sorrow increases such that) in *Pyaasa* (1957).
2. http://www.bfi.org.uk/sightandsound/filmmusic/favourites.php

Each believed he was more responsible than the other for the success of the film's soundtrack. In an industry where the lyricist traditionally played second fiddle to the music director (a near-feudalistic relation, one may suggest), Sahir's act of claiming credit didn't go down too well with Burman. The music director refused to work with Sahir thereafter.

Pyaasa is the story of a young poet Vijay (Guru Dutt), who is left disillusioned by the greedy, materialistic ways of society. The movie begins with Vijay finding it impossible to find a publisher for his poems. His own brothers also turn against him, having no appreciation for his poetic talent. Meanwhile, Vijay befriends a young prostitute Gulab (Waheeda Rehman), who is a big fan of his poetry.

While rendering a ghazal at a college reunion, Vijay meets Mr Ghosh (Rehman), the owner of Modern Publishing House. Mr Ghosh, acting on a hunch that Vijay is the former lover of his wife Meena (Mala Sinha), offers Vijay a job. Meena eventually tells Vijay that she spurned his love and affection in the college years because of his inability to deal with the practicalities of life and provide her with materialistic comforts. A livid Mr Ghosh overhears their conversation.

After this, in a quirk of fate, Vijay is mistaken for dead as his coat is discovered on a beggar who has been run over by a train. Gulab, determined to keep Vijay's memory alive, takes his poems in her possession to Mr Ghosh who has them published. The publication is an instant hit. Meanwhile, Vijay comes to his senses in a hospital after possibly being injured in the train mishap. Mr Ghosh and Vijay's flatmate deliberately fail to recognize him, for they believe that Vijay's existence is detrimental to the commercial windfall that has come their way because of his supposed death.

As Vijay continues to insist that he is indeed the real Vijay, he is committed to a mental asylum from where he breaks free with the help of his friend Abdul Sattar (Johnny Walker). He lands up at the memorial service organized for him by Mr Ghosh and denounces this corrupt and materialistic world in what is one of the finest poetic moments of Indian cinema: *'Yeh duniya agar mil bhi jaaye toh kya hai'*(What does it matter even if one has such a world at his feet?). Seeing Vijay there, those who had opportunistically declared him dead, now side with a rival publisher, once again for a monetary motive, and declare this is Vijay. Vijay, on the other hand, tired of all the hypocrisy around him, says he is not Vijay. The film ends with Vijay walking away with Gulab to start a new life.

There is no denying Burman's contribution to the success of *Pyaasa*. He got Mohammed Rafi to emphatically convey, in the absence of any accompanying instrument, the angst brimming within Vijay in *'Tang aa chuke hain kashmakash-e-zindagi se hum'* (I am tired of life's never-ending hardships). Some of his other melodies in the film, like *'Jinhe naaz hai Hind par woh kahaan hain?'* (Where are they who take pride in India), have a minimalistic quality to them, which helps shift the focus entirely on the words.

Equally, his compositions *'Hum aap ki aankhon mein is dil ko basa de toh'* (If I were to place my heart in your eyes) and *'Sar jo tera chakraaye'* (If your head feels wobbly) create the necessary romantic, frothy mood required by the film's script in those moments. His choice of Geeta Dutt, Rafi and Hemant Kumar as singers could not have been more inspired. But in terms of pushing the envelope, Burman did very little with *Pyaasa's* soundtrack.

The minimalistic quality of Burman's tunes in *Pyaasa* was a continuation of what he had done with *'Kisko khabar thi, kisko yakeen tha'* in *Devdas* (1955). Similarly, for *House No. 44* (1955), Burman composed songs that were as mellifluous (*'Phaili hui hain sapnon ki bahein'*) or melancholic (*'Teri duniya mein jeene se toh behtar hain ki mar jaayein'*) as those of a similar genre in *Pyaasa*: *'Hum aap ki aankhon mein'* or *'Jaane woh kaise log thay jinke pyaar ko pyaar mila'* (What kind of people were they whose love has been reciprocated?). Even the wonderful kirtan-style '*Aaj sajan mohe ang laga lo*' (Hold me closely, o beloved one), sung by the Baul singer in *Pyaasa*, is not very different from '*Aan milo, aan milo, shyaam saanware*' (Please meet with me, o Divine One) which Burman composed for *Devdas*.

However, '*Sar jo tera chakraaye*', which is quite unlike any other song in *Pyaasa* in terms of its theme and mood, cannot be credited to SD alone. The song is generally considered to have been composed by a precocious R.D. Burman, who assisted his father in the early stages of his career. Yet another allegation is that the song was inspired from a tune in the film *Harry Black and the Tiger* for which Burman (senior), even though he was asked by Guru Dutt to copy the song note for note, 'waved his baton effectively enough to blend the tune with his own melody in such a manner that no one really noticed the surgery'.[3]

Consequently, purely from a musical standpoint, *Pyaasa* was not a turning point in the advancement of the Hindi film song, a la *Alam Ara* (1931), *Teesri Manzil* (1966) or *Roja* (1992).

But Sahir Ludhianvi, his lyrical contribution apart, remains central to *Pyaasa*'s theme. The film is replete with references to Sahir and his life even if they happen unwittingly. For example, in the film's second scene, when the publisher refuses to publish Vijay's poems saying that poetry should be about beauty and romance instead of hunger and unemployment, the parallel to Sahir's own brand of poetry is all too familiar. Further, when Vijay rebuts the publisher's allegation of not only having read Meer and Momin, but Josh (Malihabadi) and Faiz (Ahmed Faiz) as well, one cannot help but think that Vijay is only a façade for Sahir.[4]

---

3. Sathya Saran, *Ten Years with Guru Dutt: Abrar Alvi's Journey*, Penguin Viking, 2008, pp. 71–72.
4. Refer Chapter 1.

Beyond those two moments, however, Sahir is an obvious, recurrent presence in *Pyaasa*. Take the second verse of the song that Vijay sings at the college reunion:

> *Hum ghamzada hain, laaye kahaan se khushi ke geet*
> *Dengey wohi jo paayengey is zindagi se hum[5]*

> (I am beseeched by troubles, from where do I find the inspiration
>   for cheerful songs
> I can give back only what I have got from this life)

This is nothing but a rehashed version of Sahir's philosophy about his own poetry:

> *Duniya ne tajurbaat-o-havaadis ki shakl mein*
> *Jo kuch mujhe diya hai, lauta raha hoon main*

> (Whatever the world by way of experience and accident
> Has given me, I return it now)

Likewise, when Gulab, after receiving the news of Vijay's demise, goes to have Vijay's poems published, the name on the file she hands over to Meena is *Parchhaaiyaan*. Mr Ghosh, who takes the file from Meena, subsequently has Vijay's poems published by the same name, in the form of a book. By itself, the book's title, *Parchhaaiyaan*, as published by Mr Ghosh appears innocuous. But a few scenes later, as the nurse reads a couple of lines of poetry to Vijay, who is recovering in hospital, one cannot help but notice that the two stanzas that the nurse recites are from Sahir's famous anti-war poem written in 1956, and which not coincidentally was titled 'Parchhaaiyaan' (Shadows).[6]

Through his exceptional lyrical contribution, Sahir best expresses the poet protagonist of *Pyaasa*. Poetry becomes the film's leitmotif.

---

5. From the song '*Tang aa chuke hain kashmakash-e-zindagi se hum*' (I am tired of life's never-ending hardships).
6. Refer Chapter 12.

Right from the opening scene, where Vijay hums a few lines in verse, Sahir sets the tone for Guru Dutt's self-deprecating character in *Pyaasa*:

> *Yeh hanstey hue phool, yeh mahka hua gulshan,*
> *Yeh rang mein aur noor mein doobi hui raahein,*
> *Yeh phoolon ka ras pee ke machalte hue bhanwre*
> *Main doon bhi toh kyaa doon tumhein aye shokh nazaaron*
> *Le de ke mere paas, kuchh aansoo hain kuchh aahein*

> (These flowers that blossom, this fragrant garden,
> These boulevards immersed in light and colour,
> The bees inebriated by the nectar from the flowers
> What can I possibly do to contribute to such splendorous
>   environs?
> I have nothing but a few tears, a few sighs, to offer)

His lyrics further the film's screenplay at various stages. When Vijay runs into Meena after accepting the job offer from Mr Ghosh, the film cuts to a flashback, to a dream sequence between Vijay and Meena. Sahir's song in this dream sequence, 'Hum aap ki aankhon mein', not only establishes the romance between the two but also makes dialogue redundant.

There is a remarkable economy to his words, lyrics that say so much in so little:

> *Jaane kya tune kahi*
> *Jaane kya maine suni*
> *Baat kuch bann hi gayee*

> (Who knows what you said
> Who knows what I heard
> Yet we have established a connect)

Then there is 'Jaane woh kaise log thay jinke pyaar ko pyaar mila' which articulates Vijay's angst in the face of unrequited love.

Khushiyon ki manzil dhoondhi toh gham ki gard mili
Chaahat ke naghmein chaahein toh aahein sard mili
Dil ke bojh ko doona kar gaya jo gham-khwaar mila . . .

(When I sought the route to happiness, I experienced the tinge
    of grief
When I wanted to experience love, my overtures were dismissed
    cold-heartedly
Whoever promised to share my sorrow, doubled my grief
    instead . . .)

Listeners plunged into absolute despair as Sahir resigned Vijay to
his fate:

Isko hi jeena kehtey hain, toh yun hi jee lengey
Uff na karengey, lab see lengey, aansoo pee lengey
Gham se ab ghabrana kaisa, gham sau baar mila

(If this is what you call living, I will continue to live like this
I will not complain, I will seal my lips, I will wipe my tears
Why should I fear grief any longer; it is the only thing that
    comes my way)

Sahir had dealt with this theme before, in his non-film poetry and
in his earlier films. For example, in *Devdas* (1955), he used chaste
Hindi in the song 'Mitwa' (Friend) to give a poignant depiction of
Devdas's troubled state after Paro had been separated from him:

Vyaakul jiyaraa, vyaakul nainaa
Ik ik chup mein sau sau bainaa
Rah gaye aansoo lut gaye raag
Mitwa laagi re yeh kaisi anbujh aag?

(Restless is the heart, anxious are the eyes
Every silence reveals a hundred truths
Tears remain, the songs have died
Friend, what implacable fire consumes me?)

On the face of it, 'Jaane woh kaise log thay jinke pyaar ko pyaar mila' is
also perceptively similar to 'Kisko khabar thi, kisko yakeen tha' (Devdas)

in that the latter is also defeatist in its theme. But what sets '*Jaane woh kaise log thay jinke pyaar ko pyaar mila*' apart from the two tracks in *Devdas*, and ensures its status as an evergreen number, is that the language in the *Pyaasa* song is a lot more understandable and, poetically, more appealing. The beautiful self-flagellating metaphors Sahir uses – '*Humne toh jab kaliyaan maangi, kaanton ka haar mila*' (I asked for flowers, I got a wreath of thorns instead) or '*Humko apna saaya tak aksar bezaar mila*' (Even my shadow played truant with me) – put this pathos-ridden number in a class of its own.

Having used Urdu of a very fine quality to bring out Vijay's despondency in love, Sahir switches effortlessly to chaste Hindi to express Gulab's desire to reunite with Vijay with '*Aaj sajan mohe ang laga lo*'. There is an outstanding double entendre in his lyrics in this song. The words, at once, serve as a devotional song for the character of the singer as well as a prayer by Gulab for Vijay to deliver her from a life of sleaze and suffering:

Kayee jugon se hain jaagey more nain abhaage,
Kahin jiya nahin laagey bin torey
Sukh dikhey nahin aagey
Dukh peeche peeche bhaagey, jag suna suna laage bin torey
Prem sudha itni barsa do, jag jal-thal ho jaaye

(For years together, my eyes have yearned for you
I cannot rest without you
I cannot see any happiness ahead of me
Sorrow follows my every step, this world seems lonely without
    you
Shower me with sufficient love, so that the world becomes a
    better place)

But it is with '*Jinhe naaz hai Hind par woh kahaan hain?*' and '*Yeh duniya agar mil bhi jaaye toh kya hai?*' that Sahir set a new benchmark for poetry in Hindi films. The great lengths to which Guru Dutt went to incorporate them in the film's screenplay also indicate the poet's influence on *Pyaasa*. In these songs, 'Sahir's words seem to articulate Guru Dutt's own view of the world and experience of tragedy.'[7]

'*Jinhe naaz hai Hind par*' is a minor reworking of a poem of Sahir's that had been published in *Talkhiyaan*. The poem was called 'Chakley' (Brothels), and the recurring question it raised mockingly was '*Sana-khwaan-e-taqdees-e-mashriq kahaan hain?*' (Where are they who praise the purity of the East?). For the purpose of the film, Sahir simplified this line, without taking anything away from its barbed tone, and instead asked, '*Jinhe naaz hai Hind par woh kahaan hain?*'

In *Ten Years with Guru Dutt: Abrar Alvi's Journey*, drawing on her conversations with Abrar Alvi, dialogue writer of *Pyaasa*, Sathya Saran refers to the adaptation of this poem by Guru Dutt to suit the purpose of *Pyaasa*:

> Guru Dutt's mind was like a magpie's, going by Abrar's view of the director. He would pick up bits and pieces – a scene here, a song idea there – and store them for the future. For example, he was enamoured of a '*chakla*' of Sahir Ludhianvi's, and kept saying that some day he would like to use it in one of his films. Of course, he needed the right situation for it. It was a visit to a kotha that gave Guru Dutt the right setting for Sahir's poem.[8]

The song itself comes out of nowhere in *Pyaasa*. Vijay, grieving at the demise of his mother, is shown to have drowned his sorrow in liquor, when suddenly, the screenplay segues to a courtesan dancing in a brothel with Vijay in attendance and the cries of her baby reverberating in the background. This situation sets up '*Jinhe naaz hai Hind par*' perfectly in the film.

---

7. Nasreen Munni Kabir, *Guru Dutt: A life in Cinema*, Oxford University Press, 2005, p. 128.
8. Sathya Saran, *Ten Years with Guru Dutt: Abrar Alvi's Journey*, Penguin Viking, 2008, pp. 65–66.

Fundamentally, 'Jinhe naaz hai Hind par' is an evocative commentary on the plight of women living on the margins of society, with the line used to great rhetorical effect:

Yeh koonchey, yeh neelamghar dilkashi ke
Yeh lut-tey huey karvaan zindagi ke
Kahaan hai kahaan hai muhaafiz khudi ke?
Jinhey naaz hai Hind par woh kahaan hain?

Yeh purpench galiyaan, yeh badnaam bazaar
Yeh gumnaam rahi, yeh sikkon ki jhankaar
Yeh ismat ke saudey, yeh saudon pe takraar
Jinhey naaz hai Hind par woh kahaan hain?

Yeh sadiyon se be-khauf sehami si galiyaan
Yeh maslee huwi adh-khilee zard kaliyaan
Yeh bikti hui khokhli rang-raliyaan
Jinhey naaz hai Hind par woh kahaan hain? . . .

Yahaan peer bhi aa chuke hain, jawaan bhi
Tanuumand bete bhi, abbaa miyan bhi
Yeh biwi bhi hai aur behen bhi hai maa bhi
Jinhey naaz hai Hind par woh kahaan hain?

Madad chahati hai ye Hawwa ki beti
Yashoda ki hum-jins, Radha ki beti
Payambar ki ummat Zulaikhan ki beti
Jinhey naaz hai Hind par woh kahaan hain?

Zaraa mulk ke rahbaron ko bulao
Yeh koonche ye galiyan ye manzar dikhao
Jinhe naaz hai Hind par unko lao
Jinhe naaz hai Hind par woh kahan hain?
Kahan hain, kahan hain, kahan hain?

(These lanes, these auction houses of pleasure
These looted caravans of life
Where are those guardians of self-pride?
Where are they who take pride in India?

These winding lanes, these ill-reputed markets
These anonymous travellers, with plenty to spend
These bargains of virginity, haggling leading to acrimony
Where are they who take pride in India?

These bylanes that have lived in fear for centuries
These exploited buds that have turned pale
These hollow revelries being sold by the minute
Where are they who take pride in India? . . .

Here old men have come, youngsters as well
Sons in the pink of health, fathers as well
These are wives, sisters and mothers as well
Where are they who take pride in India?

These daughters of Eve plead for help
As do the sisters of Yashodha, the daughters of Radha
The race of the Prophet, these daughters graced with such fine
    beauty
Where are they who take pride in India?

Go, call out to the leaders of the nation
Show them these streets, these bylanes, these scenes
Those who take pride in India bring them here
Where are they who take pride in India?
Where are they, where are they, where are they?)

'Yeh duniya agar mil bhi jaaye', in contrast, is a much grander disillusionment with mankind. Sathya narrates how 'Yeh duniya agar mil bhi jaaye toh kya hai?' was incorporated into the film, calling it, 'the remarkable tale about the song that *Pyaasa* is most remembered for':

> We [Guru Dutt and Abrar Alvi] had worked out the details of the scene where Guru Dutt returns to be present at his own death anniversary function. I [Abrar] had yet to write the dialogues, but I told Guru Dutt, let's get the song ready, and I will write the dialogues when I return [Abrar had gone away for some weeks for an operation].

Sahir Ludhianvi, who had written all the other songs, wrote this one too. But somewhere along the way, he seemed to have lost track of the milieu of the story. However, the song he wrote had enough punch and pathos in it to excite the director in Guru Dutt, who filmed it immediately.

I returned to the sets, fresh from my convalescence and Guru Dutt triumphantly showed me the rushes of the song. I was impressed by the wonderful way he had shot it, but the lyrics dismayed me. Guru Dutt could not understand why, so I had to explain. 'The era we have placed the film in is the mid-fifties,' I said, 'and Sahir has written about the *mahelon*, the *takhton*, the *tajon ki duniya* . . . these symbols of the Raj, royalty and the zamindari are defunct; that era is past in the period our movie is set in, we are a democratic nation. So what duniya are we referring to?

Of course, it was impossible to change the lyrics; the song had already been shot. I had to do some damage control at my end and bring relevance to the lines . . . Which is why Rehman talks about the dead poet and says that if Vijay were alive today, he would place him on a takht and place a crown (taj) on his head . . . which Vijay, standing framed in a flood of light at the door of the hall, overhears and responds to with the now-famous renunciation of the world of falsehood and hypocrisy.[9]

Yeh mahlon, yeh takhton, yeh taajon ki duniya
Yeh insaan ke dushman, samaajon ki duniya
Yeh daulat ke bhookhe, ravaajon ki duniya
Yeh duniya agar mil bhi jaaye toh kyaa hai? . . .

Yahaan ik khilona hai insaan ki hasti
Yeh basti hai murda-paraston ki basti
Yahaan par toh jeevan se hai maut sasti
Yeh duniya agar mil bhi jaaye toh kyaa hai? . . .

Yeh duniya jahaan aadmi kuchh nahin hai
Wafaa kuchh nahin, dosti kuchh nahin hai

---

9. Ibid., pp. 74–75.

Jahaan pyaar ki qadr hi kuchh nahin hai
Yeh duniya agar mil bhi jaaye toh kyaa hai

Jalaa do ise phoonk daalo yeh duniya
Jalaa do jalaa do jalaa do, ise phoonk daalo yeh duniya
Mere saamne se hataa lo yeh duniya
Tumhaari hai tum hi sambhaalo yeh duniya
Yeh duniya agar mil bhi jaaye toh kyaa hai?

(This world of palaces, thrones and diadems
This world that abhors humanity
This world that craves for prosperity
What does it matter even if one has such a world at his feet? . . .

Here man's life is no more valuable than a toy's
This is a ghetto of half-dead individuals
Here life comes cheaper than death itself
What does it matter even if one has such a world at his feet? . . .

This world where man has no value
Fidelity and friendship have no meaning
Where love has no respect
What does it matter even if one has such a world at his feet?

Burn it, annihilate such a world
Burn it, burn it, annihilate such a world
Remove such a world from before my eyes
It is yours, this world is for you to lord over
What does it matter even if one has such a world at his feet?)

Both songs are trenchant critiques of the prevailing state of affairs in society. Where one is a telling indictment of the government in power (*Jinhe naaz hai Hind par*), the other (*Yeh duniya agar mil bhi jaaye*) is an abject disapproval of its people. In both songs, Sahir had the audacity to hold a mirror to the people of India to show them at their unflattering worst.

In both songs, he used Urdu of the finest quality, where words, despite their acerbic connotations, continue to resonate within the listener. And even if the language is esoteric in parts – '*Madad chahati hai ye Hawwa ki beti*' – that the audience took to it was testimony that if great art truly appeals, people do unravel the mystique behind it.

There can be no bigger proof that Sahir touched a chord with cine-goers than in the manner in which the film's publicity underwent a change. Where initially, leading up to the film's release, advertisements in the print media focused on the presence of Mala Sinha, Guru Dutt, Johnny Walker and Waheeda Rehman in the film, with S.D. Burman's name as music director mentioned ahead of Sahir Ludhianvi's as the film's lyricist, in the weeks following the film's release, perhaps cashing in on the pulse of the masses, the focus changed entirely to the lyrics of these two songs. One advertisement even propped up *Pyaasa* as 'A LYRICAL NEW HIGH IN FILM MUSIC!'.[10] In all these advertisements after the release, Sahir Ludhianvi's name as lyricist was promoted ahead of Burman's. Both these aspects to the film's promotion, of lyrics being used to promote a film and the lyricist being mentioned ahead of the music director, were possibly novel developments in Indian film publicity and further underlined Sahir's pre-eminence over Burman's in *Pyaasa*'s success.

Still, the importance of Sahir's work in *Pyaasa* is incomplete without the mention of the jovial '*Sar jo tera chakraaye*'. Its light-hearted lyrics bring a sudden cheer to what is otherwise a very serious film:

> *Tel mera hai muski, ganj rahe na khushki*
> *Jiske sar par haath phira doon chamke kismet uski*
> *Sunn sunn sunn, arrey beta sunn, is champi mein bade bade gunn*
> *Lakh dukhon ki ek davaa hai kyun na aazmaaye, kahe ghabraaye, kahe*
> *ghabraaye*

---

10. *Hindustan Times*, Thursday, 21 March 1957.

(My oil has the qualities of musk, it is a remedy for baldness and
dandruff
Whosoever scalp I run my hands through, his luck changes for the
better
Believe me when I say that this massage has many great qualities
It is the medicine to cure all your troubles, why not give it a try,
why be afraid?)

But even here, Sahir managed to slip in a sobering thought by
advocating the merits of the socialist order:

Naukar ho ya maalik, leader ho ya public
Apne aage sabhi jhukey hain kya raja kya sainik

(Be it a servant or his master, a leader or one from the general
public
Everyone has to bow to me, be it a king or a soldier)

On every possible parameter – from the kind of language used, to
the variety of themes, to the larger implication of each song – *Pyaasa*
was not only a personal triumph for Sahir Ludhianvi, but also for
those who value the words in a song more than the melody. Never
before had a songwriter covered such a broad spectrum of themes
as Sahir had done in *Pyaasa*. Nor had the language in Indian cinema
ever been more contemptuous in its assessment of the status quo.
Sahir had synthesized the Progressive ideology, of using the literary
effort to create awareness among people, in his lyrics.

Owing to *Pyaasa*'s commercial success, Sahir never shied away
from incorporating the literary and Progressive element in his film
songs. Whenever he had the opportunity, he would comment on
society's many failings.

Take a nondescript film like *Shagoon* (1964), a love story which
dealt with the theme of blind superstition in society. Here, Sahir
urged listeners into thinking about the impoverished in India even
when the film's storyline had no such agenda:

Daulat ki qami aisi toh nahi
Phir bhi gurbat ka raaj hai kyun
Sikke toh karodo dhal dhal kar
Taksaal se baahar aate hain
Kin gaaron mein kho jaate hain
Kin purdoh mein chhup jaatein hain?

Yeh raat bahut rangeen sahi
Is raat mein gham ka zehar bhi hain
Naghmon ki khanak mein dubee huyee
Fariyaad-o-pua ki lehar bhi hai[11]

(Not that there is any dearth of wealth
Yet why is it that poverty reigns
Coins, crores of them, are shaped
And made available from the mint
Into what gaps do they disappear?
Behind what cloaks do they hide?

This night may appear beautiful
But it has a poisonous tinge to it as well
Immersed in the sound of music
It carries the cries for help as well)

In that sense, *Pyaasa* was a pioneering effort by the film's lyricist and a point of reference in the history of songwriting in Indian cinema.

The legacy of *Pyaasa's* songs lives on in our movies even today. *Gulaal* (2009), a recent film by Anurag Kashyap with a powerful political storyline, begins with a dedication to Sahir which reads 'This film is inspired by the song "*Yeh mahlon, yeh takhton, ye tajon ki duniya*" by Sahir Ludhianvi from the film "*Pyaasa*".' Even the song that plays at the climax in *Gulaal* is strongly inspired from this same song in *Pyaasa*:

---

11. From the song '*Yeh raat bahut rangeen sahi*' in *Shagoon* (1964).

Mamta ki bikhri kahaani ki duniya, oh duniya
Behnon ki siski jawaani ki duniya, oh duniya
Aadam ke Hawwa se rishtey ki duniya, oh duniya re
Shaayar ke pheeken lafzon ki duniya, oh duniya

Ghalib ke Momin ke khaabon ki duniya
Majaazo ke un inqalaabon ki duniya
Faiz, Firaaqon, Sahir, Makhdoom,
Mir ki Zauq ki Daaghon ki duniya
Yeh duniya agar mil bhi jaaye toh kya hai?

(This world that robs mothers of their children
This world where sisters spend their youth sobbing
This world based on Adam's relation with Eve
This world where poets' lyrics are without meaning

This world of Ghalib's and Momin's dreams
This world of Majaaz's call to revolution
Faiz's, Firaaq's, Sahir's, Makhdoom's,
This world as imagined by Mir, Zauq and Daagh
What does it matter even if one has such a world at his feet?)

Imagine two film-makers as different from each other as Guru Dutt and Anurag Kashyap, two eras as distinct as the 1950s and the new millennium, two films as dissimilar as *Pyaasa* and *Gulaal*, bound together by the words of a song. It is probably impossible to think of another Hindi film song that manages this feat. What greater tribute to Sahir and his poetry in *Pyaasa* can there be?

Following his acceptance in the film industry, Sahir had begun to believe that the lyricist's job was no less important than the music director's. But as more and more fame came his way, he took a superior view of the lyricist's position vis-à-vis the music director's by advocating that songwriters had to apply their mind to write a song, while the latter only had to listen to the gramophone to find inspiration for their melodies.

Abrar Alvi remembers Sahir sharing a similar sentiment one

evening in the presence of S.D. Burman when the last song for *Pyaasa* ('*Yeh duniya agar mil bhi jaaye*') still had to be written: 'One day, while we are all together, he got a bit high and aired his views on music directors being lesser mortals to writers like him. S.D. Burman, who was present, got very riled up about his statements. Dada pronounced then and there that he would never again work with Sahir, not for the rest of his life.' SD set the music for that final song in *Pyaasa* without sitting with Sahir.[12]

The part where Abrar talks about Sahir getting high is interesting, because it did become a habit with him. Having had his fill of liquor, he often became offensive towards anyone in sight. When I met the lyricist Naqsh Lyallpuri, who wrote songs for a few films in the 1970s and 1980s, in his Oshiwara residence in Mumbai's Andheri West area in late January 2010, he recalled a similar incident:

B.R. Chopra had thrown a party for a businessman friend of his who had come from South Africa. He was a crorepati. BR invited Sahir as well. Drinks were being served at the party. The businessman, a Punjabi, was a fan of Sahir's. He approached Sahir, who by then had consumed two or three pegs, and said that he would like Sahir to recite a few of his couplets. Sahir ignored the gentleman. The businessman, a little while later, repeated his request to Sahir. Sahir refused to oblige on this occasion as well. Then the businessman approached B.R. Chopra with his request. Chopra saab went to Sahir and put forth his friend's request. That got Sahir irritated. He burst out saying, '*Aapney mujhe gramophone record samajh rakha hai kya? Jahaan suyee rakhee, wahaan bolna shuru kar doon*' (Do you think I am a gramophone record? Wherever you place the needle, I will start reciting from there). He [Sahir] left the party immediately after that.

---

12. Sathya Saran, *Ten Years with Guru Dutt: Abrar Alvi's Journey*, Penguin Viking, 2008, p. 112.

Dev Anand, too, was critical of Sahir for Burman's decision to never work with him again following *Pyaasa*. 'When Sahir became big, he became egoistic. He would keep saying, "When I write a lyric, it becomes a hit." A song becomes a hit because of the tune also. Otherwise, a book of poems can also be a big hit,' Dev saab told me when I interviewed him.

Guru Dutt replaced Sahir Ludhianvi with Kaifi Azmi for his next directorial venture, *Kaagaz Ke Phool* (1959). S.D. Burman composed the music for the film. This only reinforced a popular notion that poets or lyricists require patronage whether it was in the bygone era of the Mughal kings or in the Hindi film industry of the mid-twentieth century. And Sahir, having fallen out with Burman, had to fend for himself.

But despite never working together again, the Burman–Sahir combine did enough to merit a mention every time the golden era of the Hindi film song is eulogized. The music of their films – *Baazi, Taxi Driver, House No. 44, Devdas, Funtoosh*, culminating with *Pyaasa* – is a reflection of two individuals in sync with each other, never mind their vastly different cultural lineages.

Perhaps Javed Akhtar summarizes it best when he says, 'I think aesthetically Burman-da and Sahir were on the same page. Sahir's words complemented Burman's tunes and vice versa. Burman-da is my favourite music director . . . But yes, in *Pyaasa*, Sahir's contribution is more than Burman-da's.'

7

Finding Love in the Shadow of Oedipus

Tumhaarey ahad-e-wafaa ko main ahad kya samjhoon?
Mujhe khud apni mohabbat ka aitbaar nahin[1]

(How do I believe your promises of fidelity?
When my own ability to love remains in doubt)

The great Punjabi poet and writer Amrita Pritam once told Uma Trilok, who authored *Amrita-Imroz: A Love Story,* of the following conversation involving Sahir and her:

Sahir happened to ask Amrita, 'Why don't the two of us go and live in China?'

Amrita, puzzled by Sahir's sudden suggestion of moving to China, sought an immediate explanation. 'What will we do living in China?'

'We shall write poetry,' replied Sahir, rather vaguely.

Amrita shot back, 'We can write poetry here without going to China.'

---

1. A couplet from a ghazal by Sahir in *Talkhiyaan.*

'Yes we can, but if we go to China we will never come back,' said Sahir.

It was, as Amrita told Uma, Sahir's idea of proposing a lifetime together with her.

He was that kind of man.[2]

*

One of the most intriguing aspects of Sahir's life was his liaison with Amrita Pritam. Amrita met Sahir sometime around 1944 in Preet Nagar, a village between Lahore and Amritsar. She was at this time married to Pritam Singh, who was an editor, but theirs was not the best of marriages. Husband and wife were known to be on totally different wavelengths from the very beginning.

Amrita, in her mid-twenties at the time, had come to Preet Nagar to attend a mushaira which was being attended by Punjabi and Urdu poets. It was here that she saw and heard Sahir for the first time. She was immediately smitten by him. 'I do not know whether it was the magic of his words or his silent gaze, but I was captivated by him,' writes Amrita of the moment.

The mushaira ended only after midnight following which the guests bid goodbye to each other. The next morning they were supposed to go to the neighbouring township of Lopoki, from where a bus had been organized to take them back to Lahore.

However, the following morning they discovered that it had rained the previous night and the road they had to take to reach Lopoki had been rendered slippery and hazardous. Apparently, the sky had turned cloudy during the mushaira itself and it had started drizzling by the time the mushaira had drawn to a close. Amrita

---

2. This anecdote was narrated to me by Uma Trilok when I met her at her Vasant Kunj residence in June 2009.

Chaudhri Fazl Mohammed, Sahir's father. The Chaudhri's depraved lifestyle had an adverse impact on Sahir as a child. Photograph reproduced from *Fann Aur Shaksiyat*, Sahir Ludhianvi Number.

From L to R: Sahir Ludhianvi, Sahir's mother Sardar Begum and cousin Anwar Sultana. Over the years, Sahir established a very strong bond with his mother and she became the centre of his being. Photograph reproduced from *Fann Aur Shaksiyat*, Sahir Ludhianvi Number.

Facsimile of Sahir Ludhianvi's
Admission Form

GOVERNMENT COLLEGE,

APPLICATION FOR ADMISSION TO **1st YEAR CLASS.**

1. Name, caste and religion. — Abdul Haye, Gujjar, Mohammedan.

2. Roll No. (to be left). — Registration No. (to be left blank in case of first year).

3. Date of birth as in Matriculation Examination. — Eighth March Nineteen hundred and twenty-one. — Agriculturist / Non-Agriculturist

4. Name, occupation and address of father. — Fazal Mohd., agriculturist, Vill. Talab Sekhuwali, Distt. Ludhiana.

5. Name, occupation and address of guardian. — Fl. Deen rashid, merchant, Near Jagraon Bridge, Ludhiana.

6. Home address. — Do.

7. Married or unmarried. — Un-married

8. Proposed residence in—
   (a) College Hostel.
   (b) Any other Hostel (specify name and locality).
   (c) With relatives or guardian (specify name, address and relationship).
   (d) Private lodging (specify name and locality). — (c) Abdul Rashid, maternal uncle, Near Jagraon Bridge, Ludhiana.

9. Relationship to any present or former student (state exact relationship).

	Year	Roll No.	Division	Marks	Subjects	School or College from which passed.
Matriculation Arts	1937	14553	II	451	Urdu, Persian	Khalsa High School
Intermediate Arts/Science						
B.A./B.Sc. Honours School						
M.A./M.Sc.						

10. Any Scholarships won.

12. Have you any claim to make for fee concession or other form of assistance? If so, submit full and properly certified particulars regarding your claim.

14. What subjects do you wish to study? — English, Persian, Philosophy, History, Urdu.

15. State in order of preference:—
    (a) What game or games you wish to play? (State if member of School or College First Team). — Cricket
    (b) The above time hobbies in which you are interested, or which you would like to take up. If a Sonali, give particulars. — Photography

16. Date of present admission. — Date of first admission to this College.

17. What is your intended future profession or occupation? — Law.

I certify that I am applying for admission at the wish of my parent or guardian and that the particulars given above are correct. I promise not to take part in political action of any kind whilst a student. — Signature of applicant. — Abdul Haye

Date of withdrawal (to be left blank).

Admt. — Principal, Government College,

Signed by Principal on his behalf P N Nag 27-10-8
27/

N.B.— Attach parent's character certificate or letter of recommendation, and a certified copy of the Provisional Certificate which should also show the date of birth. Also any [illegible] and certificates in connection with item No. 13 above.

Anupama Sharma

Sahir's College admission form, which shows his place of residence, his hobbies and subjects that he enrolled for at Government College.

Sahir (second from right in the third row with name given as A.H. Sahir) as a member of Government College Ludhiana photography club.

The entrance to the Sahir Auditorium at Government College Ludhiana.

From L to R: Music composer Ravi, Sahir Ludhianvi, Sajjad Zaheer and Jan Nisar Akhtar. Because of his early childhood experiences, Sahir was automatically drawn to the PWM, which was founded by Zaheer and of which Akhtar was an active member.

Sahir reciting at a mushaira. Choosing his attire for such an event would often be a hair-splitting experience for Sahir.

Imroz

Sahir and Amrita Pritam: A relationship which was defined largely by silence.

S.M.M. Ausaja

Amrita Pritam.

Hindustan Times, Delhi edition, 24 February 1957.

THE STORY OF A POET WHO WROTE AS HE WISHED AND LIVED AS HE WILLED!

GURU DUTT FILMS (PRIVATE) LTD. PRESENTS

Pyaasa

STARRING

MALA SINHA
GURU DUTT
JOHNNY WALKER
WAHEEDA REHMAN

DIRECTION
GURU DUTT

MUSIC
S. D. BURMAN

LYRICS
SAHIR LUDHIANVI

OPENING - FRIDAY, MARCH 1

REGAL Plans Open 9-30 a.m. to 8-30 p.m.
MOTI Plans Open 9-30 a.m. to 8-30 p.m.
& One more theatre   Heavy Rush Book Now

Hindustan Times, Delhi edition, 1 March 1957

Guru Dutt Films Private Ltd. PRESENT

MALA SINHA
GURU DUTT
JOHNNY WALKER
AND
WAHEDA REHMAN

Pyaasa

Directed by
DUTT

Music
S. D. BURMAN

Lyrics: SAHIR LUDHIANVI   MOTI

GALA OPENING REGAL

SONGS OF TOMORROW—
IN A PICTURE OF TODAY!

YEH KOOCHE YEH NILAMGHAR DILKASHI KE
YEH LOOTTE HUE KARWAN ZINDAGI KE
KAHAN HAIN KAHAN HAIN MUHAFIZ KHUDI KE
JINHE NAAZ HAI HIND PAR WOH KAHAN HAIN
RAHAN HAIN, KAHAN HAIN, KAHAN HAIN.........

YEH PURPECH GALIYAN YEH BADNAAM BAZAAR
YEH GUMNAM RAHI YEH SIKKON KI JHANKAR
YEH ASMAT KE SAUDE, YEH SAUDON PE TAQRAAR
JINHE NAAZ HAI HIND PAR WOH KAHAN HAIN

YAHAN PEER BHI AA CHOOKE HAI JAWAN BHI
TANO-MAND BETE BHI ABBA MIYAN BHI
YEH BIWI BHI HAI AUR BAHIN BHI AUR MAA BHI
JINHE NAAZ HAI HIND PAR WOH KAHAN HAIN

ZARA MULK KE RAHBARON KO BULAO
YEH KOOCHE YEH GALIYAN YEH MANZAR DIKHAO
JINHE NAAZ HAI HIND PAR OONKO LAO
JINHE NAAZ HAI HIND PAR WOH KAHAN HAIN

HEAR THIS
AND 6 OTHER
SONG SENSATIONS
OF SAHIR
& S. D. BURMAN
in
GURUDUTT'S
Universally Acclaimed

Pyaasa

6th Houseful Week
REGAL 12, 3-15, 6-30, 9-30
MOTI 12, 3-15, 6-30, 9-3
Ad. Bk. 9-30 A.M. to 8-30 P.M.

Hindustan Times, Delhi edition, 16 March 1957.

A LYRICAL NEW HIGH
IN FILM MUSIC !

Sheer Ecstasy You Have Never
Before Experienced !!

GURU DUTT'S

Pyaasa

Songs: SAHIR
6th Houseful Week
REGAL
12, 3-15, 6-30, 9-30
Music: S. D. BURMAN
MOTI
12, 3-15, 6-30, 9-30
Ad. Bk. 9-30 A.M. to 8-30 P.M.

Hindustan Times, Delhi edition, 21 March 1957.

Pyaasa's advertising reflected the importance of Sahir's contribution to the film. From initially being advertised with images of Guru Dutt and Waheeda Rehman, it undergoes a change, highlighting the importance of the film's songs like *'Jinhe naaz hai Hind par'* and *'Yeh duniya agar mil bhi jaaye'*.

THE SONG THAT HAS STIRRED A NATION ...

YE MAHALON YE TAKHTON YE TAJON KI DUNIYA
YE INSAN KE DUSHMAN SAMAJO KI DUNIYA.
YE DAULAT KE BHOOKE RIWAJON KI DUNIYA
YE DUNIYA AGAR MIL BHI JAYE TO KYA HAI.
YAHAN IK KHILAUNA HAI INSAN KI HASTI
YE BASTI HAI MURDA PARASTON KI BASTI
YAHAN PAR TO JEEVAN SE HAI MAUT SASTI
YE DUNIYA AGAR MIL BHI JAYE TO KYA HAI
YE DUNIYA JAHAN AADMI KUCHH NAHIN HAI
WAFA KUCHH NAHIN DOSTI KUCHH NAHIN HAI
JAHAN PYAR KI KADRA HI KUCHH NAHIN HAI.
YE DUNIYA AGAR MIL BHI JAYE TO KYA HAI
JALA-DO ISE PHOONK DALO YE DUNIYA
MERE SAMANE SE HATA LO YE DUNIYA
TUMHARI HAI TUM HI SAMBHALO YE DUNIYA
YE DUNIYA AGAR MIL BHI JAYE TO KYA HAI.

Hear It In GURU DUTT'S

Pyaasa

Starring: Guru Dutt,
Mala Sinha, Johny Walker,
Waheeda Rehman

Songs: SAHIR
Music: S. D. BURMAN
Direction: GURU DUTT

8th Houseful Week

REGAL — MOTI
12, 3-15, 6-30, 9-30
12, 3-15, 6-30, 9-30

Hindustan Times, Delhi edition, 24 March 1957.

Mr Arun Dutt on behalf of Guru Dutt Films and *Hindustan Times*

From L to R: Mahendra Nath, Sahir Ludhianvi
and Salma Siddiqui on the occasion of Sahir's
birthday. Despite his slim, tall stature and
sharp features, Sahir's biggest complex, as
Amrita Pritam suggests, was that he was not
good looking. Photograph reproduced from
Fann Aur Shaksiyat, Sahir Ludhianvi Number.

Yash Chopra

Sahir (L) and Yash
Chopra (R): Friends
for life. Sahir worked
as lyricist on each of
Yash's films, beginning
with *Dhool Ka Phool*
(1959).

saw the hand of fate in all of this as she recalls, 'Now, when I look back on that night, I can say that destiny had sown the seed of love in my heart which the rain nurtured.'

Desperate to go to Lopoki, the guests made their way ahead cautiously. It was in these circumstances that Amrita experienced her love blossoming for Sahir. She writes:

> Walking at some distance from Sahir, I noticed that where his shadow was falling on the ground, I was being engulfed by it entirely. *Uss waqt nahin jaanti thi ki baad ki zindagi ke kitne hi taptey huey saal mujhey usi ke saaye mein chalte huey kaatney hongey, ya kabhi-kabhi thak kar apne hi aksharon ki chhaya mein baithna hoga. Yeh akshar meri unn nazmo ke thay, jo maine Sahir ki mohabbat mein likhey, lekin unka koi zikr kabhi meri zabaan par nahin aaya* (At that time I didn't know I would spend so many years of my life in his shadow or that at times I would get tired and seek solace in my own words. These poems were written in Sahir's love, but I never revealed the inspiration behind them publicly).[3]

Over the course of attending several such mushairas, the acquaintance between the two grew into a mutual affection.

It was by all reckoning a most unusual relationship. The two hardly ever spoke to each other, preferring instead to let silence define their association. 'There were two obstacles between us — one of silence, which remained forever. And the other was language. I wrote poetry in Punjabi, Sahir in Urdu.'[4]

The silence that defined their relationship finds mention in her poems:

> *Kayee barson ke baad achaanak ek mulaaqat*
> *Hum dono ke praan ek nazm ki tarah kaanpey*

---

3. Amrita Pritam, *Sahir, Main aur Nau Sau Meelo ka Faasla*, Sulabh India, 1988, p. 12.
4. Ibid.

Saamney ek puri raat thi
Par aadhee nazm ek koney mein simti rahi
Aur aadhee nazm ek koney mein baithi rahi

Phir subah savere
Hum kaagaz ke fatey huey tukdon ki tarah miley
Maine apne haath mein uska haath liya
Usne apney baanh mein meri baanh daali

Aur hum dono ek censor ki tarah hansey
Aur kaagaz ko ek thandey mez par rakh kar
Us saari nazm par lakeer pher di[5]

(After many years, a sudden meeting
Both of us experienced a kind of nervousness

A whole night stretched ahead of us
But one half of the poem remained confined in one corner
The other half, in another

Then, the next morning
We met like torn pieces of paper
I took his hand in my hand
And he took my arms in his

And we both laughed liked censors
Having kept the paper on the desk beside us
We scratched out the entire poem written on it)

Even in her autobiography, *Raseedi Tikkat* (Revenue Stamp), Amrita
writes of the eloquent silence that characterized their relationship:

When Sahir would come to meet me in Lahore, it was as if an
extension of my silence had occupied the adjacent chair and
then gone away . . .
    He would quietly smoke his cigarettes, putting out each after
having finished only half of it. He would then light a new

cigarette. After he would leave, the room would be full of his unfinished cigarettes . . .

I would keep these remaining cigarettes carefully in the cupboard after he left. I would only light them while sitting alone by myself. When I would hold one of these cigarettes between my fingers, I would feel as if I was touching his hands . . .

This is how I took to smoking. Smoking gave me the feeling that he was close to me. He appeared, each time, like a genie in the smoke emanating from the cigarette.[6]

She also gives Sahir's side of the story. 'Sahir also told me, much later in life, "When both of us were in Lahore, I would often come close to your house and stand at the corner where I would sometimes buy a paan, or light a cigarette or hold a glass of soda in my hand. I would stand there for hours together watching that window of your house which opened towards the street."'[7]

Then, when the country was partitioned, Amrita moved with her husband and eventually settled down in Delhi. Sahir, as we already know, had established himself in Bombay a few years after Partition.

Amrita hit upon a novel idea to bridge the geographical distance between the two. She began to include her experiences with Sahir in her literary endeavours. His character featured prominently in the anthology of poems 'Ik si Anita' (A Girl Named Anita), the novel 'Dilli Diyaa Galiyaan' (The Bylanes of Delhi) and the collection of short stories 'Aakhari Khat' (Final Letter). Her poem 'Sunehray' (Messages), which fetched her the Sahitya Akademi Award in 1956, was also written for Sahir.

An interesting anecdote regarding their relationship can be found

6. Amrita Pritam, *Raseedi Tikkat*, Kitaabghar Prakashan, 2008, p. 28.

7. Amrita Pritam, *Sahir, Main aur Nau Sau Meelo ka Faasla*, Sulabh India, February 1988, p. 12.

in the short story 'Aakhari Khat' in the eponymous collection. It was in the year 1955 that the weekly Urdu magazine *Aayeena* was launched from Delhi. When *Aayeena* requested Amrita to write a story for them, she decided to use the publication as a conduit to get through to Sahir. She wrote of her first meeting with Sahir in the form of a story and called it 'Aakhari Khat'.

In its short life, *Aayeena* had already become an acclaimed weekly publication and was well respected amongst Urdu literary figures. This convinced Amrita that her story would reach Sahir and would probably bridge the language divide between them. Yet, many days passed with no response from Sahir.

Then, one day, Amrita ran into him. And he said: 'When I read "Aakhari Khat", I was so delighted that I wanted to take the magazine to each of my friends and tell them – look this has been written for me, but I decided to keep quiet. I thought if I told friends like Khwaja Ahmad Abbas and Krishan Chander, they would chide me and threaten to take me to the asylum.'[8]

*

Amrita was a stunningly beautiful woman. The film writer C.L. Kavish is eloquent in his description of her: 'Amrita Pritam was a chiselled piece of marble. If a sculptor's eyes had fallen on her, he would have carved a statue out of her that would have been worshipped as Radha in temples today.'[9]

Sahir Ludhianvi, as Kaifi Azmi describes him,[10] was about six feet tall. He had long, shapely legs, a slim waist, was broad-chested and had pockmarks on his face. He had a prominent nose and

8. Ibid., p. 13.
9. Saabir Dutt, *Fann Aur Shaksiyat*, Sahir Ludhianvi Number, C.L. Kavish, 'Anarkali se Parchhaaiyaan tak', p. 111.
10. Ibid., Kaifi Azmi, 'Mera Hum Asra Mera Saathi', p. 293.

beautiful eyes, which seemed lost in deep thought. His hair was long and lustrous and he walked with loose strides, often with a tin of cigarettes in his hand. There is nothing in this description to suggest that Sahir was blessed with less-than-average looks. Yet, as Amrita also observed, Sahir's biggest complex in life was that he was not good-looking.

She narrated an incident to reinforce her point.

> One day Sahir offered to tell my daughter a story. He started by saying, 'Once, there was a woodcutter who would chop wood all day long in the jungle. One day he noticed a beautiful young princess. He yearned to run away with her . . . But he was only a poor woodcutter. He kept admiring her from a distance, and then, disappointed, returned to chopping wood.'
>
> Sahir then asked my daughter, 'Is that not a true story?'
>
> 'Yes, even I have seen this happen.' I don't know why my daughter said this but she did.
>
> Sahir laughed. He looked at me and said, 'See, even she knows.' He asked my daughter, 'You saw them, didn't you?'
>
> My daughter nodded her head.
>
> 'Who was the woodcutter?' asked Sahir.
>
> Possibly under the influence of some divine power, my daughter mumbled, 'You . . .'
>
> Sahir then asked, 'And the princess, who was she?'
>
> 'Mama!' my daughter said gleefully.
>
> Sahir looked at me and said, 'See, children know everything.'[11]

But Sahir's looks weren't an issue for Amrita. Going by her account, she was deeply in love with Sahir. At various places in her autobiography, she makes fawning references to him. There is mention of Sahir in the very first few pages of her autobiography when Amrita talks about rebelling against her maternal grandmother for the first time (Amrita had lost her mother when she was only eleven years old).

11. Amrita Pritam, *Raseedi Tikkat*, Kitaabghar Prakashan, 2008, p. 27.

Amrita, only fifteen then, had noticed that her grandmother kept three glasses on a tray in one corner of the kitchen, separate from all the other vessels. These glasses would only be put to use when Amrita's father's Muslim friends came to visit and they had to be served tea or lassi. After the guests would leave, these glasses would once again find their way back to the corner.

Amrita eventually challenged her grandmother. Knowing very well that her grandmother could be bigoted but could not afford to have her granddaughter starve, Amrita insisted on having water and milk in those very same glasses. The matter eventually reached Amrita's father. Amrita succeeded in making her point and all vessels ceased to be segregated thereafter.

Amrita ends this episode with an obvious reference to Sahir. 'At that moment, neither I nor my grandmother were aware that on growing up, the individual I would love deeply for many years of my life would belong to the same faith for whom those three glasses had been put aside. He was not part of my life then, but I think, at that instant, it was his shadow that graced my childhood . . .'[12]

Later in the book, Amrita remarks that the woman in her always played second fiddle to the writer, but for three exceptions. One such exception pertained to Sahir. He had been running a slight temperature and was breathing with great difficulty. Amrita tended to Sahir with great care and even applied 'Vicks' on his neck and chest.

'I can't remember for how long, but I felt that I could stand on my feet and rub my fingers and palms gently on his chest for the rest of my life. The "woman" within me did not feel the need for any paper or pen at that time,' Amrita recalls.[13]

If this tender moment confirms Amrita's complete devotion to

---

12. Ibid., pp. 11–12.
13. Ibid., pp. 51–52.

Sahir, her single-minded obsession with Sahir also reveals itself in the autobiography.

Towards the end of 1946, Amrita was pregnant with her son. She had heard that a child resembles the kind of photographs that adorn a pregnant woman's room or the person she imagines in her mind. Convinced by this theory, Amrita started thinking about Sahir constantly. She hoped that her son would resemble Sahir. When her son, Navraj, was born on 3 July 1947, and Amrita saw his face for the first time, she was convinced that he actually looked like Sahir.

Such obsessive behaviour obviously led to speculation whether Navraj was indeed Sahir's son. Amrita even mentioned that when she visited Bombay in 1960, Rajinder Singh Bedi (the Progressive writer) even confronted her on the subject to which Amrita replied, 'This is the truth of my imagination, not the truth in reality.' [14]

Given such devotion on her part, it is not surprising that when Amrita learnt of Sahir's involvement with another woman in 1960, she was left extremely distressed.

*

Sudha Malhotra was in her early twenties when rumours of an alleged affair between her and Sahir Ludhianvi began doing the rounds in film circles in the late 1950s. Sudha had recently entered the world of playback singing and had managed to carve a niche for herself in a short time with a few songs, most of them penned by Sahir, which became enormously popular.

I met Sudha in the opulent surroundings of her bungalow in Khar (West), Mumbai, in early 2010. I must admit that I was apprehensive of asking someone of her age (now in her late seventies) details

14. Ibid., p. 27.

about a past relationship in the lead-up to the interview. Sudha, though, was most forthcoming on the subject, possibly because she saw it as an opportunity to clear the myths involving her and Sahir once and for all. Fresh from a ghazal performance in memory of the legendary Begum Akhtar the previous evening, she went about setting the record straight.

According to Sudha, her first song for Sahir, perhaps, was the hugely popular 'Mere nadeem, mere humsafar' (My friend, my companion) from Bhai Behen (1959):

> One day he [Sahir] just dropped in at the house. I had never met him. He said, 'I would like you to sing my song ['Mere nadeem, mere humsafar'] . . . In those days, I was singing in films and any new contract was good for me. And since it was coming from Sahir, it meant a lot. He was well established by then, very well known. I sang that song and then, every second day, I was singing one song for him.

Between 1958 and 1960, Sudha sang for a number of films in which Sahir wrote the songs – Bhai Behen (1959), Dhool Ka Phool (1959), Barsaat Ki Raat (1960), Baabar (1960). By itself, this was not something worthy of mention. But the circumstances – an interesting mix of Sahir's bachelor status, his failed romantic liaisons and the kind of songs that he wrote for Sudha – spawned speculation of a relationship brewing between the two. For Baabar (1960), he wrote the following song sung by Sudha:

> Salaam-e-hasrat qabool kar lo
> Meri mohabbat qabool kar lo . . .
>
> Tumhi nigaahon ki justajoo ho, tumhi khayaalon ka mudda ho
> Tumhi mere waastey sanam ho, tumhi mere waastey khuda ho
> Meri parastish ki laaj rakh lo, meri ibaadat qabool kar lo
> Salaam-e-hasrat qabool kar lo
>
> (Please accept the overture of my desires
> Please accept my proposition of love . . .

You are what my eyes yearn for, you are the subject of my
 thoughts
You are my beloved, you are the one I call God
Please uphold the nobility of my devotion, please accept my
 prayers
Please accept the overture of my desires)

Such compositions sent the rumour mills into overdrive.

Speaking to me, Sudha was candid about these developments:

He must have liked my voice . . . I don't know what it was, but
he was definitely very enamoured. He kept giving me good
songs to sing, which was my achievement . . . Every morning I
used to get a call from him, but it was always related to work.
My uncle would tease me, '*Tere morning alarm ka phone aa gaya hai*'
(Your morning alarm is at the other end of the telephone) . . . All
I know was that attention was being showered on me and I was
lapping it up. As a young girl, if somebody, such an important
person, is giving you so much attention, you enjoy it.

In the same breath, she rebutted the thought of ever having
entertained the idea of romancing Sahir:

It didn't even cross my mind once. For one thing, he was much
older and from a different kind of world. We were very different
people. I came from a very different background. My father was
a college principal. My grandfather was a Western Railway
chief officer. And remember, in those days, the film line was not
considered a good one.

The gossip, though, never went away. In fact, it increased to the
extent that the line between fact and fiction got blurred. It was
suggested that the song '*Chalo ik baar phir se ajnabi bann jaayein hum
dono*' (Come, let us be strangers once again), sung by Mahendra
Kapoor in *Gumraah* (1963), was a vicarious expression of anguish
by Sahir for Sudha. This, despite the fact that it was first published
as a poem under the title 'Khubsoorat Modh' (A Beautiful Turn) in
his book *Talkhiyaan*.

But the words of the song fitted the premise of an estranged romance between the two perfectly:

Na main tumse koi umeed rakhoon dil nawaazee ki
Na tum meri taraf dekho galat-andaaz nazron se
Na mere dil ki dhadkan ladkhadaaye meri baaton mein
Na zaahir ho tumhaari kashmakash ka raaz nazron se . . .

Taa-aruf rog ho jaaye toh usko bhoolna behtar
Taaluq bojh bann jaayein toh usko todna achchha
Woh afsaana jisey anjaam tak laana na ho mumkin
Usey ek khoobsurat modh dekar chhodna achchha
Chalo ik baar phir se ajnabi bann jaayein hum dono

(Neither will I harbour any hopes of your love
Nor should you look at me enticingly
Neither will my heart give itself away when I speak
Nor will your eyes betray your inner anxieties . . .

If an acquaintance becomes an ailment, it is best forgotten
If a relationship becomes a burden, it is best broken
A story that cannot be taken to its logical conclusion
Is best given a beautiful tinge and then left alone
Come, let us be strangers once again)

Even today, the mere mention of Sahir Ludhianvi and Sudha Malhotra draws an immediate reference to this song from those claiming to know everything about Sahir.

Sudha, on the other hand, was simply stumped by the innuendo, for she had married almost three years before *Gumraah*'s release, in 1960.

Because I got married I didn't want to get into any kind of controversy. They, the press, all of them, tried their best to malign my name in many ways. It was a bad phase in my life. I was totally oblivious initially, but when it happened, I stopped singing. Because he was such a famous writer, all the famous music directors I knew – Jaidev, Roshan – everybody sided with him. There was really nothing from my side. But what could I do about it? I felt that they should have supported me, but they chose to support him because that was their bread and butter. They all used to compose for him. How could they fight him?

Someone who worked with Sahir in those years was music director Khayyam (*Phir Subah Hogi*, 1958). My two meetings with Khayyam saab were facilitated by a common acquaintance. Diminutive in stature, Khayyam, possibly a forgotten film legend among today's generation of Hindi film lovers, stands tall with his impressive body of work, which includes composing for films like *Shola Aur Shabnam* (1961), *Kabhi Kabhie* (1976) and *Umrao Jaan* (1981). Well into his eighties when I met him, Khayyam's memory was as sharp and lucid as ever as he frequently recalled an old nazm or a couplet or the lyrics of a song by a poet or a lyricist from an earlier era in response to my questions. Speaking to me in his distinctive, rich voice, in a language peppered with a heavy dose of Urdu, Khayyam took a mature view of the Sudha–Sahir situation:

> It is possible that his [Sahir's] feelings could have been entirely one sided. She [Sudha] may have denied the whole situation, but where such a great personality like Sahir Ludhianvi was involved, it is hard to imagine that she didn't respond in some way, howsoever minutely, to his overtures. She may have been married or unmarried, but she must have had some kind of a soft corner for him. But I am only guessing, since I was never privy to the relationship between them.

Ruhan Kapoor, Mahendra Kapoor's son, whom I interviewed in May 2010 at his Bandra home, was a bit more sympathetic towards Sudha's position. He presented an interesting analogy to explain what might have transpired between the two: 'I am an artist. I am a writer. I fall in love with Madhuri Dixit and I conceive a subject. It becomes a brilliant piece of art. It becomes super successful. What does Madhuri Dixit have to do with it? Probably, Sahir saab was similarly infatuated with Sudha Malhotra.'

After 1960, the year she got married, Sudha stopped singing in Hindi films. She did not sing for Sahir or anyone else. Neither did she meet him again. Looking back, Sudha had no regrets.

> It's too far gone. It's behind me. In the first couple of years it made me very upset . . . I know I hadn't done anything wrong. I admired him as a writer . . . I am grateful. He is the one who really took me to those heights. It was because of his songs. People can't forget his songs . . . As a human being also he was very, very nice to me. Everything was good. His sisters, his mother, they were all there, very nice people . . . But there was nothing from my side.

The opening lines of one of Sahir's songs, sung once again by Sudha, probably summarize the relationship best:

> *Tum mujhe bhool bhi jao, toh yeh haq hai tumko*
> *Meri baat aur hai, maine toh mohabbat ki hai*
>
> *Mere dil ki, mere jazbaat ki keemat kya hai?*
> *Uljhe uljhe se khayaalat ki keemat kya hai?*
> *Maine kyun pyaar kiya, tumne na kyun pyaar kiya?*
> *In pareshaan sawaalaat ki keemat kya hai?*
> *Tum jo yeh bhi na batao, toh yeh haq hai tumko*
> *Meri baat aur hain, maine toh mohabbat ki hai . . .* [15]

> (Even if you forget me, you have the right to do so
> But I can't be expected to do the same for I have genuinely loved
>   you
>
> What does it matter how I feel deep within my heart?
> Of what significance are these tangled thoughts running through
>   my mind?
> Why I chose to love, and why didn't you choose to reciprocate
>   that love?

---

15. From the film *Didi* (1959).

What is the point behind all these difficult questions?
Even if you don't answer, you have every right to do so
But I can't be expected to do the same, for I have genuinely
    loved you . . .)

                                *

Needless to say, all this left Amrita distraught. She confesses in her
autobiography to having written some of her most despondent
poetry in this period. She even sought psychiatric help to address
her fragile state of mind. And while there is no direct mention of
any bitterness that she felt towards Sahir for his relationship with
Sudha, Amrita does dwell on a few dreams, one of which may have
a bearing on her tumultuous relationship with him:

> There was a white marble statue right in front of me. I kept
> looking at it, staring at it, and then I said to it, 'What do I do of
> you! Neither do you speak, nor do you breathe. Today I will
> destroy you, break you into pieces. You have wasted all my life,
> my imagination, my principles . . .' and then when I hurled that
> statue with all my strength, I woke up under the influence of my
> own fury.[16]

It was, conceivably, Amrita's way of seeking closure. In 1964,
Amrita separated from her husband. She spent the last forty-odd
years of her life (Amrita died in 2005) with Imroz, a man who
loved her unconditionally. Uma Trilok describes Amrita's love for
both Sahir and Imroz in her book:

> She expressed her views on love saying that there was one kind
> of love like that of the sky, and there was another, which was
> like a roof over one's head. Sahir Ludhianvi was 'like the sky' for
> her. A woman seeks both, she had said, and the roof eventually

---

16. Amrita Pritam, *Raseedi Tikkat*, Kitaabghar Prakashan, 2008, pp. 31, 34–35.

opens to the sky. It was chance and circumstance that she chose the roof. The sky was very distant.[17]

The last time Amrita reflects on her association with Sahir in *Raseedi Tikkat* is when she hears of his death. She recalls the time Sahir and she had met at the Asian Writers' Conference held in Delhi (sometime in the early 1950s). Those attending the conference had been given badges carrying their names. However, Sahir had interchanged their badges. When someone pointed this out, Sahir laughed. He said the people handing out the badges had made a mistake and that they (Amrita and he) could have corrected it but chose not to.

'Now, many years later, when I heard of Sahir's demise at two o'clock in the night, I feel that death had wanted to knock on my door but went to his instead, since the badge carrying my name was attached to his coat,' writes a wistful Amrita.[18]

It is indeed a travesty that the relationship between Amrita and Sahir, two doyens of literature, couldn't mature into anything more substantial, something that mirrored their beautiful individual contributions to prose and poetry. Yet, it is probably with Amrita that Sahir came closest, at least in his mind, to a long-term relationship, as revealed in a telling conversation he had with his mother.

'*Maaji, yeh Amrita thi, janti ho na? Yeh aapki bahu bhi bann sakti thi,*' (Mother, that was Amrita. She could have become your daughter-in-law) Sahir is said to have told his mother in reference to Amrita once while they were in Delhi with some of Sahir's friends.

To which his mother replied imploringly, '*Bete, bahu banao toh sahi kisi ko.*' (As long as you make someone my daughter-in-law.)

'*Chhodo, maaji, sab baatein. Chalo Aslam [driver] se kaho, gaadi start*

17. Uma Trilok, *Amrita-Imroz: A Love Story*, Penguin Books India, 2006, p. 18.
18. Amrita Pritam, *Raseedi Tikkat*, Kitaabghar Prakashan, 2008, p. 117.

kare. Khaana khaaney chaltey hain Moti Mahal mein. Aaj teetar khaayengey!'
(Forget it mother. Tell Aslam to start the car. We will eat at Moti
Mahal where we will enjoy the partridge today.)[19]

Maybe the last word on the Amrita–Sahir relationship comes
from Imroz, who first met Amrita in 1957 and almost immediately
fell in love with her. It wasn't easy asking Imroz about Amrita's
relationship with Sahir. After all, talking to someone who in a very
shallow sense was competing with Sahir for Amrita's affection at
one point could well be awkward. But my worst fears were put to
rest when Imroz readily agreed to meet me at the same Hauz Khas
residence where he had lived with Amrita for many years. He
spoke to me freely on the subject. According to Imroz, it was
Sahir's poetry that drew Amrita to Sahir. 'There is nothing
untoward or extraordinary about this. It's just that a creative woman
was drawn towards another very talented man.'

Imroz also admitted to being a huge admirer of Sahir's songs. A
remarkable man by all accounts, Imroz summarizes the Amrita–
Sahir story with an insightful poem of his own:

> *Woh bhi ek kavi thi*
> *Aur uska dost bhi ek shaayar thaa*
> *Woh aap bhi ek shehar mein rehti thi*
> *Aur uska dost bhi nau sau meel door ek shahar mein rehta tha*
>
> *Kabhi kabhi miltey thay*
> *Jab kabhi mauka mila dey*
> *Mushaira bhi ek mauka tha*
> *Aur conference bhi*
> *Khud woh kabhi mauka nahin baney*
> *Ek doosrey ko aa ja ke milney ka*

19. Saabir Dutt, *Fann Aur Shaksiyat*, Sahir Ludhianvi Number, Krishan Adeeb,
'Sahir: Yaadon Ke Aaynein Mein', p. 527.

Kabhi kabhi likhkar woh dono mauka bana letey thay
Nazmein likhkar miltey rehtey
Zyaadatar woh isi tarah miltey rahey barah saal
Woh mohabbat ki nazmein aur kavitaein aaj bhi zinda hain pathakon ke
     dilon mein

Mohabbat zindagi bhi hoti hai
Sirf kavita ya nazm nahin

Uska dost jab bhi uskey shehar aata
Jab bhi uskey paas hota, woh kuch aur hi hota
Jaisey woh isi shehar ka ho
Isi dharti ki koi nazm ho, khushboo ho
Par apney shehar jaakar, woh kuch aur ho jaata
Chup ho jaata, bhool jaata
Jis tarah woh kisi ko kabhi mila hi na ho
Mahiney, saal, viraaney ki tarah
Guzarety rehtey, guzartey rehtey

Nau so meel ka faasla koi faasla nahin hota
Aur bhi hongey andikh fasley jo taye nahin huey
Waqt ke saath uski kavita behtereen kavita tak pahunch gayee
Aur uskey nazm bhi behtereen nazm tak pahunch gaye
Par dono zindagi tak nahin pahunchey
Pahunch jaatey, toh dono ki zindagi bhi
Kavita kavita ho jaati, nazm nazm ho jaati.

(She was a poet
And her friend was a poet, too
She lived in a city
And he, too, lived in a city nine hundred miles away

They seldom met
Whenever an opportunity presented itself
Mushairas were an opportunity
So too were conferences
Yet, they individually never became the reason
To visit each other

Sometimes their writings became a conduit for them to meet
They would meet through their poems
Mostly, they met like this for twelve years
Those poems of love are fresh in the hearts of readers even today

Love is life as well
Not just a poem or a song

Whenever her friend would visit her city
Whenever he would meet her, he would behave differently
Like he belonged to this city itself
Like he was this city's creation, part of this city's ambience
But as soon as he returned to his own city, he would become
    someone else
He would stop talking and soon forget
Like he had never ever met her
Months, years, like a great emptiness
Passed by

A distance of nine hundred miles can be bridged
There may have been other distances that weren't bridged
With time, her poems got her fame
And his songs earned him a reputation
But both couldn't reach each other
Had they done so, their lives
Would have resembled a beautiful poem)

Besides Amrita and Sudha Malhotra, Sahir's name was linked with
a few other women. He was allegedly engaged to Hajra Masroor,
an Urdu writer, sometime around 1946, but abruptly broke all ties
with her. There are detailed descriptions of a short but intense
affair with a married lady in Hyderabad. But with none of these
women, nor with anyone else, could Sahir conjure a lasting
companionship.

Possibly, it was Sahir's fear of unrequited love, as expressed in
his poem 'Hiraas' (Fear), that eventually led him to part ways with
all these women:

Tere hothon pe tabassum ki woh halki see lakeer
Mere takhaiyul mein rah-rah ke jhalak uth-ti hai
Yoon achaanak tere aareez ka khayaal aata hai
Jaisey zulmat mein koi shamaa bhadak uth-ti hai . . .

Main sulagtey huey raazon ko ayaan toh kar doon
Lekin in raazon ki tash-heer se jee darta hai
Raat ke khwaab ujaaley mein bayaan toh kar doon
In haseen khwaabon ki taabeer se jee darta hai . . .

Kahin aisa na ho, paaon mere thar-raa jaayein
Aur teri marmari baahon ka sahaara na miley
Ashk behtey rahein khaamosh siyah raaton mein
Aur tere reshmi aanchal ka kinaara na miley

(That hint of a smile appearing on your lips
Keeps emerging from within my imagination
When suddenly I think of your cheeks
It is like a light has filled the darkness . . .

I can declare openly these intense desires
But I am afraid of disclosing these secrets publicly
I could discuss the night's dreams in the morning light
But I am frightened what these dreams will bare . . .

It shouldn't happen that I find my feet paralysed
And that I do not get the support of your beautiful fair arms
My tears flow unabated into the silent dark night
And I don't even get the edge of your silken clothing to hold on to)

But his failure to convert any of his relationships into something more meaningful went far beyond his anxiety of being rejected. There was a deeper, more profound explanation for Sahir's self-imposed state of bachelorhood. An explanation best articulated by Imroz:

Owing to his troubled childhood, Sahir had developed a special place for his mother in his heart. He was unwilling to share her with anyone. He was like the protagonist from one of Amrita's novels who explained his distressed upbringing and continued aversion to get married by saying, '*Meri maa ki zindagi mein ek hi mard hai, aur main usko kisi aur ke saath baant nahin sakta*' (There is only one man in my mother's life and I cannot afford to share myself with anyone else). He was so dependent on his mother that even when he went for a mushaira all the way to Allahabad, he would take her along.

Indeed, Imroz's opinion on the relationship between mother and son finds resonance with people who knew Sahir from close quarters. According to Javed Akhtar, 'He was heavily obliged towards his mother. She was the centre of his universe. And if the mother becomes such a dominating figure in a man's life, he feels guilty thinking about any other woman. And perhaps, that was the problem. So, the moment he would get involved with another woman, he would feel guilty that maybe he was letting his mother down. It was strange, unhealthy, even complicated, but then that is how it was.'

Even Khushwant Singh, who claims to have met Sahir only twice, doesn't mince words in this aspect: 'Sahir developed a strong mother-fixation and loathing for his father: the relationship was an example of the Greek Oedipus complex, which made him incapable of consummating the few love affairs he had in the short life of 59 years.'[20]

Sahir, though, explained his bachelor status taking shelter in filial ties:

No, I am not against the institution of marriage, but as far as I am concerned, I have never felt the real need to get married. In my opinion, the relationship between a man and a woman may not necessarily be confined to a relation between husband and wife.

20. Khushwant Singh, 'Sahir's tortured soul', *The Tribune*, Saturday, 10 January 2004 (http://www.tribuneindia.com/2004/20040110/windows/above.htm).

It can also be similar to a mother's love or affection for one's sister.[21]

Yet, the various relationships served their purpose at least from a poetic perspective in Sahir's life. Without them, we might have been robbed of some of his best romantic songs, be it 'Chalo ik baar phir se ajnabi bann jaayein hum dono' or 'Tum mujhe bhool bhi jao, toh yeh haq hai tumko' or 'Jaane woh kaise log thay jinke pyaar ko pyaar mila'.

He needed a muse to spur his creativity and these women, at various stages in his life, brought out the romantic in him. These associations gave him a nuanced understanding of the many seasons of love and longing. How else could he have given expression to the despondency of Bharat Bhushan's character in 'Mehfil se uth jaaney waalo' (Dooj Ka Chaand, 1964), a song he allegedly wrote immediately after a meeting with Amrita and Imroz.[22]

> Mehfil se uth jaaney waalo, tum logon par kya ilzaam?
> Tum aabaad gharon ke waasi, main aawaara aur badnaam
> Mere saathi khaali jaam
>
> (You who leave an evening of celebration, how can I blame you?
> You are destined for happier times, I am a vagabond, much maligned
> Empty liquor glasses now keep me company)

These romantic liaisons allowed him to articulate the state of bliss one experiences in love ('Yeh raat, yeh chandni phir kahaan?'),[23] write songs of everlasting romance ('Jo waada kiya woh nibhaana padega'),[24] and turn sensual to describe the blossoming love between two individuals ('Neele gagan ke taley').[25]

---

21. Saabir Dutt, Fann Aur Shaksiyat, Sahir Ludhianvi Number, Balwant Singh, 'Hum Ke Thehere Ajnabee', p. 50.
22. Amrita Pritam, Raseedi Tikkat, Kitaabghar Prakashan, 2008, p. 87.
23. Jaal (1952).
24. Taj Mahal (1963).
25. Humraaz (1967).

Likewise, having been spurned on a few occasions, he was able to take a gentle dig at these stone-hearted women:

Jo inki nazar se khele
Dukh paaye, museebat jhele
Phirte hain yeh sab albele
Dil leke mukar jaane ko[26]

(Those who lock eyes with them
Are doomed, in deep misery
They walk around, all these beauties,
Having stolen your heart, they then turn truant)

These remarkable compositions led Aale Ahmed Saroor, the eminent Urdu poet, critic and scholar, to dedicate the very lines, from which Sahir chose his takhallus, to Sahir on his demise:

Hoo bahoo kheinchega lekin, ishq ki tasveer kaun?
Uth gaya nawak fagan, marega dil par teer kaun?[27]

(But who will sketch such a vivid portrayal of love?
Who will enchant the heart, now that the marksman is gone?)

No wonder then that in the absence of a muse, Sahir's romantic songs in the 1970s and after, barring 'Kabhi kabhi mere dil mein' (*Kabhi Kabhie*, 1976), didn't create much of an impression. This might have also been a reflection of the changing times in Hindi cinema, with scripts tailor-made to suit the persona of the 'Angry Young Man' at the turn of the 1970s.

But given that his dreamy compositions in these years – 'Waada karo nahin chhodogi tum mera saath' (*Aa Gale Lag Jaa*, 1973), the title song of *Ek Mahal Ho Sapnon Ka* (1975) or 'Aapki mehki hui zulf ko kehtey hain ghata' (*Trishul*, 1978) – lacked the beauty of his songs

---

26. From the song *'Jeevan ke safar mein raahi milte hain bichad jaaney ko'* (On the path of life we meet people only to get separated), *Munimji* (1955).
27. See Chapter 1.

from the 1950s and early 1960s, one wonders what a steady female companion would have done for him and his poetry.

Haafiz Ludhianvi, in the context of the Mahinder Chaudhary episode from Sahir's college years, perhaps best explains Sahir's fleeting romantic trysts:

> Sahir did not linger with one issue for very long. His emotions and experiences were momentary. He would get influenced by a particular episode with such passion that his friends would get amazed, but Sahir, having given the incident a poetic form, would feel that he had fulfilled his objective. All his poems are written in response to some personal tragedy or romantic liaison.[28]

He really was that kind of man.

---

28. Saabir Dutt, *Fann Aur Shaksiyat*, Sahir Ludhianvi Number, Haafiz Ludhianvi, 'Rumaan Aur Inquilaab Ka Shaayar', p. 132.

8

The Chopras Come Calling

Umra ka rishta jodney waaley
Apni nazar mein deewaane hain[1]

(Those who strike relations for life
Are, in my opinion, of a higher disposition)

The only thing I was certain of while working on this book was that if I didn't get an audience with Yash Chopra, this endeavour would be bereft of substance. After all, Sahir had written the songs for each of Yash Chopra's films beginning with *Dhool Ka Phool* (1959) up until his death in 1980. He had also written the songs for most of B.R. Chopra's (Yash's elder brother) films starting with *Naya Daur* (1957). With BR having passed away in November 2008, it was pretty clear to me that a book on Sahir without inputs from Yash Chopra would be like a book on Sanjeev Kumar without a perspective from Gulzar, or one on Robert De Niro without Martin Scorcese's point of view. It would simply be incomplete.

---

1. From the song '*Pal do pal ka saath hamaara*' (Ours is but a momentary acquaintance), *The Burning Train* (1980).

And so from mid-March 2010, I dedicated myself solely to the purpose of seeking an interview with Yash. It finally came to fruition two-and-a-half months later, following several rescheduled appointments, including the one time I reached Yash's office only to be told by the veteran film-maker himself that he had suddenly taken ill and that our meeting would have to wait for another time.

But when the interview did take place, on 4 June 2010, it was an extremely unnerving experience. Not just because the man lays claim to, arguably, being Hindi cinema's most successful producer-director ever, but because his humility was at odds with the high-strung behaviour of most film personalities, even when their achievements aren't anywhere near as great as Yash Chopra's.

Then there was the matter of meeting Yash Chopra in his office.

The entrance to his chamber itself fills one with a sense of reverential awe, covered as it is by photographs of Yash's many blockbusters that are an integral part of the legacy of popular Hindi cinema. Once you get over that and past the door, you find yourself in an office whose size not only mirrors the stature of the person sitting in it, but also makes you wonder about the hue and cry about space in the city. Situated on the fourth floor of YRF Studios, Andheri (West), Mumbai, Yash's office is probably the size of a king's durbar with a beautiful garden beyond the glass partitioning on one side adding to the grandeur. It is so huge that when you mixed sugar in the tea that Yash offered so kindly to every visitor, you could hear the distinct echo of the spoon clattering against the inside of your teacup.

Yash sat at one end of the room, with his many trophies and awards placed behind him, a very visible reminder of his achievements in the film industry. Towards the other end of the room was a large flat-screen television, neatly tucked away in a wall unit, with a sofa set placed in front, possibly, for Yash to entertain his guests or watch the rushes of one of his many films under production.

Despite the intimidating surroundings, I found myself engrossed in conversation with Yash for close to ninety minutes. The grand old man, who had served Indian cinema for over five decades, opened up on his long-time friend and associate, Sahir, in his trademark style – a delightful mix of English, Punjabi and Hindi.

'I was a fan of Sahir's poetry. I had read all his poetry when I was in college [in Jalandhar],' Yash began. Accordingly, when he came to Bombay in the early 1950s, Yash wanted to meet Sahir. B.R. Chopra, who had already established himself in the film industry by this time, thought that his younger brother might be excited to see some stars. He asked Yash whom he would like to meet.

'Sahir,' said Yash.

'He was staying in a place called Four Bungalows. I met him. We became, I can't say friends, but we began on a positive note towards each other,' said Yash Chopra of his first encounter with Sahir.

The first movie that Sahir worked with B.R. Films was *Naya Daur* (1957). The film was produced and directed by B.R. Chopra. Yash played a prominent part in securing the role of the songwriter for Sahir in this film. 'We were very good friends. I had confidence in Sahir's poetry. When I came into B.R. Films, as an assistant to Mr Chopra, I suggested his name. That was the beginning of Sahir's journey in B.R. Films.'

Naya Daur released in the same year as *Pyaasa*. The film had a strong socialistic flavour in keeping with the ideology of the Nehruvian era. It championed the cause of manual labour in the face of modernization and mechanization. It had a predominantly rural setting, with a tangewala, Shankar (Dilip Kumar), playing the central character in the film. Vyjayanthimala starred as the female lead.

Naya Daur's soundtrack, like the movie, was a runaway hit. Like in *Pyaasa*, the songs serve a variety of purposes and address a number of themes. 'Ude jab jab zulfein teri' (Whenever your locks blow in the

wind) ever so beautifully brings out the budding romance between
the film's protagonists while retaining a strong, yet innocuous,
flirtatious flavour. There are two remarkable aspects to this song.
Firstly, the word 'zulfein' is used by Vyjayanthimala's character to
describe Dilip Kumar's locks. This is surprising as 'zulf' has
traditionally been used by the hero in Hindi cinema to describe the
heroine's beauty. The other is the use of the word 'yaar' in the
second stanza of the song:

> *Us gaaon pe swarg bhi sadke*
> *Ke jahan mera yaar basta*

> (I forsake heaven too for the village
> Where my beloved lives)

The word 'yaar', which literally means 'friend', has at times been
used with a negative connotation – '*Bahut yaaraana lagta hai*' (There
is great chemistry between the two of you)[2] – in Hindi cinema to
insinuate an illicit relationship between a man and a woman.
Eventually, though, the word did find a place in hit romantic
numbers shot on female characters: '*Poocho na yaar kya hua*' (Ask my
dear what the matter is)[3] and '*Yaar bina chain kahaan re*' (There is no
peace in the absence of a soulmate).[4] But for Sahir to have given
Vyjayanthimala's character this word to use for her beloved in the
1950s, even when it was not in direct reference to Dilip Kumar's
character, was both pioneering and brave.

Equally inspiring is the song '*Yeh desh hai veer jawaano ka*':

> *Yeh desh hai veer jawaano ka*
> *Albelon ka, mastaano ka*
> *Is desh ka yaaron kya kehna, yeh desh hai duniya ka gehna*

---

2. Gabbar Singh's (Amjad Khan) legendary remark to Basanti (Hema Malini) and
Veeru (Dharmendra) in *Sholay* (1975).
3. From *Zamaane Ko Dikhana Hai* (1981).
4. From *Saaheb* (1985).

Yahaan chaudi chhaatee veeron kee
Yahaan bholi shakley Heeron kee
Yahaan gaate hai Raanjhein masti mein
Machti hain dhoomein basti mein

Pedon pe bahaarein jhuloon ki
Raahon mein kataare phoolon ki
Yahaan hansta hai saawan balon mein
Khilti hain kaliyaan gaalon mein

(This is the land of spirited youth
Of beautiful, carefree inhabitants
What does one say in praise of this nation, this country is the
    pride of the world

The brave here are strapping lads
The maidens are blessed with innocent faces
Here, love-struck men sing with gay abandon
The neighbourhood comes alive with joy

The trees swing in the glory of spring
The streets are lined with beautiful flowers
Here, the rain shimmers in the maidens' hair
Their cheeks glowing like buds)

The website upperstall.com captures the true essence of this composition when it says, 'A certain pride in the still-developing nation is seen as embodied by the song.'[5]

But going beyond that observation, one needs to juxtapose 'Yeh desh hai veer jawaano ka' vis-à-vis another great Sahir song which ruled the waves that year: 'Jinhe naaz hai Hind par woh kahaan hain' in Pyaasa. It is noteworthy that both songs address the same subject so to speak, the nation state, and yet are at complete odds with each other. Where the former, with its vibrant character, paints a heartening picture of India, the song in Pyaasa expresses

5. http://www.upperstall.com/films/1957/naya-daur.

disillusionment with the nation state. Both songs are true to their respective characters. Where Shankar and Krishna of *Naya Daur* are virile, self-confident boys, Vijay of *Pyaasa* is a defeatist hero. Where *Naya Daur*'s protagonists are not afraid to challenge their fate, Vijay is resigned to his.

For Sahir to have penned two such contrasting songs with totally different moods on the same subject was nothing short of remarkable. Then there is 'Saathi haath badhana'. The song, with its call for unity amongst the proletariat, has since become a rallying cry for Indians when faced with seemingly insurmountable odds:

> Saathi haath badhaana, saathi haath badhaana
> Ek akela thak jaayega, milkar bojh uthaana
>
> Hum mehnat waalon ne jab bhi mil kar kadam badhaaya
> Saagar ne rasta chhoda, parbat ne sees jhukaaya
> Faulaadi hain seeney apne, faulaadi hain baahein
> Hum chaahein toh paida kar de chattaanon mein raahein
> Saathi haath badhaana

(Oh friend, extend your helping hand
One alone will easily tire, let us share each other's burden instead

Whenever we, the working class, have worked together
The seas have parted way for us, the mountains have bowed
    their heads
Our chests are made of steel, our arms full of zeal
If we wish we can create our own path even through rocks and
    stone
Oh friend, extend your helping hand)

Like in *Pyaasa*, Sahir also slipped in yet another plea for the socialist order through the Johnny Walker ditty '*Main Bambai ka babu*' (I come from Bombay) in *Naya Daur*:

> Kuch hain daulat waaley, kuch hain taaqat waaley
> Asli waaley woh hain jo hain himmat waaley
> Sun lo aji sun lo yeh jadoo ka taraana

Aaya hoon main bandhu
Roos aur Cheen mein jaake
Kaam ki baat bata di arrey comedy gaana gaakey
Sun lo aji sun lo yeh jadoo ka taraana

(There are some who are wealthy, there are some who are powerful
But the people with character are those who have courage
Listen, listen carefully, to this magical song

I have come over here, my friend,
Having travelled to Russia and China
My message of great significance comes to you in jest
Listen, listen carefully, to this magical song)

There is the usual song of love and romance, '*Maang ke saath tumhaara*' (Having asked for your companionship), as also a hymn in praise of the Almighty, '*Aana hai toh aa raah mein kuch pher nahin hai*' (Come if you wish to come, the path is without obstacles). But what set *Naya Daur* apart from what Sahir had done in his brief career in the film industry so far was the distinct rustic element to his lyrics in the film. Songs like '*Ude jab jab zulfein teri*', '*Yeh desh hai veer jawaano ka*' and '*Reshmi salwaar kurta jaali ka*' (The maiden dressed in silk salwaar and gossamer kurta) are rich with words like 'kotwaali' (police station), 'phool jhadiyaan' (fire crackers), 'saawan' (month in the Hindu calendar associated with the rains, the monsoon), 'Raanjhein' (Romeo-like Punjabi folk character), 'kawaariyon' (nubile young maidens) which augment the film's rural setting. In doing this, Sahir charted new territory successfully.

Javed Akhtar brings out the contrast between *Pyaasa* and *Naya Daur*:

One is the story of a poet. The other is the story of a tangewala. One story is extremely urban, in the other there is a village. You can see the total difference of metaphor, of language, of vocabulary, of style.

In one he wrote '*Jaane woh kaise log thay jinke pyaar ko pyaar mila*, *humne toh jab kaliyaan maangi kaaton ka haar mila'* and in the other he is saying *'Reshmi salwaar kurta jaali ka, roop saha nahi jaayein nakhre waali ka'*. There is an earthiness to the songs in *Naya Daur*, whereas the poetry in *Pyaasa* is of cultivated, sophisticated, polished and educated expressions.

Even in the bhajan in *Pyaasa*, *'Aaj sajan mohe anj laga lo'*, there is a certain sophistication. In *Naya Daur*, the character is of a villager and the songs are also suitably rustic.

If 1957 was the year in which Sahir produced his finest work through *Pyaasa* and *Naya Daur*, it was also the year that saw him part ways, first with S.D. Burman, and then with O.P. Nayyar. There was *Sone Ki Chidiya*, which released a year later and in which Nayyar and Sahir worked together, but the songs for that film had been written before *Naya Daur* released. Nayyar and Sahir went their separate ways immediately after *Naya Daur*.

To get further insights into Sahir's relationship with the Chopra family, I met Ravi Chopra, B.R. Chopra's son and a producer-director in his own right, in April 2010 at the B.R. Films' office in Mumbai's Khar (West) neighbourhood. The B.R. Films' office is a pale shadow of its once glorious past, a phase that lasted for almost fifteen years from the mid-1950s to the late-1960s. Even during the 1980s, when B.R. Films produced and directed a couple of successful commercial potboilers – *Insaaf Ka Taraazu* (1980), *Nikaah* (1982) and *Tawaif* (1985) – and the popular television serial, *Mahabharat*, the banner was a name to be reckoned with. However, in the last decade, with the passing of B.R. Chopra in 2008, the failure of films like *Baabul* (2006) and *Bhoothnath* (2008) at the box office, and the family having to contend with several court cases, B.R. Films hit its lowest ebb. This decline in fortunes is what many believe to be the reason for Ravi Chopra's ill health since late-2009. In fact, when I met Ravi, he had just returned from hospital, having temporarily recovered from a breathing ailment which had severely constrained his ability to speak. Despite his condition,

Ravi was gracious enough to tell me all that he knew about Sahir from what he had heard from his father and what he had noticed of the man on the basis of his own working relationship with him.

Ravi spoke of the severing of ties with O.P. Nayyar: 'After finishing *Naya Daur*, O.P. Nayyar said he didn't want to work with Mr Sahir Ludhianvi any more. Dad told him [Nayyar], "He [Sahir] has not told me that he does not want to work with you. If you say that you do not want to work with him, so be it, but I will work with him."' Yash Chopra corroborated Ravi's version. He said BR was unwilling to turn his back on Sahir Ludhinavi because of Nayyar's unwillingness to work with him. At the same time, Yash believed that if it was Sahir who had said that he didn't want to work with Nayyar, BR would have reacted no differently. 'I think this was a matter of personal egos. *Kabhi kabhi koi loose sentence bol dena, artistic people ko hurt bahut karti hai* (At times a casual remark can hurt artistic people very badly),' said the veteran producer-director.[6] Nayyar and Sahir worked together in very few films. Their partnership was nowhere as prodigious as the S.D. Burman–Sahir combine. But their all-too-brief association did result in a timeless classic in *Naya Daur*, for which Nayyar won his only Filmfare Award for Best Music Director.

Following the triumph of *Naya Daur*, Sahir entrenched himself firmly under the B.R. Films' umbrella. Over the next ten years, his partnership with the Chopras resulted in quality cinema enhanced by fine lyrics.

It is important to understand here what B.R. Chopra, very much the patriarch in the Chopra family and the man behind B.R. Films, stood for in terms of his cinematic vision. Before he turned director with *Afsaana* (1951), BR had established himself as a successful film journalist in the early 1940s. In that role he was severely critical of

---

6. Yash told me that Sahir felt that Nayyar's tunes were copied.

film producers. From his perspective, they 'were wasting their time with comedies and mythologicals, dancing and songs, thus avoiding dealing with any serious social issues'.[7] Accordingly, when BR started producing his own films, he saw it as an opportunity to address issues of social reform.

BR's philosophy found immediate resonance with Sahir. Because of his Progressive leanings, and then through his songs in *Pyaasa* and *Naya Daur*, Sahir had already committed himself to using the film medium to air his views on matters of social importance.

Sadhana (1958), the next film under the B.R. Films' banner, dealt with the subject of an educated young man, Mohan (Sunil Dutt), falling in love, unknowingly, with a courtesan, Champabai (Vyjayanthimala), and his subsequent dilemma in offering her a new life by agreeing to marry her. Sahir set the tone for Champabai's character early in *Sadhana* with the song 'Kaho ji tum kya kya khareedoge?':

> Mohabbat bechti hoon main, sharaafat bechti hoon main
> Na ho gairat toh le jao, ki gairat bechti hoon main
> Nigahein toh milao, adaayein na dikhao, yahaan na sharmao
> Kaho ji tum kya kya khareedoge?
>
> (I am in the business of selling love, I sell propriety as well
> If you have no self-respect, you may buy that, too, for I sell my
>   own self-respect as well
> Look me in the eye at least, do not be high handed, do not play coy
> Tell me what all is it that you have come to buy?)

Closer to the climax of the film, he produced the song that summarized the courtesan's troubles and articulated BR's directorial vision:

7. Rachel Dwyer, *Yash Chopra: Fifty Years in Indian Cinema*, The Lotus Collection, Roli Books, 2002, p. 29.

Aurat ne janam diya mardon ko, mardon ne usay bazaar diya
Jab bhi chaaha masla kuchla, jab bhi chaha dhutkaar diya

Tulti hain kahin dinaaro mein, bikti hain kahin baazaaro mein
Nangi nachwayee jaati hai, ayyaashon ke darbaaron mein
Yeh woh beizzat cheez hai jo bant jaati hai izzatdaaron mein . . .

Jin hothon ne inko pyaar kiya, un hothon ka wyaapaar kiya
Jis kokh mein inka jism dhala, us kokh ka kaarobaar kiya
Jis tann se ugey kopal bankar, us tann ko zaleelo-khwaar kiya . . .

Sansaar ki har ek besharmi, gurbat ki godh mein palti hai
Chaklon heen mein aakar rukti hai, faakon se jo raah nikalti hai
Mardon ki hawas hai jo aksar aurat ko paap mein dhalti hai[8]

(Woman gave birth to man, men confined her to the brothel instead
Whenever he wishes he tramples over her, whenever he wishes
        he treats her contemptuously

At places she is valued in money, sold in many a brothel
She is paraded naked in the drawing rooms of the depraved
She is that disgraced commodity that is feasted upon by the self-
        respecting . . .

The very lips that gave men love, those very lips have been bargained
The wombs in which their bodies were nourished, those very
        wombs have been trafficked
The bodies they were raised from, the same bodies they have
        now brought disrepute to . . .

Every immoral act in this world, owes its genesis to impoverished
        circumstances
In brothels they come to an end, those roads that begin from poverty
It is the lust of men which often drives women to a life of sin)

Where '*Jinhe naaz hai Hind par*' in *Pyaasa* is a subtle lament on the
plight of women, '*Aurat ne janam diya mardo ko*' is scathing, almost

---

8. From the song '*Aurat ne janam diya mardon ko*'.

melodramatic, in its tone. This isn't a bystander's cynical view of proceedings, like Vijay's in *Pyaasa*. Instead, it is a courtesan's first-hand account of man's twisted ways. Yash Chopra remarked in reference to this song: 'Sahir was very, very bitter about certain things. Where even certain dialogue writers could not write so powerfully, his poetry did that magic.'

Next up were *Dhool Ka Phool* (1959) and *Dharamputra* (1961). The first of these marked Yash's debut as director. Both films complemented each other perfectly. *Dhool Ka Phool* deals largely with the topic of an illegitimate child, while broaching the subject of communal harmony between Hindus and Muslims. Partition and the ensuing communal hatred remain at the core of *Dharamputra*'s storyline even as the film begins with Husn Bano (Mala Sinha) getting pregnant out of wedlock.

There are some beautiful ballads that suit the romantic subtext of both films. '*Tere pyaar ka aasra chahta hoon*' (I seek the succour of your love) from *Dhool Ka Phool* deserves special mention. It is a lovely duet, which doubles up as a battle of wits between the film's protagonists. For Rajendra Kumar (Mahesh), Sahir's lyrics are an obvious attempt at wooing Mala Sinha (Meena), while for Sinha, his words rebut Kumar's overtures with youthful impudence. It involves an outstanding play of words by a lyricist in absolute control of his craft:

> *Tere narm baalon mein taare saja ke*
> *Tere shokh kadmon mein kaliya bithake*
> *Mohabbat ka chhota sa mandir banake*
> *Tujhe raat din poojna chaahta hoon*
> *Wafaa kar raha hoon wafaa chahta hoon*
>
> *Zara soch lo dil lagane se pehle*
> *Ki khona bhi padhta hai paane se pehle*
> *Ijaazat toh le lo zamaane se pehle*
> *Ki tum husn ko poojna chahte ho*
> *Bade na samajh ho, yeh kya chahte ho*

(I shall adorn your silky hair with the stars
Your beautiful feet I shall embellish with flowers
I will make a small temple of love
Where I will worship you night and day
I am making my vows, I expect the same from you

Spare a moment's thought before you give away your heart,
That you have to lose before you win anything
Seek the consent of this world
That you wish to worship beauty
You lack common sense, what is this that you seek)

But the two songs that really stand out are '*Tu mere pyaar ka phool hai*' (You are the symbol of my love) from *Dhool Ka Phool* and '*Naina kyun bhar aaye?*' (Why do my eyes brim with tears?) from *Dharamputra*. Both numbers present a truly distressing picture of a mother's plight as she grapples with the issue of bearing a child out of wedlock. Possibly, the experiences of his childhood, with his mother often at the mercy of his father's depraved behaviour, helped Sahir write such songs of extraordinary empathy for the mother figure.

The words of '*Tu mere pyaar ka phool hai*' bluntly articulate the stigma attached with being illegitimate:

Poochhega koi toh kisey baap kahega
Jag tujhe fenka hua paap kahega
Bann ke rahegi sharmindagi, teri zindagi, jab tak tu jeeyega
Aaj pilaaon tujhe doodh main, kal zehar peeyega

Tu mere pyaar ka phool hai ki meri bhool hai kuch keh nahi sakti
Par kisi ka kiya tu bhare, yeh seh nahin sakti

(If someone asks, whom will you refer to as your father
The world will consider you an abandoned sin
Your life will be an embarrassment, for as long as you live
Today I give you milk to drink, tomorrow it will be venom that
    you consume

Are you the fruit of my love or an accident of my actions, I am
    yet to decide
But that you should have to pay for someone else's doing, I
    simply cannot bear)

'*Naina kyun bhar aaye*', on the other hand, is more forlorn. Expressing a mother's grief at having been separated from her child, the words are capable of moving even the most stone-hearted:

Jee bhi saki toh jeetejee yeh sog rahega mujhko
Bolega par mera munna maa na kahega mujhko
Maa kehalaana bann gaya gaali, naina yuun bhar aaye
Kokh bhari aur godh hai khaali, naina yuun bhar aaye

(Even if I live, I shall have this regret all my life
That my son will be able to speak but will not call me his mother
Being a mother has become a curse, and so tears well up in my eyes
The womb was full but my lap is empty, and so tears well up in
    my eyes)

The music director of *Sadhana*, *Dhool Ka Phool* and *Dharamputra* was N. Dutta. Dutta had served as an assistant to S.D. Burman in films like *Jaal* (1952), *Lal Kunwar* (1952), *Jeevan Jyoti* (1953), *Shahenshah* (1953) and *Angaarey* (1954), all films for which Sahir had written lyrics. Perhaps it was this that led Dutta to forge a working relationship with Sahir when he debuted as music director for *Milaap* (1955) and *Marine Drive* (1955). In terms of the number of films on which the two worked together, the Sahir–Dutta combine was almost as prolific as Sahir's association with music directors S.D. Burman, Ravi and Roshan. According to Yash, 'They were very good friends. N. Dutta had great respect for Sahir. He felt that Sahir knew music and that they could work peacefully without any conflicts.'

However, both Yash and Dev Anand (who starred in *Milaap*) agreed on one thing regarding Dutta: he was not of the same class as Naushad or S.D. Burman when it came to the quality of his music.

But it is Dev Anand's discerning observation of N. Dutta that points to Sahir's stature in the film industry at the time and the accompanying problems that came in dealing with him. 'N. Dutta to my mind was very ordinary. But because Sahir started feeling that he is indispensable, he could give a break to any composer, so he gave a break to Dutta. That was his ego. I'm not underestimating N. Dutta, but Dutta has no contribution [legacy] at all,' remarked Anand.

Dutta died in 1987. Some of his other films with Sahir include *Chandrakaanta* (1956), *Bhai Behen* (1959), *Didi* (1959), *Chaandi Ki Deewaar* (1964) and *Chehre Pe Chehra* (1980). Although there were some lilting and vintage Sahir tracks in these films – '*Maine chaand aur sitaaron ki tamanna ki thi*' (I have yearned for the moon and the stars) in *Chandrakaanta*; '*Ashqon mein jo paaya hai, woh geeton mein diya hai*' (What I got in tears, I return through my songs) in *Chaandi Ki Deewaar*; and '*Mere nadeem, mere humsafar*'[9] in *Bhai Behen* – the reason Sahir's association with N. Dutta is largely relegated to a footnote is because the bulk of their films didn't do well commercially. Barring *Sadhana* and *Dhool Ka Phool*, their films together had no impact at the box office, with the result that the songs too were quickly forgotten.

If Sahir's initial films under the B.R. banner highlighted matters of social concern, the next few films had a greater romantic flavour. Be it *Gumraah* (1963), *Waqt* (1965) or *Humraaz* (1967), human relationships are at the centre of the storylines in these movies. Even *Aadmi Aur Insaan* (1969), ostensibly dealing with bribery and corruption, is a tale of two friends who love each other like brothers. B.R. Chopra roped in Ravi to compose the music for these films.

My meeting with Ravi, who passed away in March 2012, was made possible by Manohar Iyer. The music composer had declined

---

9. Refer Chapter 7, the section on Sudha Malhotra where she says this was the first song offered by Sahir to her.

to meet me on the couple of occasions I contacted him. His initial reluctance may have stemmed from the fact that various newspaper reports at the time suggested that Ravi was facing severe domestic problems over matters concerning his property. However, when Manohar eventually took me along to meet Ravi in his Santacruz (West) bungalow, the genial man gave no indication of any tumultuous events unfolding in his life.

Ravi had been acquainted with Sahir from much before. As the composer recalled:

> I was struggling in the film industry and even Sahir saab was new to the industry. I had come to become a singer and to achieve this end, I would go to meet all the music directors, beseeching them to hear me sing. They would say, 'You cannot get an opportunity to sing solo now, first sing in the chorus.' Initially, I was reluctant to do so, but then considering my desperate circumstances, I decided to take the opportunity. I started meeting music directors on the pretext of singing in the chorus.
>
> I went to meet Burman-da. I asked him if there was a chorus song that he was composing. He said, 'Yes, it should be due anytime now. Sahir is writing it for me.' That is when I first met Sahir saab, at Kardar Studio, while he was writing a song for Burman-da for the film *Naujawaan* (1951).

Ravi went on to narrate how the opportunity to work under the B.R. banner and his professional association with Sahir Ludhianvi came about:

> When *Chaudhvin Ka Chaand* [1960] became a big hit, HMV organized a party at the Taj Hotel. A lot of film personalities attended the function. B.R. Chopra also came. I first met B.R. Chopra while working in *Ek Hi Raasta* [1956] where Hemant Kumar was the music director and I was his assistant. And so [because BR was the director of *Ek Hi Raasta*], I used to interact with him a lot.

At this party, Chopra saab grabbed me aside. He congratulated me and asked me why I didn't work with them, for B.R. Films. I said I had never refused. He said he would come the next day and narrate a story to me. True to his word, he came the next day. Sahir saab was there with him as well. This first film was *Gumraah*.

Both *Gumraah* and *Humraaz* have some truly memorable romantic numbers.

With '*In hawaaon mein, in fizaaon mein*' (In this gentle breeze, in this ambience) in *Gumraah* and '*Neele gagan ke taley*' (Beneath the azure sky) in *Humraaz*, Sahir returned to familiar territory – using nature's breathtaking splendour to draw a parallel with the many emotions one experiences in love.

However, what makes '*Neele gagan ke taley*' stand out, is the way it hints at, in keeping with the film's storyline, the budding physical intimacy between Raaj Kumar (Captain Rajesh) and Vimi (Meena):

Shabnam ke moti phoolon pe bikhrey, dono ki aas phale
Balkhaati bele, masti mein khele, pedon se mil ke gale
Nadiya ka paani dariya se milke, saagar ki ore chaley
Neele gagan ke taley, dharti ka pyaar paley

(Pearl-shaped dewdrops gather on flowers, both nursing their
    desires
The gleaming vines are entwined teasingly around the barks of
    trees
The waters of two rivers meet and head towards the ocean
Beneath the azure sky, love blossoms on earth)

There are few songs in Hindi cinema that so subtly convey the physical aspect of love while talking of nature.

'*Kisi patthar ki murat se*', from the same film, is another inspired piece of lyrical genius. The words of the song, given Meena's reticence and Kumar's (Sunil Dutt) fervent love for her, are those of a devotee indulging in idol worship while paying little heed to societal norms:

Suna hai har jawaan patthar ke dil mein aag hoti hai
Magar jab tak na chhedo, sharmagi purdeh mein soti hai
Yeh socha hai ki dil ki baat uskey roo-baroo keh de
Nateeja kuch bhi nikley aaj apni aarzoo keh de
Har ek beja takaloof se bagaavat ka iraada hai

Kisi patthar ki murat se mohabbat ka iraada hai
Parastish ki tamanna hain, ibaadat ka iraada hai

(It is said that every stone brims with passion
But till one doesn't tap into it, its coyness remains asleep behind
   the veil
I have decided that I will declare what my heart feels in her presence
Whatever be the end result, today I shall express what I desire
I intend to declare rebellion against every unwarranted social norm

I intend to romance an idol made of stone
I desire to worship it, I yearn to revere it)

Yet, it is the anguish in 'Chalo ik baar phir se' and 'Aap aaye toh khayaal-e-dil-e-nashaad aaya' (Your arrival makes the heart feel despondent), both from *Gumraah*, that resonates with listeners the most. There is something cathartic about these songs which give expression to the spurned lover's abject state of mind. The very thought of distancing oneself from one's lover, as expressed in 'Chalo ik baar phir se', is novel:

Chalo ik baar phir se ajnabi bann jaayein hum dono
Na main tumse koi umeed rakhoon dil nawaazee ki
Na tum meri taraf dekho galat-andaaz nazron se
Na mere dil ki dhadkan ladkhadaaye meri baaton mein
Na zaahir ho tumhaari kashmakash ka raaz nazron se

(Come let us become strangers once again
Neither will I harbour any hopes of your love
Neither should you look at me flirtatiously
Neither will my heart give itself away when I speak
Neither should your eyes betray your inner anxieties)

Ravi Chopra acknowledged this ability of Sahir's to provide a fresh perspective. 'His strength was seeing a different aspect to the same thing. He would take a different angle altogether. He would think on a tangent. That's what I liked about him.'

As mentioned earlier, '*Chalo ik baar phir se*' was not an original composition for *Gumraah*. It had been included under the title '*Khubsoorat Modh*' in Sahir's anthology *Talkhiyaan*. Ravi remembered the time he was asked to compose a melody around it. 'Chopra saab told me, "This poem has been published in Sahir's book. I really like it. Please compose a song for this." I did. The song became a super hit.'

Gumraah, with its premise of the sanctity of marriage prevailing at all cost, was B.R. Chopra's favourite Sahir film. According to Ravi Chopra, 'He was really very happy with *Gumraah*. Every song had meaning to it. Every song took the story forward.'

'*Chalo ik baar phir se*' and '*Neele gagan ke taley*' earned playback singer Mahendra Kapoor his first two Filmfare Awards. Ruhan Kapoor recalls the abiding gratitude his father felt towards Sahir for having contributed towards his success. 'I cannot remember a show in my life which my father has done where he has not taken his [Sahir's] name, has not remembered him, has not spoken about him.'

Since *Dharamputra*, Yash's second film as director, did not do well at the box office, even as *Gumraah* became a big success, 'B.R. decided to boost Yash's spirits . . . by giving him the banner's first colour production, *Waqt*.'[10]

Waqt (1965) was a pioneering effort by the younger Chopra on several fronts. Apart from the element of colour, a first for B.R. Films, it popularized the 'lost and found' theme in Hindi cinema. It

10. Rachel Dwyer, *Yash Chopra: Fifty Years in Indian Cinema*, The Lotus Collection, Roli Books, 2002, p. 56.

is also one of the earliest multi-starrers in the industry. With *Waqt*, Yash introduced a new aesthetic in his cinema, one that he used in most of his films subsequently: larger-than-life stars who became fashion statements, gorgeous locations, opulent settings, with little or no reference to the Indian middle class.

Once again the Sahir–Ravi pairing proved to be a winning one as the soundtrack of *Waqt* became an instant hit. Most of the songs – '*Kaun aaya ki nigaahon mein chamak jaag uthi*' (Whose arrival cause the eyes to light up?), '*Din hai bahaar ke*' (It is the time of spring), '*Chehre pe khushi chhaa jaati hai*' (The face brims with joy) – deal with love and longing between the young couples in the film. Then there is '*Aye meri zohrajabeen*' which has Balraj Sahni (Lala Kedarnath) gushing over his wife's beauty (Laxmi Kedarnath played by Achala Sachdev) even when she had become a mother of three:

> *Aye meri zohrajabeen, tujhe maloom nahin*
> *Tu abhi tak hai haseen aur main jawaan*
> *Tujhpe qurbaan meri jaan, meri jaan . . .*
>
> *Tu meethe bol jaanemann jo muskara ke bol de*
> *Toh dhadkano mein aaj bhi sharaabi rang ghol de*
> *Oh sanam, oh sanam, main tera aashiq-e-jaanvida*
>
> (Oh my radiant beauty, you may not know
> But you are still so beautiful and I so young
> That I would willingly lay my life down for you . . .
>
> When you smile and say something sweet to me
> It causes the blood to rush through my veins even today
> Oh beloved, I am still so madly in love with you)

To this day, almost fifty years after it was released, this song reminds many married couples of the romance they shared in an earlier time before getting caught up in the monotony of family life. Even Yash Raj Films' 1995 blockbuster production *Dilwale Dulhaniya Le Jaayenge* reaffirmed the effect of this song as an anthem for rekindling love when it had the stern and uptight Chaudhry Baldev Singh (Amrish Puri) serenading his lovely wife, Lajwanti (Farida Jalal), at Simran's (Kajol) wedding in the film with this number.

'*Aage bhi jaane na tu*' became as big a hit. The beauty of the song is its lilting melody, but the lyrics run deep:

> *Is pal ke saaye mein, apna thikaana hai*
> *Is pal ke aage hi, har shai fasaana hai*
> *Kal kisne dekha hai, kal kisne jaana hai*
> *Is pal se paayega jo tujhko paana hai*
> *Jeene waale soch le yahi waqt hai kar le puri aarzoo*
>
> *Aage bhi jaane na tu, peechhe bhi jaane na tu*
> *Jo bhi hai bas yahi ik pal hain*
>
> (In the shadow of this moment, we all have an identity
> In the presence of this moment, every entity becomes a story
> Who has seen the future, who knows what might happen tomorrow
> In this moment, you will get what you seek
> Think, the time is now, fulfil what you desire
>
> What lies ahead, you do not know, what is gone, you do not know
> The only thing that matters is this very instant)

This emphasis on the present is a thought Sahir had previously expressed in *Taxi Driver* (1954) with:

> *Ae meri zindagi*
> *Aaj raat jhoom le, aasmaan ko choom le*
> *Kisko pata hai kal aaye ke na aaye?*
>
> (Oh this life of mine
> I must enjoy every bit of it tonight
> Who knows if there is another dawn destined for me?)

The philosophy echoes Ralph Waldo Emerson's words: 'With the past, I have nothing to do; nor with the future. I live now.' Sahir repeated the idea in '*Zindagi hasne gaane ke liye hai*' in *Zameer* (1975), a B.R. Films' production:

Zindagi hasne gaane ke liye hain pal do pal
Ise khona nahin, kho ke rona nahin

(Life is but a few moments of joy and merriment
Don't let it go by, lest it makes you cry)

The popularity of the other songs notwithstanding, the highlight of *Waqt* is the film's title song. Sung brilliantly by Mohammed Rafi, the song conveys the gist of the film while stressing on the whimsical nature of time:

Waqt se din aur raat, waqt se kal aur aaj
Waqt ki har shai ghulam, waqt ka har shai pe raj

Waqt ki gardish se hai, chaand taaron ka nizaam
Waqt ki thokar mein hain, kya huqumat kya samaaj

Waqt ki pabandh hain aati jaati raunaqey
Waqt hai phoolon ki sej, waqt hai kaaton ka taaj

Aadmi ko chahiye waqt se darr kar rahe
Kaun jaane kis ghadi waqt ka badley mizaaj?

(Night and day are a function of time as are tomorrow and today
Every entity is a slave of time, time lords over every being

The sun and the moon too move according to time
Time also decides who rules and who forms society

Even the good days are governed by time
It is time that is a bed of roses; a crown of thorns

Man should learn to fear time
Who knows at what instant time will change for the worse?)

It is this last stanza that drew Yash Chopra's appreciation, though it went against Sahir's grain. As Yash remembered, 'He didn't believe in destiny. He believed in man's efforts. He would say I do not believe in all this. I would tell him you are not writing your biography but some songs in the film . . . And then he would write as per the occasion.'

Aadmi Aur Insaan (1969) was the last film involving the Yash, Ravi and Sahir combine. While the film's music was a resounding success, there is not much to it lyrically. Save perhaps a few lines from '*Jaagega insaan zamaana dekhega*' (Man will arise, the world will see) which, in keeping with the government's philosophy at that time and the success of the Green Revolution, were a bold declaration of India's march towards self-sufficiency:

> *Phirte thay mulko mulko jholi pasaarey*
> *Ab se jeeyenge hum bhi apne sahaarey*
> *Chamkega desh hamaara mere saathi re*
> *Aankhon mein kal ka nazaara mere saathi re*
> *Bharey huey khaliyaan zamaana dekhega*
> *Kal ka Hindustaan zamaana dekhega*

> (We used to seek aid from nation to nation
> From now on we too shall live through our means
> Our nation too will prosper, my friend
> Our eyes visualize that better tomorrow
> The world will see our fields abundant with grain
> This India of tomorrow will be the pride of the world)

Through this song Sahir presented a third visual of India. Where '*Jinhe naaz hai Hind par*' lamented the decadence creeping into the nation state, '*Yeh desh hai veer jawaano ka*' had a decidedly patriotic ring to it. '*Jaagega insaan zamaana dekhega*', on the other hand, held out a note of optimism. Neither did it have the disillusionment of Vijay's intellectual character in *Pyaasa*, nor did it share Shankar's brazen enthusiasm in *Naya Daur*'s rural setting. Instead, it hoped India would break free of its shackles to emerge as a nation to reckon with in the international arena.

There was good reason for Sahir to pen such a song. 'The years after 1962 were a period of crises for India and not only on account of the Chinese debacle [the Indo-China war] but also because of the failure of two successive monsoons in 1965 and 1966, leaving the economy vulnerable . . . Indian popular cinema reacted to the crises by retreating into a kind of social "unresponsiveness" . . .'[11] But where a socially aware poet like Sahir was concerned, it is entirely possible that he wanted to give Indians reason to be positive and, consequently, through '*Jaagega insaan zamaana dekhega*' dreamt of a better tomorrow.

The end of the 1960s saw an end to the golden era of the film song. This was mostly in response to the changes taking place in popular cinema, with the emergence of the 'Angry Young Man' and a new era of film music that saw songwriting take a back seat. It wasn't surprising then that by the end of this period, Sahir's best as a lyricist was behind him.

---

11. M.K.Raghavendra, *Seduced by the Familiar: Narration and Meaning in Indian Popular Cinema*, 'The 1950s and 1960s', Oxford University Press, 2008, p. 156.

9

Good but Only *Kabhi Kabhie*

Main pal do pal ka shaayar hoon, pal do pal meri kahaani hai
Pal do pal meri hasti hai, pal do pal meri jawaani hai[1]

(I am a transient poet, my story is fleeting
My existence is momentary, my youth evanescent)

The early 1970s saw Yash Chopra move out of B.R. Films. Sahir was among the few people who followed Yash from B.R. Films when the latter set out to make his first independent film, *Daag* (1973). Yash recalled Sahir's magnanimity at that critical time in his own career: 'He said, "Don't give me any money. First, you make your film, release it. If it is successful, give me whatever you want. In your film, I don't work purely as a lyricist that I have to take this much of money." By God's grace, the film was successful and I paid him eventually.' But in comparison with the quality of Sahir's work in the 1950s and '60s, the years that followed were distinctly unremarkable.

Besides *Daag*, the other film made by Yash after he parted ways with B.R. Films was *Joshila* (1973). While *Daag* was produced by

---

1. From the song '*Main pal do pal ka shaayar hoon*' (I am a transient poet), *Kabhi Kabhie* (1976).

Yash Chopra, Gulshan Rai produced *Joshila*. The music for *Daag* was composed by Laxmikant–Pyarelal and *Joshila* marked Sahir's first film with S.D. Burman's son, R.D. Burman. Both films had some eminently hummable songs, but the emphasis was more on beats and rhythm than on the words. In fact, with the trademark RD cabaret number in *Joshila*, 'Kaanp rahi main', Sahir even plumbed a new low as the lyrics bordered on the ridiculous:

> *Kaanp rahi main, abhi zara tham janam*
> *Baaki hai raat abhi*
> *Haanf rahi main, le lu zara dum janam*
> *Na kariye baat abhi*
>
> (I quiver, hold on for a while, my dear
> The night is still long
> I am exhausted, let me gather my breath
> Do not talk right now)

Although he had penned some successful club numbers for S.D. Burman in the 1950s – '*Tadbeer se bigdi huyee*' (*Baazi*, 1951), '*Dil jale toh jale*' (*Taxi Driver*, 1954), '*Ae Johnny jeene mein kya hai*' (*Funtoosh*, 1956), Sahir let himself down with the line '*Haanf rahi main, le loon zara dum janam*' in the *Joshila* song. The word 'haanf' literally translates to 'gasping', 'out of breath' and is used, generally, to express one's state after a strenuous bout of athleticism. Using it, instead, to describe a night filled with passion caricatured the whole song and introduced an element of lewdness which undermined Sahir's poetic roots.

The few songs that did have some poetic merit – '*Jab bhi ji chahe nayee duniya basa lete hain log*' (Whenever people want they start new lives) and '*Mere dil mein aaj kya hai*' (What is in my heart today) from *Daag* and '*Kiska rasta dekhe*' (Who does the heart seek) in *Joshila* – didn't do enough to further Sahir's legacy. They were the usual songs of romance, melancholy and infidelity, subjects which Sahir had given better expression to previously.

Sahir's work with the B.R. Chopra camp fared no better as *Dhund* (1973), *Dastaan* (1972) and *Zameer* (1975) produced, largely, ordinary music and lyrics, barring the odd song like the philosophical '*Sansaar ki har shai ka itna hi fasaana hai*' (The story of every individual in this world, *Dhund*) and the meditative '*Tum bhi chalo, hum bhi chalein*' (You go along, I too will come, *Zameer*). It was as if the well of creativity within Sahir, which could so eloquently express even the most banal moment, had dried up.

Speaking to me, Yash disagreed. 'I never felt this way. I feel a commercial writer needs a strong situation to write. How long can a lyricist write a love song? The situation must be different. The director's demand must also be different.'

Ruhan Kapoor too rules out the possibility of Sahir's creative juices ever drying up. He, instead, points towards the declining quality of music in the industry in the 1970s to explain Sahir's decline. 'The fifties and sixties were a beautiful time for film music. In the seventies, things changed. Literary value went down a couple of notches compared to the standard of the preceding decades. There was a downward trend in the industry by and large which couldn't match up to Sahir Ludhianvi,' says Kapoor.

As if to prove both these gentlemen right – that given the right screenplay he could, at any time, conjure lyrical utopia – *Kabhi Kabhie* (1976) came along.

Kabhi Kabhie is the story of a poet Amit (Amitabh Bachchan), who falls in love with a fellow college student Pooja (Rakhee). But bowing to her parents' wishes, Pooja marries Vijay Khanna (Shashi Kapoor). Ironically, Vijay is a big fan of Amit's poetry and even asks Pooja to recite Amit's poem 'Kabhi Kabhi' on their wedding night. Amit, heartbroken by Pooja's decision, gives up on his poetry and joins his father's construction business. He marries Anjali (Waheeda Rehman) and the two have a daughter, Sweetie (Naseem).

Years go by. Vikram 'Vicky' Khanna (Rishi Kapoor), Pooja and Vijay's son, falls in love with Pinky (Neetu Singh), the daughter of Mr and Mrs Kapoor (Parikshit Sahni and Simi Garewal). However, Pinky turns out to be the illegitimate child borne by Anjali before her marriage to Amit. When Pinky gets to know of this, she decides to go and confront Anjali before taking her relationship with Vicky any further. Vicky follows her. He meets Sweetie who falls for him. Vicky entertains Sweetie's advances to make Pinky jealous. Meanwhile, Amit and Pooja meet once again by way of a television interview. Pooja's husband Vijay gets to know of Amit's love for Pooja but accepts the fact with great grace. Amit, in contrast, is extremely upset when he finds out that his wife had Pinki from a relationship before their marriage.

The film's climax addresses all these complex situations in a rather dramatic fashion. In trademark Hindi film style, a happy ending ensues.

With the theme of unrequited love at the core of the film, Yash asked Sahir if he could make use of the latter's poem 'Kabhi Kabhi' that had been published in *Talkhiyaan*. 'I liked his poem. I told Sahir, "I want to use your poem in my movie. The name of my movie is also *Kabhi Kabhie*. It is based on a poet's life. Your poem suits the purpose of my film." He agreed.'

A few verses of this original poem are recited by Amit when he meets Pooja after many years. The words succinctly express the character's pathos:

Kabhi kabhi mere dil mein khayaal aata hai
Ki zindagi teri zulfon ki narm chhaaon mein
Guzarney paatee toh shadaab ho bhi sakti thi
Yeh ranj-o-gham ki siyahi jo dil pe chhaayee hai
Teri nazar ki shuaaon mein kho bhi sakti thi

Magar yeh ho na saka aur ab yeh aalam hai
Ki tu nahin, tera gham, teri justaju bhi nahin

Guzar rahi hai kuch iss tarah zindagi jaisey
Isey kisi ke sahaarey ki aarzoo bhi nahin

Na koi raah, na manzil, na roshni ka suraag
Bhatak rahi hain andhero mein zindagi meri
Inhi andheron mein reh jaoonga kabhi kho kar
Main jaanta hoon meri hum-nafas, magar yoonhi
Kabhi kabhi mere dil mein khayaal aata hai

(Sometimes my heart wonders pensively
That had I lived in the cool shade offered by your tresses
My life may have blossomed a lot more
This despondency that plagues my heart
Could have been obliterated in the warm glow of your eyes

Alas this could not happen and now such is the situation
That even though you are no longer there,
I feel no pain or desire to be with you
My life passes by such that
It no longer yearns for the company of someone else

There is no path, no end, not a glimmer of light
My life wanders aimlessly in such darkness
I shall soon exist having lost myself in this darkness
I know this is my fate, my beloved, yet
Sometimes my heart wonders pensively)

However, the song picturized on Pooja and Vijay Khanna in the film was written completely as per the demands of *Kabhi Kabhie*'s screenplay.

Sahir played a prominent role in finding the music director for *Kabhi Kabhie*. Ramesh Talwar, Yash Chopra's chief assistant director from *Ittefaq* (1969) onwards, and whom I met in his Andheri office one afternoon in March 2010, elaborates:

We first went to Laxmikant–Pyarelal. They were very busy in those days. This film [*Kabhi Kabhie*] was about a poet and Yash-ji thought that he would largely use poetry for the songs and the tunes would be composed later, around the lyrics. However, we went there and gave them [L–P] a song. But it took time because they used to do a lot of films and all the big film-makers were working with them.

Sahir and Laxmikant–Pyarelal had worked together for Yash Chopra on *Daag*. The film's music had done exceedingly well and so it made sense to continue with the hit pairing of music director and lyricist. However, knowing L–P's hectic schedule and Yash's anxiety to get on with the making of the film, Sahir told Yash to move past Laxmikant–Pyarelal.

'Sahir told Yash-ji, "You talk to L–P, tell them your problem and let's part with them politely. This is a poet's picture and so we should take a man who is, firstly, available and then composes music around the lyrics." He [Sahir] then recommended Khayyam saab's name,' says Talwar.

However, the problem with Khayyam was that he wasn't as saleable a proposition as Laxmikant–Pyarelal or R.D. Burman. In the 1970s, Burman junior and L–P were quite the flavour of the industry with a string of hits backing both music directors. This was in contrast to Khayyam who, while being an excellent composer, wasn't anywhere near as prolific or successful as RD or L–P.

Ramesh Talwar then proffered the explanation that eventually saw Khayyam come on board for *Kabhi Kabhie* despite not matching up to L–P on the saleability scale. 'We had the stars. Amitabh Bachchan was there. Shashi Kapoor was there. Rakhee too. Waheeda Rehman as well. And Yash Chopra himself was the biggest star. He had a regular set of distributors. And so Yash-ji agreed to Sahir's suggestion and the sittings with Khayyam began.'

But there was more to Sahir's suggestion of switching to someone other than Laxmikant–Pyarelal.

Ruhan Kapoor mentions Sahir's unwillingness to work with music directors whose understanding of the Urdu language was limited:

Sahir had immense respect for the Urdu language. There were people he refused to work with because they did not understand what he was saying. He would say, 'When they cannot understand what I am saying, what are they going to compose.' An odd word here and there everyone has a problem. Literature is such a vast subject that it is not possible for a layperson to have full knowledge of it. But he felt that unless the composer was inspired by his poetry, he would not do justice to it. The music director could be inspired only if he understood his poetry. He did not want to work with people who did not have an aptitude for Urdu literature.

Ravi Chopra mentions the souring of relations between Sahir and L–P. 'He was not very happy to work with certain people. We worked with Laxmikant–Pyarelal and he was not happy with them at all. They had a fight in our house. We had given a wrap-up party for *Dastaan* and *wahaan pe dono ka jhagda ho gaya* [both parties ended up having a fight there]. Sahir felt that they were doing only *tu-ta-tu* [creating cacophony] and were not helping him make the right song for the film.'

The decision to work with Khayyam having been made, the matter of *Kabhi Kabhie*'s title song came up next. Khayyam passes on an invaluable nugget on this front:

Chetan [Anand] saab was making a film, *Kaafir*. Dev [Anand] saab was working in it. Geeta Bali as well. We had recorded this poem ['Kabhi Kabhi'] for *Kaafir*. For some reason it did not get completed. But Chetan saab always wanted to make that film involving the song. Whenever we would meet him he would say, 'Sahir saab, Khayyam saab, I want to make that film. As soon as the arrangements are made we will make that film.'

A lot of time went by. One day I was sitting at Sahir saab's house. He said, 'Yaar Khayyam, Chetan saab has been wanting to make that film but it has still not been made. Those songs we recorded will unnecessarily get wasted. Let us both go and ask Chetan saab if he wants to make use of them. Otherwise, we will use them somewhere else.' I agreed.

Accordingly, we met Chetan saab one evening at his house. There was a party hosted in our honour. Kaifi Azmi was there and so was Shaukat aapa [Kaifi's wife]. There were others as well. These songs, the *'Kabhi Kabhi'* song as well as four other songs which we had recorded, were to be played over there. However, the tape couldn't be found. It had been misplaced and so the songs couldn't be played. Sahir saab then said to Chetan saab, 'It's okay if the tape got misplaced, but are you making any use of those songs?' Chetan saab replied, 'No Sahir saab, those songs are now outdated.' Those were his very words. He said it in front of everyone. So Sahir saab asked, 'Can we make use of them in that case?' And he said, 'Yes, I do not have a problem.'

Yash Chopra was making *Kabhi Kabhie* at the time. It was obvious that since the film's title itself was *Kabhi Kabhie*, it borrowed from the poem. So I had to take the original song that I had recorded [for *Kaafir*] and tweak it according to how the poet would sing it in a melody.

Interestingly, this original version of 'Kabhi Kabhi' for Chetan Anand's film was recorded by Khayyam in the voices of Geeta Dutt and Sudha Malhotra, the lady who had once been romantically linked with the poet.

The poem 'Kabhi Kabhi' published in *Talkhiyaan* has a feel of profound suffering to it. In contrast, Sahir's song in Yash Chopra's film overflows with sensuous appeal. It is a celebration of love, of a man's enchantment with his lover's beauty:

Kabhi kabhi mere dil mein khayaal aata hai
Ki jaise tujhko banaaya gaya hai mere liye
Tu ab se pehle sitaaron mein bas rahi thee kaheen
Tujhe zameen pe bulaaya gaya hai mere liye

(Sometimes my heart wonders pensively
That you were created solely for me
You who resided among the stars
Have been called down to earth for me)

Sahir had previously written lyrics referring to a married couple's first night. 'Aaj ki raat muraadon ki baaraat aayee hai' (Dharamputra) or 'Muddat ki tamannaaon ka sila' (Kaajal, 1965) were both equally mesmerizing compositions:

> Har gunaah aaj muqaddas hain farishton ki tarah
> Kaanptey haathon ko mil jaane do rishton ki tarah
> Aaj milney mein na uljhan hai na ruswayee hai
> Aaj ki raat muraadon ki baaraat aayee hai

> (Every sin today is sacred like the angels
> Let quivering hands meet like they are related to each other
> Today brings with it neither stigma nor any shame
> Tonight a plethora of desires overwhelm me)

Or

> In paak gunaahon ki ghadiyaan
> Aati hain magar har raat nahin
> Is raat mein sab kho jaaney do
> Is raat mein sab mil jaaney do
> Muddat ki tamannaaon ka sila
> Jazbaat ko ab mil jaane do

> (These moments of holy sin
> Come but not every night
> Let's lose everything this night
> Let's find everything this very night
> The desire that has been nursed forever
> Let it be quenched tonight)

But the language in both these songs is largely metaphorical. It makes the experience of the first night appear surreal, far too exotic. In *Kabhi Kabhie*, on the other hand, Sahir's approach is more direct, the language far simpler:

> Kabhi kabhi mere dil mein khayaal aata hai
> Ki yeh badan yeh nigaahein meri amaanat hai
> Yeh gesoo-on ki ghani chhaaon hai meri khaatir
> Yeh honth aur yeh baahein meri amaanat hain

(Sometimes my heart wonders pensively
That this body, these eyes are in my safekeeping
The thick shade offered by your tresses is for my benefit
These lips and these arms are for me alone)

And yet, after taking the listener through this beautiful, mildly erotic journey, Sahir makes a dramatic volte-face to lay bare the heart of the distraught lover:

*Main jaanta hoon ki tu gair hai magar yoonhi
Kabhi kabhi mere dil mein khayaal aata hai*

(I know that you are no longer mine, yet
Sometimes my heart wonders pensively)

'*Kabhi kabhi*', immortalized in the voices of Lata Mangeshkar and Mukesh, became a big hit. It fetched Sahir and Mukesh Filmfare Awards for Best Lyricist and Best Male Playback Singer respectively. Khayyam, who won his first Filmfare Award for Best Music Director for *Kabhi Kabhie*, mentions that when the song became popular, Chetan Anand sent both Sahir and him a legal notice on the use of the song, claiming it was his property. 'Sahir saab replied to the notice through his lawyer. I replied to it through my lawyer. And our replies were factual. I told him that you [Chetan Anand] had said that you no longer had any use for them . . . We also told him that we hadn't even taken our payment for the songs,' recalls Khayyam.

'*Mere ghar aayee ek nanhi pari*' (A little angel comes to my house), also from the same film, is a beautifully written lullaby. It is picturized on Anjali when her daughter Pinky comes to meet her. Here, Sahir once again deftly merged the film's screenplay into his lyrics. He used the song to allow Anjali to acknowledge Pinky's existence, while subtly admitting that Pinky was her own flesh and blood. All this without giving anything away to the rest of the characters:

Maine poochhaa usay ke kaun hai tu
Hans ke bolee ke main hoon tera pyaar
Main tere dil mein thee humesha se
Ghar mein aayee hoon, aaj pehalee baar

(I asked her who are you
She said, smilingly, I am the fruit of your love
I was always there in your heart
Today, though, I come home for the first time)

There are other melodious tracks as well. *'Tera phoolon jaisa rang'* (Your flower-like complexion) and *'Tere chehre se nazar nahin hathti'* (I cannot take my gaze away from you) picturized on Rishi Kapoor and Neetu Singh bring out the vivacity of their relationship, as indeed the spark of youth. Yash Chopra revealed an interesting aspect to these songs. He admitted that it was a deliberate ploy to keep these songs frothy. 'Amitabh's songs in the film had to be poetic. Those songs had to be written first and then the music would be composed. Because Amit was a poet, the level of poetry had to be good. The other songs would be sung by Chintoo [Rishi Kapoor].'

Though Yash did not say so in as many words, it is probably safe to assume that Rishi Kapoor's songs were written to tunes composed by Khayyam. Also, it is hard to imagine Sahir writing *'Tera phoolon jaisa rang'* or *'Pyaar kar liya toh kya'* in the absence of a musical hook.

While these songs convey the youth and spirit of the character Rishi plays, Yash sought one of Sahir's earlier poems, 'Main pal do pal ka shaayar hoon', for Amitabh's melancholic poet. Its self-deprecating lines are at complete odds with the man who had fallen out with music directors because he considered his own contribution greater. Instead, they bring out Amit's brooding disposition:

Mujhse pehle kitne shaayar aaye aur aakar chale gaye
Kuch aahein bhar kar laut gaye, kuch nagmein gaa kar chale gaye

Woh bhi ek pal ka kissa thay, main bhi ek pal ka kissa hoon
Kal tumse juda ho jaaonga jo aaj tumhaara hissa hoon

Kal aur aayengey nagmon ki khilti kaliyaan chun-ney waaley
Mujhse behtar kehne waaley, tumse behtar sunney waaley
Kal koi mujhko yaad karey, kyun koi mujhko yaad karey
Masroof zamaana mere liye kyun waqt apna barbaad karey

(Countless poets have come and gone before me
Some left with a heavy heart, others delighted with their art
They were with us for a while, I, too, am here for a short time
Tomorrow I'll be out of style, though, today I am very much in
    vogue

Tomorrow, other lyricists will come, adding beauty to every song
There will be better writers than me, better listeners than you
Who will remember me tomorrow, why should I be remembered
    tomorrow?
The busy inhabitants of this world, why should they waste their
    time for me?)

The use of Sahir's poems from his earlier days, the protagonist Amit's struggles with love and his depiction as a poet have often led to the suggestion that Amitabh's character in *Kabhi Kabhie* was inspired by Sahir.[2] And even though Yash Chopra vehemently denied this ('*Kabhi Kabhie* is not at all based on Sahir Ludhianvi'), there can be no refuting that Bachchan's first real attempt at playing the romantic hero owed immensely to Sahir's lyrical contribution.

A little before *Kabhi Kabhie* was released, Yash Chopra made the first of his trilogy of 'Angry Young Man' films with Amitabh Bachchan, *Deewaar* (1975). This was followed by *Trishul* (1978) and *Kaala Patthar* (1979).

The tight, action-oriented scripts of these films offered Sahir

---

2. Rachel Dwyer, *Yash Chopra: Fifty Years in Indian Cinema*, The Lotus Collection, Roli Books, 2002, p. 116.

little opportunity to enthral listeners with his lyrics. He even complained to Yash Chopra about *Deewaar*. 'He would say, "Why yaar? Why don't you give me a powerful situation, which you are portraying in dialogue, and then see if I can do justice or not. Is this any situation to write a song? *Ek mein ladke ko naukri nahin mil rahi hain aur ek mein ladki mil gayee* (in one situation the boy does not get a job and in the other he gets the girl),"' said Yash, laughing at the memory.

The film-maker responded to Sahir's grouse by having a couple of serious songs written for the film. One was a comment on Bombay, '*Yeh deewaaron ka jungle, aabaadi jiska naam*' (These jungles of concrete, which we call homes), and the other a satire on customs officers, '*Idhar ka maal udhar jaata hai, udhar ka maal idhar aata hai*'[3] (Smuggling is the order of the day). Unfortunately, by Yash's own admission, these could not be included in the film as, 'we thought it hampered the storyline'. The qawwali, '*Koi mar jaaye kisi pe yeh kahaan dekha hai*' (Who has ever seen one get smitten by another), was incorporated reluctantly, 'since the song could be passed off as being played in the company of smugglers'. Apparently, the decision to omit the songs in the film's final cut offended composer R.D. Burman so much that he never worked with Yash Chopra again.[4]

Trishul, in comparison, was a bigger musical success. Yet, Sahir's songs '*Jaan-e-mann tum kamaal karti ho*' (Darling, you really amaze me) or '*Kabhi kasmein na tode*' (Never shall we break our promises) didn't push the envelope on the creativity front. They were based, largely, on staid romantic themes. Yash, however, claimed that Sahir was happier with *Trishul* because he got the opportunity to write at least one powerful song: '*Tu mere saath rahega munney*'.[5]

3. As given on http://www.saavn.com/Nz8uWUwdfFg.
4. Vinay Lal, *Deewaar: The Footpath, the City and the Angry Young Man, 'Deewaar in Its Times'*, HarperCollins, 2011, p. 27.
5. Refer Chapter 1, 'A Bittersweet Inheritance'.

Khayyam comments on the peculiarity of this song:

> While the song presented the entire premise of *Trishul*, the heroine's difficulties, her travails, it created a lot of difficulty for me since it was written in free verse. Every couplet didn't carry the same weight. They varied greatly. For example, the first couplet '*Tu mere saath rahega munney / Taaki tu jaan sakey*' was short and very different from the next, '*Tujhko parwaan chadhane ke liye / Kitni sangeen marahil se teri maa guzri*'. This was not the language of a song. I had to struggle for many days, even seeking recourse to the Almighty, to find an appropriate way to fit this into a melody.

Khayyam offers another amusing anecdote regarding the genesis of '*Gapuchi gapuchi gam gam, kishiki kishiki kam kam*'. Although the stanzas of the song were written by Sahir, the opening lines were given by Yash.

> Yash had asked me to begin the song with these lines bearing in mind the taste of the youth in those days. I told him, 'Yash-ji, neither do these lines appeal to my sensibilities, nor will Sahir saab approve of them.'
>
> But Yash-ji was not willing to listen. He told me to get them approved by Sahir. I went to Sahir saab. He said, '*Oye nahin yaar. Gaana kharaab ho jaayega*.' (Nothing doing. The song will only get ruined.) I said patronizingly, 'Sahir saab, the youth today talk like this. Even Yash-ji wants this included in the song.' He disagreed saying, '*Main Yash se baat karta hoon.*' (I will talk to Yash.) I replied, 'It doesn't matter Sahir saab. See, this is how I've arranged the lines to fit the song.' He listened and finally relented saying, '*Chal, kar le yaar.*' (Okay, go ahead.) This is how it came into being.

Khayyam, nonetheless, remains apologetic about the frivolous nature of the lines. 'I apologize. Sahir saab is not here to defend himself, but I apologize on behalf of both of us for this opening couplet. And even if it was Yash-ji who wanted us to use these lines, I don't blame him. *Sharmindigi humey hai* [We are embarrassed]. But yes, the song did become very popular.'

The taut storyline and the setting of *Kaala Patthar* too offered very little scope for poetic endeavours. And while Rajesh Roshan's music held the listener's attention, there is very little to them lyrically. The only thing to note is that with songs like '*Meri dooron se aayee baaraat*' (My wedding procession comes from a great distance), '*Dhoom mache dhoom*', '*Ik raasta hai zindagi*' (This life is a journey) and '*Jaggeya Jaggeya*', Sahir remained in sync with the film's setting, a small industrial town. Words like 'balma' (sweetheart), 'maike' (mother's house), 'raseele' (tender), 'kateele' (razor-sharp), 'maiyaa' (mother), 'saajan' (beloved), 'raina' (night), 'toka/tohri' (you), 'bitiyaa' (daughter), 'sang' (together), 'piya' (dear), 'bideswa' (abroad), 'chaand' (moon), bring the film's rustic characters to life.

Kaala Patthar marked the end of Sahir's partnership with Yash Chopra as the poet passed away a year later.

Sahir Ludhianvi was associated with the Chopras for over two decades. In this period he worked on every one of the films directed by either of the Chopra siblings barring *Kanoon* (1960), *Ittefaq* (1969), *Karm* (1977) and *Pati, Patni Aur Woh* (1978). Of these, *Kanoon* and *Ittefaq* are songless films.

Sahir's professional relationship with the Chopras far outlived his working tenure with any music director. For their part, the Chopras too set an exemplary trend of seldom undertaking any film without Sahir. Though Sahir clashed with music directors repeatedly, he was always in sync with the Chopras.

Ravi Chopra, with whom Sahir worked in *Zameer* (1975) and *The Burning Train* (1980), sums up Sahir's significance for the banner:

> He was a great poet. No question about it. He used to think of the situation before he actually wrote the song. He would always tell us, '*Yaar, yeh toh situation nahin hai, yeh toh aisa hi hai.*' (This is no situation, this is how the situation must be.) He would sit

with us and mould the situation so that the songs would be better.

Ramesh Talwar narrates a charming idiosyncrasy in the poet to illuminate the extent to which Sahir was valued in the Chopra camp.

Sahir, it seems, was scared of taking the elevator and never used one all his life. Consequently, whenever Yash Chopra recommended a particular music director to Sahir, the lyricist would measure the person's suitability for the film according to this quirk in his own personality. 'Arrey nahin nahin, woh gyaaraveh floor pe rehta hain. Jaane dijiye, chhodiye. Yeh ground floor pe rehta hai. Yeh first floor pe.' (Forget him. He lives on the eleventh floor. This one lives on the ground floor. He on the first floor. Let us go to them instead.) And the Chopras went with him.

Speaking about what Sahir meant to Yash Chopra, Talwar says: 'When Sahir Ludhianvi died, Yash-ji thought, "Main film kaise banaoonga. Mere filmon mein gaana kaise aayega."' (How will I make films? Who will write the songs for my films?)

The final word, however, belonged to Yash:

> We were Punjabis. We became good friends. We could tell each other what we couldn't tell others. I could tell Sahir saab, 'Aap ye galat kar rahe ho. Kyun kar rahe ho?' (You are doing a wrong thing. Why are you behaving like this?) He would say, 'Nahin yaar, mann nahin kar raha.' (I don't feel like it.) I would reply, 'Sahir saab, mann ki baat nahin, yeh kariye aap.' (It is not about how you feel, please do it in the larger interest.) I never had any problems with him. He respected me because I spoke the truth. I had the confidence and faith that he loved me very much. He would do anything for me. Is liye bond zyaada strong ho gaya (That is why our bond grew stronger).

10

New Peaks, New Associations

Jo mil gaya usi ko muqaddar samajh liya
Jo kho gaya main usko bhulaata chala gaya[1]

(Whatever came my way, I accepted as my destiny
Whatever I lost out on, I never stopped to think about it)

Following the success of *Pyaasa* and *Naya Daur*, both of which released in 1957, Sahir became a force to reckon with in the film industry. Suraj Sanim writes, 'By now Sahir had acquired a status where producers wanted him at any cost. If he could not be teamed with the "A"-grade music directors, the "B"-grade music directors were hired. This came as a blessing for music directors like Khayyam, N. Dutta, Ravi and Roshan who were languishing in the wings.'[2]

With success also came a temperamental attitude which often rubbed people the wrong way, leading to his falling out with stalwarts like S.D. Burman. In fact, among the many ego tussles Sahir Ludhianvi had with people in the film industry, Javed Akhtar

---

1. From the song *'Main zindagi ka saath nibhaata chala gaya'* (I made my compromise with life), *Hum Dono* (1961).
2. Suraj Sanim, *Filmfare*, 16–31 August 1985, p. 79.

recalls one with Lata Mangeshkar. 'A couple of years before *Pyaasa* and *Naya Daur*, Sahir had a misunderstanding with Lata Mangeshkar. Lata stopped singing his songs. There was some kind of ego clash between them.'

Prakash Pandit, Sahir's friend, details the discord between the two:

> Once, in the presence of both Lata Mangeshkar and Sahir Ludhianvi, a film-maker said, '*Sahir saab, agar Lata ki aawaaz na ho toh aapke geet bejaan hain!*' (Without Lata's voice your lyrics carry no weight.) On hearing this, Sahir, a self-respecting and literary poet, got angry and undertook a solemn oath in their presence: '*Jab tak main yeh saabit na kar dikhaaoonga ke achhee, adbee shaayari Lata Mangeshkar ki awaaz ki mohtaaj nahin hain, Lata Mangeshkar mera ek geet bhi nahin gaayegi.*' (Until I prove that good, literary poetry does not need Lata Mangeshkar, she will not sing even one of my songs.)[3]

From that point on, narrates Pandit, Sahir insisted that Lata would not sing any of his songs while taking up a film. However, no film-maker could afford to ignore Lata Mangeshkar. They could, on the other hand, disregard Sahir. But Sahir never lost hope. For two years, Lata Mangeshkar did not sing any of his songs. Despite this, Sahir's songs continued to scale the peaks of success through the voice of the lesser-known Sudha Malhotra.

'Finally, one day,' recalls Pandit, 'while we were travelling in his car, Sahir smiled and said to me, "*Ab Lata Mangeshkar ke saath meri phir se dosti ho gayee hai. Ab dosti sahi maaino mein ho gayee hai. Dosti darasl do barabar ke aadmiyon mein hoti hai.*"' (Now Lata Mangeshkar and I are friends once again. Now the friendship exists in real terms for friendship can only be between equals.)[4]

---

3. Saabir Dutt, *Fann Aur Shaksiyat*, Sahir Ludhianvi Number, Ibrahim Jalees, 'Abdul Hayee Se Sahir Tak', p. 504.
4. Ibid.

Coincidentally, the three films predominantly remembered for Sahir's magical touch – *Pyaasa* (1957), *Naya Daur* (1957) and *Phir Subah Hogi* (1958) – did not have a single song by Lata Mangeshkar. Whether this was a vindication of Sahir's pledge or pure happenstance we shall never know, but it was clear that the poet managed to hold his own even without the nightingale. Lata Mangeshkar's name once again finds mention in films for which Sahir wrote the lyrics beginning with B.R. Chopra's *Sadhana* (1958).

*

Phir Subah Hogi was based on Fyodor Dostoevsky's novel *Crime and Punishment*. It had Raj Kapoor (Ram Babu) in the lead with Mala Sinha (Soni). In need of some money, Ram accidently murders a moneylender. But the police are unable to nail Ram for his crime as someone else claims to have done it. The film deals with Ram's subsequent internal struggle of coming to terms with the punishment meted out to this other person for his own wrongdoing.

The film gave music director Khayyam, still looking for his first big commercial success, his maiden opportunity to work with Sahir. Khayyam had read Sahir's poetry and had a fair idea of the poet based on his anthology of poems, *Talkhiyaan*. The music director had also seen Sahir attend the meetings of the Progressive Writers' Movement held once a month at Red Flag Hall in Khetwadi, Bombay. But the two hadn't met at any of these meetings. It was when Khayyam was working at Shaheed Lateef and Ismat Chughtai's house for the music of their film *Lala Rukh* (1958) that the music director met Sahir for the first time.

'Kaifi [Azmi] saab, who was writing the lyrics of the film, was also present at their house. It so happened that Sahir saab and Jan Nisar Akhtar dropped by at that time. Everyone, including Sahir saab, was very impressed by what they heard of our work that afternoon,' recalls Khayyam.

It was at this point that Khayyam took the opportunity to introduce himself to Sahir. 'You may have heard of me but, today, for the first time, you have seen how I conduct my work,' he told the poet. He went on to add, 'Sahir saab, perhaps nobody knows, but I have composed songs for all the poems in your anthology, *Talkhiyaan.*'

> Sahir saab was shocked. He asked, 'Is that right?' I said, 'Yes. Every poem, every ghazal.' I told him, 'I would like you to listen to one of my compositions on your poems.' He agreed. The poem was 'Fankaar' (The artiste) and the lines were:
>
> *Maine jo geet tere pyaar ki khaatir likhey*
> *Aaj un geeton ko bazaar mein le aaya hoon*
>
> (The songs that I had written in your love
> Today, I bring them to the marketplace)
>
> Sahir saab was so impressed, he said, '*Bhai, aisa lag raha hai ki is nazm ko likha bhi aapney hai.*' (It appears the poem as well has been written by you.) He even said, '*Bhai, kabhi mauka mila toh ikkathay kaam bhi karengey.*' (If we get an opportunity, we will surely work together.)
>
> That was our first real meeting. We developed a mutual admiration for each other from thereon. It was the ideal platform for an association between a music director and a poet.

Khayyam recalls the role Sahir played in securing *Phir Subah Hogi* for him:

> Director Ramesh Saigal went to Sahir saab's house and told him that he wanted Sahir to write the lyrics for his film which was based on Dostoevsky's *Crime and Punishment.* Sahir saab agreed readily. But he asked Saigal who would do the music for the film. Ramesh-ji replied, 'If Raj Kapoor is the hero, it is obvious that Shankar—Jaikishen will give the music. They are a team.' To this, Sahir saab said, 'There is no doubt they are a very successful and competent team. But the music director should be someone

who has *read* and *understood* Crime and Punishment. Read and understood.' Saigal asked, 'Who do you have in mind?' Sahir saab replied, 'Khayyam.'

The songs of *Phir Subah Hogi*, like the film itself, had a very sombre feel to them. And like *Pyaasa*, Sahir's lyrics here too were distinctly poetic. Every word, every line, every couplet packed a punch, broached the subject of human suffering and lampooned the status quo in the same breath. Sample this stanza from 'Do boondein saawan ki' (Two drops of rain):

> *Do sakhiyaan bachhpan ki*
> *Ek singhaasan par baithay aur roopmati kehlaaye*
> *Dooji apney roop ke kaaran galiyon mein bik jaaye*
> *Kisko mujrim samjhey koi, kisko dosh lagaaye*
> *Do sakhiyaan bachhpan ki*

> (Two girls, friends from childhood
> One sits on a throne and is termed the beautiful one
> The other, owing to her beauty, is sold in the streets
> Whom do we blame for these inequities, whom do we hold guilty?
> Two girls, friends from childhood)

'Aasman pe hai Khuda' criticized the Almighty for his lackadaisical attitude:

> *Aasman pe hai Khuda aur zameen pe hum*
> *Aaj kal woh is taraf dekhta hai kum*

> *Aaj kal kisiko woh tokta nahin*
> *Chahe kuchh bhi kijiye rokta nahin*
> *Ho rahi hai loot maar, phat rahe hain bum*

> (God sits in the skies while we humans languish on earth
> These days, He hardly gives us enough attention

> These days, He doesn't chastise anyone any more
> Whatever people do, He doesn't stop them
> Even when larceny is afoot, bombs explode everywhere)

While heroes and heroines in Hindi films usually seek recourse to the Almighty in troubled times – 'Aye Maalik tere bandey hum' (Oh Almighty, we are your children; Do Aankhey Baaraah Haath, 1957), 'Allah megh de' (God, let the rains pour; Guide, 1965), 'Itni shakti humey dena, Daata' (Give us the strength, o Lord; Ankush, 1986) – Sahir vented his ire, mockingly, at God for the deteriorating state of affairs on earth. Right at the end of the song, he even urged humanity to stop persecuting themselves for Him:

> Jo bhi hai woh theek hai zikr kyun kare
> Hum hi sab jahaan ki fikr kyun kare
> Jab usay hi gham nahin kyun humey ho gham

> (Whatever is happening why talk about it
> Why should we alone bother about the world?
> When He does not seem to care, why should we?)

Equally scathing was 'Cheen-o-Arab humaara'. The song is a satirical take on two of Allama Iqbal's poems, 'Taraana-e-Hind' (Anthem of Hindustaan) and 'Taraana-e-Milli' (Anthem of the Community). The former goes 'Saare jahaan se achcha, Hindustaan humaara' (Better than the entire world is this India of ours), while the latter's opening lines are the same as the song in Phir Subah Hogi, namely, 'Cheen-o-Arab humaara':

> Cheen-o-Arab hamaraa, Hindustaan humaara
> Muslim hain hum; watan hai saara jahaan humaara

> Parbat woh sab se ooncha, hamsaaya aasman ka
> Woh santari humaara, woh paasbaan humaara

> Ay gulsitaan-e-andalus, woh din hai yaad tujh ko
> Thaa teri daaliyon par jab aashiyaan humaara[5]

---

5. The first and third couplets are from 'Taraana-e-Milli' (Anthem of the Community), while the second couplet is from 'Taraana-e-Hind' (Anthem of Hindustaan).

(China and Arabia are ours, Hindustaan is also ours
We are Muslims, this entire world is our home

The tallest mountain, the one that shares space with the sky
Keeps watch over us, it stands guard over us

Oh gardens of Spain, do you remember the days
When we had made our nest in your branches?)

Sahir, instead, lampooned Iqbal's poems with barbed lyrics of his own:

Cheen-o-Arab humaara, Hindustaan humaara
Rahne ko ghar nahin hai, saaraa jahaan humaara

Jeben hain apni khaali, kyun deta varna gaali
Woh santari humaara, woh paasbaan humaara

Jitnee bhi buildingey thi, sethon ne baant lee hain
Footpaath Bambai ke hain aashiyaan humaara

(China and Arabia are ours, India is also ours
There is no roof over our heads, yet the entire world is ours

Our pockets are empty, why else would they abuse us
They who are meant to protect us, they who are meant to guard us

Whatever buildings were there, the wealthy have divided among
    themselves
These footpaths of Bombay now remain our only source of
    shelter)

This was vintage Sahir, expressing the woes of the poor and the homeless while the rich and wealthy live their lives of excess, oblivious to the plight of the former. With that singular couplet *'Jeben hain apni khali . . . woh paasbaan humaara'* he indicted the long arm of the law for only being available to suit the purpose of these aristocrats. It was this ability to show us a mirror to our worlds without in any way compromising the intellectual and poetic quotient of a song that made Sahir peerless. That he said these things fifty-five years ago also showed he was a poet much ahead of his time. Khayyam compliments Sahir's working style that allowed him to produce songs of such high calibre:

> Sahir saab would take a really long time to write a song. This was because he used to immerse himself in the film's story and the situation for which he was writing. He would put himself in the character's shoes, think of the circumstances and write accordingly. And this was a special quality because when he would complete the song and present it, there was hardly an instance where the producer or director had to ask for any kind of revision. He was that kind of poet.

Indeed, it is such dedication to his art that led Sahir to produce the definitive title song for *Phir Subah Hogi*. 'Woh subah kabhi toh aayegi' provides a comprehensive view on all that ails society. Here, Sahir does not limit himself only to the cause of exploited women like he does in 'Jinhe naaz hai Hind par'. Neither does he restrict himself only to censuring the increasingly materialistic ways of man as in 'Yeh duniya agar mil bhi jaaye toh kya hai'. Instead, with 'Woh subah kabhi toh aayegi', Sahir articulates his vision of a utopian state:

> *Woh subah kabhi toh aayegi*
> *Maana ki abhi tere mere armaano ki keemat kuchh bhi nahin*
> *Mitti ka bhi hai kuchh mol magar insaano ki keemat kuchh bhi nahin*
> *Insaano ki izzat jab jhootey sikkon mein na toli jaayegi . . .*
>
> *Woh subah kabhi toh aayegi*
> *Daulat ke liye jab aurat ki ismat ko na becha jaayega*
> *Chaahat ko na kuchla jaayega, gairat ko na becha jaayega*
> *Apni kaali kartooton par jab yeh duniya sharmaayegee*
>
> *Woh subah kabhi toh aayegi*
> *Beetengey kabhi toh din aakhir, yeh bhookh ke aur bekaari ke*
> *Tootengey kabhi toh buut aakhir, daulat ki ijaaradaari ke*
> *Jab ek anokhi duniya ki buniyaad uthaayee jayegi*

Woh subah kabhi toh aayegi
Majboor budhaapa jab sooni raahon ki dhool na phaankega
Masoom ladakpan jab gandi galiyon mein bheekh na maangega
Haq maangney waalon ko jis din sooli na dikhayee jaayegi[6]

(That dawn shall come some day
Agreed that our aspirations have no meaning today
Even dust has some value, mankind none at all
When man's self-respect is not determined by his wealth . . .

That dawn shall come some day
When women will no longer be sold for money
When love will not be crushed, self-respect no longer bartered
When man will be ashamed of his wrongdoings

That dawn shall come some day
These days of hunger and unemployment will pass someday
These statues of pelf and wealth shall be destroyed somehow
When the foundation of a unique world will be laid

That dawn shall come some day
When hapless aged will no longer be coerced on to the desolate
    streets
When innocent kids will not have to beg on dirty roads
When those who ask for what is theirs will no longer be
    subjected to the gallows)

Unlike the two songs in *Pyaasa*, 'Woh subah kabhi toh aayegi' is not just a poet crying out loud in isolation. Here, Sahir fixes the responsibility of ushering in a better tomorrow squarely on mankind:

Woh subah hum hi se aayegi
Jab dharti karvat badlegi, jab qaid se qaidi chootengey
Jab paap-gharaundey phootengey, jab zulm ke bandhan tootengey
Us subah ko hum hi laayengey, woh subah hum hi se aayegi

6. Verses 2, 3 and 4 included here were not part of the film but were part of the whole song written by Sahir.

(That dawn will come from us
When this earth will change for the better, when prisoners shall
    be set free
When houses of sin will be shattered, the shackles of persecution
    broken
That dawn we only shall bring, that dawn will come from us
    alone)

'He was always on the lookout for an opportunity to incorporate
the pain and torment of this country's workers and peasants in his
songs. He carried the suffering of each and every poverty-stricken
individual in his heart,' says Khayyam of Sahir's inspiration for this
song.

It is this strong socialist-humanist content in the songs that puts
Phir Subah Hogi in the same league as *Pyaasa*. The film gave Sahir the
scope to do what he did best. In between his contemptuous view of
the rich, '*Chin-o-Arab humaara*', and his sacrilegious take on God,
'*Aasman pe hai Khuda*', '*Woh subah kabhi toh aayegi*' stands out like a
beacon, giving hope to the disillusioned human race. Later films
too gave him the opportunity to address issues close to his heart,
but in terms of the number of songs that mirrored his socialist stand
and their impact, *Pyaasa* and *Phir Subah Hogi* remain Sahir's signature
films.

Khayyam credits his own rise in the film industry, following the
musical success of *Phir Subah Hogi*, entirely to Sahir:

> I was working in films at that time but I needed a big break. And
> credit goes to Sahir saab for this. The manner in which he
> promoted me by saying that only someone who has read and
> understood *Crime and Punishment* could do justice to the film.
> Instead of propping me up as just another music director who
> carried a harmonium around, he highlighted my strong literary
> and educational background.

Another music director who came into prominence with Sahir is Jaidev. The composer had been an assistant to S.D. Burman right through the 1950s and is unofficially credited with many of the maestro's popular ditties. As part of S.D. Burman's troupe, he had been part of Dev Anand's Navketan banner, and with Sahir and SD no longer working together, when the appointment of a composer came up for Navketan's 1961 venture *Hum Dono*, it fell upon Jaidev to don the mantle.

Here, Sahir's songs, all mesmerizing compositions, were an offshoot of the film's unfolding storyline, blending smoothly with the narrative. All the romantic, tragic, devotional, introspective moments in the film inspired him to produce an exemplary all-round performance. The very first song in the film, '*Abhi na jao chhod kar*' (Do not leave just yet), became an enduring hit and remains one even now, over fifty years later.

'The metering of the opening lines of the song was inspired by the Pakistani poet Hafeez Jalandhari's famous poem "*Abhi toh main jawaan hoon*" (I am still young),' remarked Dev Anand, sharing some valuable trivia behind the origins of what is perhaps one of the finest duets in Hindi cinema. A closer examination of the song, vis-à-vis another popular number of the 1970s, also reveals the difference between the golden era of the Hindi film song, in the 1950s and early 1960s, and the period that followed.

'*Achchha toh hum chalte hain*' (So I take your leave) from the film *Aan Milo Sajna* (1970), written by Anand Bakshi, is a popular duet with a premise not very different from Sahir's song in *Hum Dono*. Where *Hum Dono*'s duet has the hero imploring his lover not to leave, Bakshi's song has the hero seek another meeting with the heroine given that she is taking his leave. Where the former has an ethereal feel to it, the latter is more matter of fact, more conversational. For instance, when Rajesh Khanna expresses regret on how time flies during his meetings with Asha Parekh in '*Achchha toh hum chalte hain'*, he does so in a single line: *'Kitni jaldi yeh din dhalte hain'* (How soon do these days pass us by).

Sahir, in contrast, is caught in the beauty of the moment with *'Abhi na jao chhod kar'*. He lets himself drown in it:

> *Abhi abhi toh aayee ho, bahaar bann ke chhaayee ho*
> *Hawa zara mehak toh le, nazar zara behak toh le*
> *Yeh shaam dhal toh le zara, yeh dil sambhal toh le zara*
> *Main thodi der jee toh loon, nashey ke ghoont pee toh loon*

> (You have only just come, your presence is like the spring
> Let the air turn a little fragrant, let me lose hold over my senses
> Let the evening melt away, let the heart get a grasp of itself
> Let me live a little longer, let me drown in your intoxicating
>   beauty)

Bakshi had the ability of simplifying lyrics which brought his songs within the reach of the common man. It took a man of his talent to simplify what was before him a largely intellectual art. Yet, Bakshi's song, wonderful for its conversational element, does not engage or stimulate the mind to the extent Sahir's does.

The bhajans, *'Allah tero naam'* and *'Prabhu tero naam'* too mirror *Hum Dono's* narrative progression. What is particularly noteworthy is that for both compositions Sahir switched to Hindi. Just as significant is the fact that *'Prabhu tero naam'* is addressed to a faith that was not Sahir's (as was the case in the devotional songs of *Devdas, Pyaasa, Naya Daur*). Despite these challenges, Sahir produced an exemplary composition. His lyrics remain absolutely in sync with the language and form of a bhajan:

> *Tu daanee, tu antaryaami,*
> *Teri kripa ho jaaye toh swami*
> *Har bigadi bann jaaye, jeevan dhan mil jaaye*

> *Prabhu tero naam, jo dhyaaye phal paaye*
> *Sukh laaye tero naam*

(You are benevolent, You the almighty
If You bless us then oh Master
Every wrong is corrected; living is fulfilled

Oh God, whoever takes your name, is blessed
Peace comes with invoking Your name)

Gone is the disapproving tone of *Phir Subah Hogi*'s '*Aasman pe hai Khuda*'. Instead, Sahir, in keeping with the general nature of human beings, looks to the Almighty as the only saviour in both songs. However, it is the pacifist nature of '*Allah tero naam*' – particularly with the 1962 war with China looming on the horizon – that makes it special. Here, Sahir delicately expresses the anguish and sorrow of women who lose their sons, brothers and husbands to war:

Allah tero naam, Eeshwar tero naam
Sab ko sanmatee de Bhagwaan

Maangon kaa sindoor na chhoote
Maa behano kee aans na toote
Deh binaa bhatake na praan

(You are called Allah, Ishwar as well
Give everyone the wisdom

Let wives not lose their husbands
Let mothers and sisters not despair
Let the soul not wander without a body)

But it is the sheer poetry of '*Kabhi khud pe kaabhi haalat pe*' and '*Main zindagi ka saath*' that makes *Hum Dono* a reference point in any study on Sahir Ludhianvi. The former is cathartic, pensive, and raises some very profound existential questions:

Kisliye jeetey hain hum, kiske liye jeete hain?
Baarha aise sawaalat pe rona aaya

Kaun rota hai kisi aur ki khaatir aye dost?
Sabko apni hi kisi baat pe rona aaya

Kabhi khud pe kabhi haalat pe rona aaya
Baat nikali toh har ik baat pe rona aaya

(Why is it that we live, who is it that we live for?
Sometimes, I cry at the thought of these questions

Who sheds a tear for another human being?
Everyone frets over their own petty considerations

At times I cry at myself, at times at the circumstances
When the memory is refreshed, I cry for everything)

Yet, with 'Main zindagi ka saath nibhaata chala gaya' Sahir does a complete about-turn. In this song, he brims with optimism even in the face of loss. Dev Anand appropriately called the song his 'philosophy for life':

Main zindagi ka saath nibhaata chala gaya
Har phikra ko dhuey mein udaata chala gaya

Barbaadiyon ka sog manaana fazool thaa
Barbaadiyon ka jashn manaata chala gaya . . .

Gham aur khushi mein fark na mehsoos ho jahaan
Main dil ko us mukaam pe lata chala gaya

(I partnered life on its roller-coaster course
Deflecting every worry with a song on my lips

I felt it unnecessary to mourn the devastations
I chose to celebrate them instead . . .

Where there is no difference between happiness and sorrow
I strive to attain that utopian state)

According to the veteran star, there is just one reason for the enduring popularity of both songs: 'Simplicity of language. They went straight to the heart. It was the language of the common man.'

Sahir had previously worked in Navketan right at the beginning of his career in films like *Baazi, House No. 44* and *Funtoosh*. However, the commercial success of *Hum Dono* notwithstanding, this was the last time Sahir worked in a Navketan film. Dev Anand paid a glowing tribute to him: 'Sahir was a creation of Navketan. We were very proud of Sahir. If today someone is writing the history of Navketan, Sahir will feature very importantly in it. When I talk of my own films, Sahir takes a very prominent place.'

Which brings us to Jaidev. Interestingly, his first film as music director was also for a Sahir film, *Joru Ka Bhai* (1955). It is lamentable that the composer never received the same commercial appreciation that S.D. Burman or Shankar–Jaikishen received, although his compositions for films like *Anjali* (1957), *Kinare Kinare* (1963), *Reshma Aur Shera* (1972) and *Gharonda* (1977) remain unmatched. The few instances that his work was truly well received were when he worked with Sahir in films like *Hum Dono* and *Mujhe Jeene Do* (1963).

But with Jaidev, too, Sahir fell out during the making of *Mujhe Jeene Do*. Lyricist and poet Naqsh Lyallpuri details the episode:

They used to drink regularly. They were both from Ludhiana and knew each other very well. But they fell out during the making of *Mujhe Jeene Do*. Actually, Sahir used to frequently say, 'What good is the music director without the lyricist?' This eventually reached the ears of Jaidev. One day, Jaidev confronted him saying, 'Just like you take pride in your talent as a poet, similarly, we music directors, too, feel proud of our work. Therefore, it is wrong of you to say that the music director is of no use without the lyricist. We have never said anything like this.'

To make his point, Jaidev even recommended doing a film with Sahir where he would compose three songs to Sahir's words and that Sahir should write the lyrics to three of his compositions. But the matter never came to that because Sahir had already been offended. Sunil Dutt [also the producer of

Mujhe Jeene Do] even tried to patch things up between the two. A few months went by in this process. But Jaidev recorded a couple of folk songs for the film ['*Moko pihar mein mat chhed*' and '*Nadi naare na jao*'] in this period. When Sahir got to know this, all hopes of a patch-up between the two were ruined.

11

On His Own Terms

Kaza ke rastey pe jaaney waalon ko bach ke aaney ki raah dena
Dilon ke gulshan ujad na jaayein, mohabbaton ko panaah dena
Jahaan mein jashn-e-wafaa ke badle, yeh jashn-e-teer-o-tafang kyun hai?[1]

(Save those who walk on the path of death
Let love blossom so that those dear to the heart do not die
Why, instead of celebrating civility, do we celebrate war instead?)

R ight through the 1960s, Sahir continued to be at his peak
with composers who were never quite regarded as
belonging to the top bracket. He had no films with A-list
composers like Shankar–Jaikishan, Naushad, S.D. Burman or O.P.
Nayyar, but it did not seem to matter as he courted success with
composers like Ravi and Roshan. This is what leads Javed Akhtar
to remark, 'After 1957, Sahir for a very long time survived and
made his presence felt with newcomers or second-rung music
directors. He proved his worth with them. N. Dutta was just a
newcomer then, as was Jaidev. Khayyam and Roshan were not
successful music directors at that point of time. Ravi was not a big

---

1. From the song 'Khuda-e-bartar' (Oh Superior One), *Taj Mahal* (1963).

name. Then he became big. Roshan became big. But they were not
as big when they started with Sahir. And film after film, he produced
great work with them.'

Roshan came to the film industry in the late 1940s. Although he
composed the music for several films in the 1950s, it was only when
he worked with Sahir in *Barsaat Ki Raat* (1960) that he tasted
commercial success. Thereafter, Roshan worked with Sahir in about
half a dozen films. These films were largely Muslim socials – *Dil Hi
Toh Hai* (1963), *Dooj Ka Chaand* (1964), *Bahu Begum* (1967) – or
period films – *Baabar* (1960), *Taj Mahal* (1963) and *Chitralekha*
(1964). Accordingly, the music was oriented towards mujras,
qawwalis and ghazals with a strong emphasis on poetry.

Of these films, *Barsaat Ki Raat* (1960), *Taj Mahal* (1963) and
Chitralekha (1964) best epitomize Sahir's work with Roshan. With
the title song of *Barsaat Ki Raat*, Sahir paints a most exquisite
portrait of the heroine's good looks. Even Madhubala's most ardent
admirer wouldn't have done as much justice to her beauty as when
Sahir writes:

> *Haaye woh reshmi zulfon se barasta paani*
> *Phool se gaalon pe rukaney ko tarasta paani*
>
> *Dil mein toofan uthaatey huey jazbaat ki raat*
> *Zindagi bhar nahin bhoolegi woh barsaat ki raat . . .*
>
> *Surkh aanchal ko dabaakar jo nichoda usney*
> *Dil pe jalta hua ek teer sa chhoda usney*
>
> *Aag paani mein lagaatey huey lamhaat ki raat*
> *Zindagi bhar nahin bhoolegi woh barsaat ki raat*

> (Oh that silken hair from which water drips
> Those flower like cheeks on which drops of water yearn to stay
>
> This night in which a plethora of desires originate in my heart
> All my life I shall never forget that rainy night . . .

The red cloth that she squeezed to drain the water out
She let loose a flaming arrow straight at my heart

It was a night on which water was beset by fire
All my life I shall never forget that rainy night)

Yet, it is the qawwali, 'Yeh ishq ishq hai', in Barsaat Ki Raat that stands out. While Sahir had written to this genre of music before – 'Aaj kyun hum se purdaah hai?' (Why do you shy away from me today?) in Sadhana (1958), it is his rousing description of love as the omnipotent force that makes the song evergreen:

Na toh kaarvaan ki talaash hai, na toh humsafar ki talaash hai
Mere shauq-e-khaana kharaab ko, tere rehguzar ki talaash hai . . .

Wehshatey dil rasno-daar se roki na gayee
Kisi khanjar kisi talwaar se roki na gayee
Ishq Majnu ki woh aawaaz jis ke aagey
Koi Laila kisi deewaar se roki na gayee . . .

Allah aur Rasool ka pharmaan ishq hai
Yaani Hadees ishq hain, Quraan ishq hai
Gautam ka aur Maseeha ka armaan ishq hai
Yeh kaayanat jism hai aur jaan ishq hai
Ishq sarmad, ishq hi mansoor hai
Ishq Musa, ishq kohinoor hai
Khaak ko buut aur buut ko devtaa karta hai ishq
Intiha yeh hai ki bandey ko Khuda karta hai ishq

Yeh ishq ishq hai

(I seek no company of travellers, nor a regular life partner
This passion which has ruined me completely, only yearns for
    your company . . .

It hasn't been stopped by evil hearts even when it has been
    crucified
No dagger or sword has been able to stop it as well
It is that voice of Majnu before which
No wall appears high enough to stop Laila . . .

What is decreed by Allah and his messengers is love
Which means what is written in the Quran is love
What was wished by Gautam and Christ is love
This entire universe, in flesh and soul, is love
Love is limitless, love is essential
Love is God's messenger, love is the brightest light
It is love which makes an idol out of dust, a deity out of an idol
That trial by which a common man turns into God is love

This is love)

Although addressing a completely different subject, *'Jinhe naaz hai Hind par'* from *Pyaasa* (1957) has a few things in common with *'Yeh ishq ishq hai'*. Both songs are replete with Islamic religious references. Where the former uses words like *Hawwa, payambar, ummat* and *zulaikhan*, the latter had words like *Rasool, Hadees* and *Musa*. The language, replete with a heavy texture of Urdu (*sarmad, mansoor, ismat, zard, peer, hum-jins*), possibly put both songs beyond the understanding of the common man. Javed Akhtar offers an explanation:

Once I talked to Sahir about this language thing. He had an interesting take. He said, 'Even in folk songs people do not understand every word. What is important is that out of two lines, one line should be totally understood by everybody and it is okay if one line is understood by only those who are familiar with such words. As long as the average listener understands one line of a couplet it is good enough. But if both lines are beyond his comprehension, he will get alienated.' And that makes sense. And it worked.

For example, *'Na toh kaarvaan ki talaash hai, na toh humsafar ki talaash hai, mere shauq-e-khaana kharaab ko, tere rehguzar ki talaash hai'*. Now not many people will understand what is the meaning of *'shauq-e-khana kharaab ko'*, but in totality they understand *'kisi rehguzar ki talaash hain'*, meaning he is looking for a *rehguzar* (your company) . . . Similarly, in *Jinhe naaz hai Hind par*, *'madad chahati hai ye Hawwa ki beti'*, ab Hawwa nahin samjho toh koi nahin, *magar yeh maloom hai ki aurat madad chahti hai* (if you do not understand Hawwa it does not matter, but you do understand that a woman needs help). '*Yashoda ki hum-jins, Radha ki beti'* — ab *hum-jins ka matlab nahin maloom logo ko, koi baat nahin. Lekin Yashoda maloom hai kaun hai aur Radha ki beti maloom hai* (You may not understand hum-jins, doesn't matter. But you know who is Yashodha, who is Radha's daughter). *Toh totality mein* (So, in totality) people understand it.

Just as striking is the manner in which Sahir switches to a doha in Hindi during '*Na toh kaarvaan ki talaash hai*':

Jab jab Krishna ki bansi baaji nikli Radha saj ke
Jaan ajaan ka gyaan bhoolake lok laaj ko tajke
Ban-ban doli janak dulaari pehan ke prem ki maala
Darshan jal ki pyaasi Meera pee gayee vish ka pyaala

(Whenever Krishna's flute called out to her, Radha appeared in
  full splendour
Forgetting all norms of propriety
She wandered, this cynosure of every eye, wearing the garland
  of love
And thirsting for His vision, Meera drank the chalice of poison)

Javed deconstructs this interplay of languages midway through the song:

If you listen to a good qawwal, while he may have one main theme, he will take detours. In these detours, he includes different stanzas, different couplets, dohas, shers, whatever. The qawwal may use some doha of Kabir or Meera or use some Hindi poetry. He may quote a Persian couplet also. This is the liberty he takes and then he returns to the original theme. This is a form that is accepted and this is what Sahir also did.

There are more songs about love and longing with Roshan, each better than the other. For *Taj Mahal* (1963), Sahir penned '*Jo waada kiya woh nibhaana padega'*, an exquisite ode to fulfilling all that had been promised in love. The song fetched him his first Filmfare Award for Best Lyricist:

> *Jo waada kiya woh nibhaana padega*
> *Rokey zamaana chahe rokey khudayee*
> *Tumko aana padega . . .*
>
> *Yeh maana humey jahaan se jaana padega*
> *Par yeh samajh lo tumney jab bhi pukaara*
> *Humko aana padega*
>
> (What has been promised ought to be honoured
> Be it this world or all of God's creation that stops you
> You will have to come to meet me . . .
>
> I agree that I will take leave of this world someday
> But do understand, whenever you call out to me
> I will have to come)

In the same film, he ups the ante towards the enemies of love with the bold '*Jurm-e-ulfat pe humey log*':

> *Jurm-e-ulfat pe humey log sazaa dete hain*
> *Kaise nadaan hain, sholo ko hawa dete hain? . . .*
>
> *Takht kya cheez hain, aur laal-o-jawaahar kya hain*
> *Ishq waaley toh khudayee bhi luta dete hain*
>
> (People punish us for the crime of falling in love
> How naive are they, don't they stoke the fire instead? . . .
>
> Of what value are thrones and precious gems?
> Those in love are willing to sacrifice everything in this world)

This avowed commitment to the cause of love is a marked departure from Sahir's willingness to walk away from his beloved if things turned sour, as seen in '*Chalo ik baar phir se ajnabi bann jaayein hum dono*' in *Gumraah* (1963). He handled this flip-flop deftly, bearing in mind the demands of the script.

If he wrote '*Tum mujhe bhool bhi jao, toh yeh haq hai tumko / Meri baat aur hai, maine toh mohabbat ki hai*' (Even if you forget me, you have every right to do so, / But I can't be expected to do the same, for I have genuinely loved you) in *Didi* (1959), he could convey quite the contrary emotion with '*Tum agar mujhko na chaho toh koi baat nahin / Tum kisi aur ko chahogi toh mushkil hogi*'[2] (Even if you do not grant me your affection, it will not matter / But if you love someone else instead, it will hurt).

Years later, he even put forth a 'for and against' argument on love in a song from *Trishul* (1978). Where Shekhar Gupta (Shashi Kapoor) sang '*Mohabbat bade kaam ki cheez hai*' (Love is of great value) in praise of love, Sahir had the simmering Vijay (Amitabh Bachchan) downplay its worth by saying, '*Zamaaney ke bazaar mein yeh woh shay hai ki jis ki kisiko zaroorat nahin hai, yeh bekaar, bedaam ki cheez hai*' (In the marketplace of the world it is a commodity for which one has no real need, it is worthless, of no value at all). In this respect, Sahir is no different from a skilled dialogue writer who writes dialogues relevant to each character in a film as per the demands of the screenplay.

Chitralekha (1964) has to be the high point of the Sahir–Roshan partnership. It is a period film about a Hindu prince and so Sahir introduced chaste, impeccable Hindi for all the songs in the film. But it is the manner in which Sahir presents his full repertoire as a lyricist while tackling the themes of the songs – ranging from seduction to love and longing to attacking the custodians of religion – that makes *Chitralekha* a special album. He conveys the seductive charms of Chitralekha, the film's title character, through the highly erotic '*Aye ri jaane na doongi*':

> *Madhur milan ki durlabh bela, yoon hi beet na jaaye*
> *Aisi rain jo vyarth gavaaye, jeevan bhar pachtaaye*

---

2. From the film *Dil Hi Toh Hai* (1963).

Sej sajao mere saajan ki
Le aao kaliyaan goond goond

Aye ri jaaney na doongi,
Main toh apne rasik ko naino mein rakh loongi
Palake moond moond

(Let this fleeting moment of a sweet reunion not pass us by
Whosoever lets such a night go waste, will regret it all his life
Adorn the bed for my beloved
With flowers carefully kneaded

I will not let him go
I will imprison my lover in my eyes
My eyelashes locked around him)

'Mann re tu kaahe na dheer dhare', rendered soulfully by Mohammed Rafi, has Sahir turn philosophical about unrequited love. Where he had gallantly promised to cross the boundaries posed by life and death in *Taj Mahal* (1963) – *Yeh maana humey jahaan se jaana padega, par yeh samajh lo tumney jab bhi pukaara, humko aana padega* – Sahir hits a more circumspect note in this song:

Mann re, tu kaahe na dheer dharey
Woh nirmohi moh na jaaney, jinn ka moh karey . . .

Utna hi upkaar samajh, koi jitna saath nibhaa de
Janam-maran ka mel hai sapna, yeh sapna bisra de
Koi na sang mare . . .

(Oh impatient heart, why do you not show a little patience
The callous one, whom you dote over, knows nothing about
     affection . . .

Consider it a favour, whatever little time one gives
Partnering together in life and death are mere dreams, forget
     about them
Nobody dies together . . .)

In a poll conducted by *Outlook* magazine on the '20 Best Hindi Film Songs Ever', the results of which were featured in their 26 June 2006 edition, and the jury for which consisted of eminent film music personalities like Gulzar, Javed Akhtar and Prasoon Joshi among others, '*Mann re*' was ranked as the number one song.[3]

No mention of *Chitralekha* is ever complete without '*Sansaar se bhaagey phirtey ho*'. It is, as Manohar Iyer observes, 'An iconoclast putting forth his views that taunted the torch-bearers of spirituality':

> *Sansaar se bhaagey phirte ho, bhagvaan ko tum kya paaoge?*
> *Is lok ko bhi apna na sake, us lok mein bhi pachtaaoge*
>
> *Yeh paap hai kya, yeh punya hai kya? Reeton par dharm ki mohre hain*
> *Har yug mein badalte dharmo ko kaise aadarsh banaaoge?*
>
> (You run away from all worldly matters, how will you reach the
>   Almighty?
> You couldn't accept this world, you will regret even when you
> reach the heavens
>
> What is sin, what is virtue? All rituals have the sanction of
>   religion
> These religions which change in every era, how do you base
>   your principles upon them?)

According to Javed Akhtar, 'As an Urdu poet, Sahir had developed such a fine sense of phonetics that when he wrote in Hindi, he applied the same sensitivity. Not many Hindi writers could have written songs like the *Chitralekha* songs.'[4]

*

3. http://www.outlookindia.com/article.aspx?231648.
4. Nasreen Munni Kabir, *Talking Films: Conversations on Hindi Cinema with Javed Akhtar*, Oxford University Press, 1999, p. 128.

Besides Roshan, the other winning partnership Sahir forged in the 1960s was with Ravi. Not only did Sahir and Ravi taste success within B.R. Films but outside it as well. The same year that the two joined hands for the first time in B.R.'s *Gumraah* (1963), they produced a memorable soundtrack for *Aaj Aur Kal* (1963).

'Itni haseen, itni jawaan raat kya karein' (The night is so young and beautiful, what do we do?) and 'Yeh waadiyan, yeh fizaayein, bula rahi hain tumhe' (These valleys, these environs call out to you) are similar to Sahir's 'In hawaaon mein, in fizaaon mein' from *Gumraah* (1963) and 'Neele gagan ke taley' from *Humraaz* (1967). In both songs, Sahir makes use of nature's stunning vistas to detail the budding romance between the film's protagonists.

Then, with 'Mujhe gale se laga lo', Sahir strikes a solemn note. The song is not very different from *Pyaasa*'s 'Aaj sajan mohe ang laga lo'. Where the baul singer in *Pyaasa* is a façade for Gulab's pleas to Vijay to deliver her from her misery, 'Mujhe gale se laga lo' is more in your face. Here Nanda (Rajkumari Hemlata) looks to Sunil Dutt (Dr Sanjay) to rescue her from the depression that was killing her steadily:

> Mujhe gale se laga lo bahut udaas hoon main
> Gum-e-jahaan se chhuda lo, bahut udaas hoon main . . .
>
> Har ek saans mein milne ki pyaas palti hai
> Sulag raha hai badan aur rooh jalti hai
> Bacha sako toh bacha lo, bahut udaas hoon main

> (Take me in your arms, I am very depressed
> Free me of this woeful world, I am very depressed . . .
>
> Every breath I take thirsts for a union with you
> The body and the soul burn with desire
> Save me if you can, I am very depressed)

Sahir turns even more forlorn with 'Maut kitni bhi sangdil ho magar':

Maut kitni bhi sangdil ho magar
Zindagi se toh meherbaan hogi . . .

Maut se aur kuchh mile na mile
Zindagi se toh jaan chhootegi
Muskuraahat naseeb ho ki na ho
Aasoon ki ladi toh tootegi

Hum na hongey toh gham kisey hoga?
Khatam har gham ki dastaan hogi

(No matter how callous death is
It is still more benevolent than life . . .

Even if one does not get anything from death
At least it delivers us from living
We may not be able to smile in death
But we will be freed from the saga of crying

Who is there to lament when we are gone?
It will bring an end to every tale of misery)

This romanticization of death is a motif Sahir used with regular frequency, for example, 'Teri duniya mein jeene se toh behtar hai ki mar jaayein' (*House No.* 44, 1955). Not only is death an escape from life's struggles for him, he also thought of it as the only alternative to a passionate romantic disposition:

Mere na-muraad junoon ka hai ilaaj koi toh maut hai
Jo dawaa ke naam pe zehar de usi chaaragar ki talaash hai[5]

(If there is a cure for my worthless passion, it is death
He who gives poison as medicine, I seek to be treated by that
   physician)

Aaj Aur Kal (1963) was by no means a runaway success. It had an average run at the box office. However, owing to Sahir's lyrics the

---

5. From the song 'Yeh ishq ishq hai', *Barsaat Ki Raat* (1960).

film continues to find mention among cine buffs. A similar fate awaited films like *Ghazal* and *Shagoon* both of which released in 1964. Both films fared poorly at the box office. Sahir's lyrical contribution alone managed to save both films the embarrassment of oblivion.

Coincidentally, it was Madan Mohan, also known as 'Ghazalon ka Shehzaada' (Prince of Ghazals), who was the music director for *Ghazal*. Sahir had worked with Madan earlier in *Railway Platform* (1955) where the composer had given music to one of Sahir's finest poems on love and the heartache that comes with it:

Chaand madham hai, aasmaan chup hai
Neend ki godh mein jahaan chup hai

Door waadi mein dudhiya baadal
Jhuk ke parvat ko pyaar kartey hain
Dil mein nakaam hasratey lekar
Hum tera intezaar kartey hain . . .

Roz ki tarha aaj bhi taare
Subah ki gard mein na kho jaaye
Aa tere gham mein jaagti aankhen
Kam se kam ek raat toh so jaayein

(The moonlight has dimmed, the sky is silent
The world is silent in the embrace of sleep

In the valley far away, white clouds
Descend lovingly to embrace the mountains
Keeping worthless desires alive in my heart
I wait patiently for you . . .

Like every day, before the stars
Are lost in the din of the morning
Come, so that my eyes, anxious about your absence
Get some sleep for a night at least)

According to Yash Chopra, 'The song was one of his earlier poems. He didn't write it for the film. But director Ramesh Saigal liked it so much, he incorporated it into the film. I think it is Sahir's most beautiful poem. The song didn't suit the film. The female character who sang the song in the film couldn't count from one to twenty and yet she was singing such a beautiful, poetic number. But because Ramesh Saigal liked Sahir's poem so much, it was used in the film.'

Similarly, in *Ghazal*, Sahir and Madan Mohan combined to produce an eternal classic with the song '*Rang aur noor ki baaraat kise pesh karoon?*':

Rang aur noor ki baaraat kise pesh karoon?
Yeh muraadon ki haseen raat kisey pesh karoon?

Mainey jazbaat nibhaein hain usoolon ki jagah
Apne armaan piro laaya hoon phoolon ki jagah
Tere sehre ki yeh saugaat kise pesh karoon?

Yeh mere sher mere aakhree nazraaney hain
Main un apno mein hoon jo aaj se begaaney hain
Betaaluk-si mulaaqat kise pesh karoon?

(To whom do I present the procession of light and colour?
To whom do I gift this beautiful night of many desires?

I have followed emotions instead of principles
Instead of threading flowers, I have crushed my dreams and
        brought them here
To whom do I present this gift that will embellish your tiara?

These couplets of mine are my parting gift
I am amongst those familiar faces who are strangers to me from
        today
Whose company do I seek without establishing a relationship?)

The music for *Shagoon*, on the other hand, was composed by Khayyam with whom Sahir had last worked in *Phir Subah Hogi* (1958). Here again, the duo created a beautiful soundtrack though the film had a far lighter storyline (a love triangle with the subtext of blind superstition in society) than Saigal's *Phir Subah Hogi*. In all the songs, be it '*Tum chali jaogi parchhaaiyan reh jaayengi*' (You will go away, your reflections will stay), '*Bujha diye hain khud apne haaton mohabbaton ke diye jala ke*' (The candles of love I lit with my own hands I have stubbed them out) or '*Tum apna ranjh-o-gham, apni pareshaani mujhe de do*' (Hand over your worries, troubles, anxieties all to me), the emphasis on poetry with an array of metaphors is discernible. Take, for example, the song '*Parbaton ke pedon par*':

> *Parbaton ke pedon par shaam ka basera hai*
> *Surmayee ujaala hai, champayee andhera hai . . .*
>
> *Thehre thehre paani mein geet sarsaraate hain*
> *Bheege bheege jhonko mein khushbuon ka dera hai*
>
> *Kyun na jazb ho jaaye, is haseen nazaarey mein*
> *Roshni ka jhurmut hai, mastiyon ka ghera hai*
>
> (The tress on the mountains, where the evening nests
> Where the light is of a dark-blue hue, the night a flaming red . . .
>
> The music resonates in the still waters
> The air is fragrant
>
> Why not drown ourselves in this beautiful scenery?
> Where there is a cluster of light, an abundance of nature's
>   intoxicants)

This poetic element in Sahir's songwriting draws praise from Javed Akhtar: 'It is to his credit that Sahir wrote many songs which can be recited without singing and people will still think it is good poetry.'

As pointed out earlier, in his songs Sahir often used chaste Urdu words which did not find a place in everyday use. In *Shagoon*'s songs, words like *ranaaiya* (beauty), *jazb* (drown), *nigahbaani* (guard over), *pashemaani* (regret), are examples of this. Similarly, in *Gumraah* or *Humraaz*, *taaruf* (acquaintance), *maazi* (past), *nashaad* (despondency), *paristish* (worship) were used. Words like *khudayee* (God's creation), *deed* (worship), *rehguzar* (companion), *taabeer* (description) and *karaho* (unhappy) find their way into his songs. This is not to suggest that other poet-lyricists of that time – Shakeel Badayuni, Majrooh Sultanpuri or Kaifi Azmi – did not use such words. But as Ravi Chopra observes of Sahir's inclination to work with Khayyam, Roshan and Ravi, 'They were the kind of music directors who helped focus on his lyrics whereas the others [music directors] didn't.'

Khayyam concurs: 'Sometimes, there were words in his [Sahir's] poetry that did not find use in everyday language. In such situations, I would try and keep the tune simple so that people could hum the tune. When people start humming the tune, they are naturally curious to find the meaning of the difficult words.'

Ravi too admitted to keeping the focus on Sahir's lyrics as the reason for his prodigious working relationship with Sahir. 'People would tell him that Sahir-saab you have worked with so many music directors. But the way Ravi enhances the beauty of your poetry no other music director does. There is such a clear focus on the words. He would then feel obligated to me. Accordingly, when a producer approached him for a film, he would say the music has to be Ravi's.'

What is also true about Khayyam, Roshan and Ravi is that they largely composed tunes to Sahir's lyrics. This explains the minimalistic quality of their tunes in songs like 'Cheen-o-Arab humaara' or 'Mehfil se uth jaane waalo' (*Dooj Ka Chaand*, 1964). This is different from S.D. Burman, who, generally, first composed a tune and then asked the lyricist to fit his words to the tune. Sahir had experienced this aspect of Burman's working when he had written his first song for Burman: 'Thandi hawaein, lehra ke aayein' (*Naujawan*, 1951).

Occasionally though, even Burman, like in *Pyaasa*'s 'Jinhe naaz hai

Hind par' and *'Yeh duniya agar mil bhi jaaye toh kya hai'*, had to compose his tunes around Sahir's poems. But because Khayyam, Roshan, Ravi and even N. Dutta took their cue mostly after Sahir had written his lyrics, Sahir was able to work with these music directors with greater creative freedom, without the melody acting as an inconvenient, limiting factor.

Accordingly, if one compares Sahir's films with Burman – *Baazi, Jaal, Taxi Driver, Munimji, Funtoosh* – with those that the lyricist undertook with Khayyam, Roshan or Ravi up until the mid-1960s – *Phir Subah Hogi, Dil Hi Toh Hai, Gumraah, Aaj Aur Kal, Taj Mahal, Shagoon* – the poetic quality of the songs in the latter set of films is discernible.

If Sahir's work with Roshan revolved essentially around qawwalis, mujras and ghazals, it is, to quote Manohar Iyer, 'His lighter and romantic side that came through in the simple and hummable ditties in films with music director Ravi.' Outside of his work under B.R. Films (*Gumraah, Waqt, Humraaz*), Sahir continued to wax lyrical over the many seasons of love in his other films with Ravi: *Kaajal* (1965), *Neel Kamal* (1968), *Aankhein* (1968), *Do Kaliyaan* (1968) and *Ek Mahal Ho Sapnon Ka* (1975).

He went from the first stage of courtship, *'Tumhari nazar kyun khafa ho gayee'* (Why do you look at me in anger; *Do Kaliyaan*), to devout commitment, *'Agar mujhe na mili tum'* (If I do not get to be with you; *Kaajal*), to voicing the despair of unrequited love, *'Dil mein kisike pyaar ka jalta hua diya'* (The lamp of love that is lit in my heart; *Ek Mahal Ho Sapnon Ka*) with the elan of having experienced it all. He also continued with his contrasting stands in these songs. Where *'Aapke paas jo aayega'* (Whoever comes close to you; *Kaajal*) is a heady description of a woman's beauty by her lover, *'Dekha hai zindagi ko kuchh itna kareeb se'* (I have seen life from such close quarters; *Ek Mahal Ho Sapnon Ka*) is a bitter critique of women who choose materialistic comforts of life over love.

Similarly, if *'Aaja tujhko pukaare mera pyaar'* (Come, my love calls

out to you; *Neel Kamal*) is a distressed lover's cry to be reunited
with his beloved, '*Gairon pe karam apnon pe sitam*' (Benevolence
towards strangers, injustice to your own; *Aankhein*) is the heroine's
lament at the hero having spurned her love for someone else's.

But the one thing that remained a constant in his work even with
Ravi was his willingness to tackle weightier matters even in a
seemingly frivolous song. In *Neel Kamal*, for instance, he took issue
with adulteration in the song '*Khaali dabba khaali botal*':

> *Khaali ki guarantee doongi*
> *Bharey huey ki kya guarantee*
> *Shehad mein gudh ke mel ka darr hai*
> *Ghee ke andar tel ka darr hai*
> *Tambaaku mein ghaas ka khatra*
> *Scent mein jhooti baans ka khatra . . .*

> *Khaali dabba khaali botal le le mere yaar*
> *Khaali se mat nafrat karna khaali sab sansaar*

> (I can guarantee something that is empty
> How do I guarantee that what is full
> Honey is mixed with jaggery, I fear
> Ghee is adulterated with oil
> There is danger of grass being blended with tobacco
> As there is of perfume being nixed with an odour far inferior . . .

> Take the empty container, the empty bottle, my friend
> Do not hate what is empty, this whole world is of a similar
> nature)

In *Aadmi Aur Insaan* (1969), a B.R. Films' endeavour, he makes a
similar jocular comment on corruption, nepotism and bribery
prevailing in India, issues that resonate even today:

> *Kaun si file kis daftar se kaisey ho gayee chori*
> *Kisne kitni gaddari ki, kitni bhari tijori*
> *Kis mill maalik ke paisey ne kitne vote kamaaye*

Kursi mili toh desh bhakt ne kitne note kamaaye?
Rishvat hi se chupe huey thay sab kaaley kartoot
Nangey ho kar saamney aayengey ab sabhi sapoot

Duniya bhar ke mulkon mein hoga Bhaarat badnaam
Bacha le aye Maula, aye Ram!

(How did a particular file disappear mysteriously from a certain
    office?
Who cheated the nation, how much did he fill his coffers?
Which industrialist's money fetched how many votes?
On getting positions of power how much did the nationalists
    gain?
Bribes have kept everyone's vices wrapped under covers
Eventually the truth will prevail to reveal all these men

Among the nations of the world India will be shamed
Save us Master, save us Ram)

He spoke his mind even in a children's song like *'Bachche mann ke
sachche'* (Children speak the truth; *Do Kaliyaan*):

Tann komal mann sundar hain, bachche badon se behtar hain
Inmey chhoot aur chhaat nahin, jhooti zaat aur paat nahin
Bhaasha ki takraar nahin, mazhab ki deewaar nahin
In ki nazron mein ek hain, mandir, masjid, gurudwarey

(Their bodies soft, their hearts clean, children are better than
    adults
They do not have issues like untouchability, or matters pertaining
    to race and caste
No disagreements over language, no boundaries concerning
    religion
In their eyes all are the same, the temples, the mosques and the
    gurudwaras)

It is easy to lose sight and significance of these three songs since
they were picturized on comedians Mehmood (*'Khaali dabba khaali
botal'*), Johnny Walker (*'Bacha le aye Maula, aye Ram'*) and a child

artiste (Neetu Singh, '*Bachche mann ke sachche*') in what were essentially lighter moments. But Sahir's unique ability to marry poetry and philosophy and take a contemptuous view of the world, even in a light number, places him several echelons above other songwriters. The famous ditty '*Chhoo lene do nazuk hothon ko*' (Kaajal) is a perfect embodiment of his genius in this regard:

Achchon ko bura saabit karna, duniya ki puraani aadat hai
Is mai ko mubaarak cheez samajh, maana ki bahut badnaam hai yeh
Chhoo lene do nazuk hothon ko, kuch aur nahin hai jaam hai yeh
Kudrat ne jo humko baksha hai, woh sabse haseen inaam hain yeh

(Belittling the good is an old trait of humanity
Think of this liquor as a blessing, even if it is much maligned
Let your delicate lips sip from this cup full of liquor
Whatever nature has given us, it remains the best of its gifts)

'Sahir was a very well-known poet when he entered the film industry. Generally, when people who are recognized names in literature come to films, they come with a certain kind of contempt. They feel they are coming down a few rungs. But Sahir did not feel that way. He took songwriting extremely seriously and made it his identity. This is why you see that his film songs were not very distinct from his literary poetry,' sums up Javed Akhtar.

12

The Poet as a People's Conscience

Tank aagey badhey ki peechey hatein, kokh dharti ki baanjh hoti hai
Fateh ka jashn ho ki haar ka sog, zindagi mayyaton pe roti hai[1]

(Whether the tanks march on or withdraw under attack, it is mother
earth whose womb is destroyed
Be it the victory parade or the dirge accompanying defeat, the living
grieve over the many who die)

'An Exemplary Progressive' is what Ali Husain Mir and Raza Mir call Sahir in their book, *Anthems of Resistance*. The book, an insightful account of the contributions of the Urdu poets to the Progressive Writers' Movement, analyses Sahir's work over the course of an entire chapter. The authors comment on Sahir's famous anti-war poem 'Parchhaaiyaan':

> While Sahir's poetry is a call for social justice of various kinds, his most poignant and heartfelt work was written in the cause of peace, or more specifically against the cry of war. Growing up

---

1. From the poem 'Aye Shareef Insaano' (Oh Dignified Humans), published in
Aao Ki Koi Khwaab Bunein (Come, Let Us Weave Together a Dream)

in the aftermath of the First World War, and as a youth seeing the destruction caused by the Second World War, Sahir wrote his best poems when he advocated against conflict. In 1956, following the Suez Canal crisis, when the British forces invaded Port Said, threatening to escalate the Arab-Israel conflict into yet another global holocaust, he wrote his magnum opus 'Parchhaaiyaan' (Silhouettes), which is without doubt the finest anti-war poem in the entirety of Urdu literature. This incredibly moving nazm is simple in its language, powerful in its imagery and devastating in its ability to bring home the depravity of war.[2]

'Parchhaaiyaan' begins on a wistful note, with a man revisiting the scene where he used to meet his lover:

Haseen phool, haseen pattiyaan, haseen shaakhen
Lachak rahi hain kisi jism-e-nazneen ki tarah
Fiza mein ghul se gaye hain ufak ke narm khutoot
Zameen haseen hai, khwaabon ki sarzameen ki tarah . . .

Inhi ke saaye mein phir aaj do dhadaktey dil
Khamosh hothon se kuch kehne-sunney aaye hain . . .

(Beautiful flowers, shimmering leaves, stunning branches
Sway like the body of a beautiful maiden
The horizon's delicate features have merged with the ambience
The earth is beautiful like the landscape of dreams . . .

In this ambience today, two lovers
With their lips sealed, have come to speak to and listen to each other . . .)

The voice goes on to describe the state of romantic bliss in which the lovers find themselves:

Mere galey mein tumhaari gudaaz baahein hain
Tumhaarey hothon pe mere labon ke saaye hain
Mujhe yakeen hai ki hum ab kabhi na bichhdengey
Tumhein gumaan hai ki hum milke bhi paraaye hain . . .

---

2. Raza Mir and Ali Husain Mir, *Anthems of Resistance*, IndiaInk 2006, p. 157.

(Your dainty arms are wrapped around my neck
Your lips are covered by my own
I am sure that we will never be separated again
You remain anxious, even though we have met, we are strangers
    yet . . .)

All of a sudden, this ethereal state is shattered. War breaks out and
society plunges into a state of ruin, both materially and morally:

Naagaah lehaktey kheton se taapon ki sadaayein aaney lagi
Baarood ki bojhal boo lekar paschim se hawaayein aane lagi
Taameer ke roshan chehrey pe takhreeb ka baadal phail gaya
Har gaon mein vahshat naach uthi, har shehar mein jungle phail
    gaya . . .

Iflaas-zada dehkaano ke hul-bail bikey, khaliyaan bikey
Jeeney ki tamanna ke haathon jeeney hi ke sab saamaan bikey
Kuch bhi na raha jab bikney ko, jismo ki tijaarat honey lagi
Khalvat mein bhi jo mumnoo thee veh jalvat mein jasaarat honey lagi . . .

(Suddenly, from across the fields, heavy treading sounds were
    heard
The air, blowing in from the west, was rife with the smell of
    gunpowder
The remarkable façade of construction was shrouded by clouds
    of destruction
Devastation ran amok in every village, every city was besieged
    by anarchy . . .

The impoverished farmers had to sell their ploughs, cattle and
    fields
For the purpose of living, the very means to earn a living were sold
When nothing was left to sell, bodies were offered for sale
What was shunned in private once was exposed in public
    now . . .)

The situation worsens with the news of the narrator's lover's
brother being declared a casualty of the war:

Tumhaarey ghar mein qayaamat ka shor barpa hai
Mahaaz-e-jung se harkaara taar laaya hai
Ki jiska zikra tumhein zindagi se pyaara thaa
Woh bhai 'nargaa-e-dushman' mein kaam aaya hai . . .

(Your house is beset by the cries of grief
From the battlefield the messenger brings a letter
He whose mention was dearer to you than life itself
That brother has died at the hands of the enemy . . .)

Confronted by the destruction, and the depths to which society has plunged as a result of it, a new realization dawns on the narrator:

Us shaam mujhe maaloom hua, jab bhai jung mein kaam aaye
Sarmaaye ke kehbakhaaney mein behno ki jawaani bikti hai
Suraj ke lahu mein lithdi hui woh shaam hai ab tak yaad mujhe
Chaahat ke sunherey khwaabon ka anjaam hai ab tak yaad mujhe . . .

(I realized that evening, when brothers sacrifice themselves in
      war
In the brothels of capitalism, the youth of sisters is put on sale
Doused in the colour of blood, I still remember that dusk
All the cherished dreams of love, which came to naught, I still
      remember . . .)

Scarred by these memories, the protagonist notices another couple at the same place where he and his lover used to meet. However, with the threat of another war looming on the horizon, the narrator is scared that their love will suffer the same fate as his own:

Aur aaj in pedon ke neeche phir do saaye lehraaye hain
Phir do dil milney aaye hain
Phir maut ki aandhi uthi hai, phir jung ke baadal chaaye hain

Main soch raha hoon inka bhi apni hi tarah anjaam na ho
Inka bhi junoon badnaam na ho
Inkey bhi muqaddar mein likhi, ik khoon mein lithdi shaam na ho . . .

(And today, under these trees, love blossoms once again
Two lovers unite once again
And again a deadly storm blows, yet again the clouds of war
    gather

I worry that their fate could be similar to ours
That their passion could get shattered
In their destiny too, there could be an evening doused in
    blood . . .)

Accordingly, the narrator urges mankind to rise and raise their voices against another war:

Chalo ki chal ke siyaasi mukamiron se kahey
Ki hum ko jung-o-jadal ke chalan se nafrat hai
Jisey lahu ke siwa koi rang raas na aaye
Humey hayaat ke us pairhan se nafrat hai . . .

(Come, let us tell these powerbrokers,
That we hate the jingoism that leads to war
What appreciates no other colour but that of blood spilled
We hate that facet of life . . .)

Sahir concludes his magnum opus with a fervent pacifist plea:

Kaho ki aaj bhi hum sab agar khaamosh rahey
Toh is damaktey huey khaakdan ki khair nahin . . .

Guzishta jung mein ghar hi jaley magar is baar
Ajab nahin ki yeh tanhaiyaan bhi jal jaayein
Guzishta jung mein paikar jaley magar is baar
Ajab nahin ki parchhaaiyaan bhi jal jaaye

Tasavvuraat ki parchhaaiyaan ubharti hain

(Speak up, for if we remain silent today
There is no saving this wonderful planet . . .

In the previous war, only houses were burnt, but this time
It will be no surprise if our entire existence is wiped out

In the previous war, only bodies were burnt, but this time
Shadows will burn as well

Silhouettes of memories arise!)

Through this incredibly moving poem, Sahir makes his case against war. Traversing the myriad emotions of nostalgia, love, despair and anxiety, he creates a vivid panorama that arrests the reader's attention from start to finish. Gauhar Raza calls it one of the best anti-war poems, adding, 'Sahir is very conscious that even individual misery is a subset of a bigger doom and therefore opposition to it has to be collective.'

Sardar Jafri, the famous Progressive writer, explains the reason for the widespread acclaim the poem has received:

> Before reading 'Parchhaaiyaan', I had heard Sahir reciting it several times at various functions and mushairas and I feel that the admiration for it is not restricted to any one generation or demographic of people.
>
> There are two reasons for this: The first and primary reason is that the subject of the poem is the most important question facing this generation, which has to be answered by entire mankind collectively. And the 'movement for world peace' is proof of the fact that every nation, every community, every race, every group of people has given the same answer to this question. More than half the world's population has declared their desire for world peace. Sahir Ludhianvi, by writing this poem, has only endorsed that stand.
>
> The second reason is that Sahir has presented his thoughts in the form of a story. A story makes a poem less esoteric. Most of our good poems are incapable of being understood by the common man. But Sahir's poem 'Parchhaaiyaan', because of its simple story and easy narration, will be understood by many people. More than ninety per cent of the words used in this poem are what we use in everyday language . . . It is to Sahir's credit that he has incorporated most of the harsh realities of our

time in his verses by using language which is both simple and straightforward. These verses are easily understood and tug at the heart as well.

Through this poem, Sahir has added to the beautiful legacy of great works in the Urdu language and the literature on world peace . . . I am convinced that Sahir's poem will help further the movement for world peace and nourish the feelings of brotherhood and love in the hearts of people.[3]

Even in his work in films, Sahir makes his opposition to war clear. In *Taj Mahal* (1963), he questions man's very desire to go to war for petty possessions:

Khuda-e-bartar! teri zameen par, zameen ki khaatir, ye jung kyun hai?
Har ek fatah-o-zafar ke daaman pe khoon-e-insaan ka rang kyun hai?

Zameen bhi teri, hai hum bhi tere, yeh milkiyat ka savaal kyaa hai?
Yeh qatl-o-khoon ka rivaaz kyun hai? Yeh rasm-o-jung-o-jadaal kyaa
hai?
Jinhe talab hain jahaan bhar ki unhi ka dil itnaa tung kyun hai?

(Oh Superior One! On Your land, why is war waged for the
sake of land?
Why is every victor's garment tainted by blood?

The land is Yours, we are Yours, why this fight for possession?
Why this tradition of murder and bloodshed? Why these rituals
of war and battle?
They who desire the whole world, why are their hearts so
troubled?)

A few years before *Taj Mahal*, in *Hum Dono* (1961), he answered this very question by putting the onus of war squarely on the powerful. In the song '*Allah tero naam*', he pleaded with the Almighty to confer some sanity on them:

---

3. In the introduction to 'Parchhaaiyaan', *Sahir Rachnawali*, Hindi Book Centre, 2007, p. 40, p. 43.

O saare jag ke rakhwaale
Nirbal ko bal dene waale
Balwaano ko de de gyaan
Sab ko sanmatee de bhagawaan
Allah tero naam, Eeshwar tero naam

(Oh Guardian of the entire world
He who gives strength to the weak
Bestow the mighty with good sense
Give everyone the wisdom
You are called Allah, Ishwar as well)

This line of thought is very similar to his poem 'Badi Taaqatey'[4] (Powerful Nations) where Sahir mocks the dominant powers of the world:

Tum hi tajweez-e-sulah laatey ho
Tum hi saamaan-e-jung baant-tey ho
Tum hi kartey ho qatl ka maatam
Tum hi teer-o-tufang baant-tey ho

(You are the harbingers of peace
You provide the reason for war as well
You grieve over the dead
Yet you distribute the arms and ammunition as well)

Having outlined the hazards of war through 'Parchhaaiyaan', while holding the prevailing powers of his time responsible for it, Sahir ultimately summarizes his views on war with his poem 'Aye Shareef Insaano' (Oh Dignified Humans) on a calmer note. The poem was written on the occasion of the Indo-Pak war of 1965 and the ensuing Tashkent agreement between the two nations in early 1966.

Jung toh khud hi maslaa hai ek
Jung kya maslon ka hul degi?
Aag aur khoon aaj bakshegi
Bhook aur ehtiyaaj kal degi

---

4. Published in *Aao Ki Koi Khwaab Bunein*.

Is liye, aye shareef insaano
Jung talti rahe toh behtar hai
Aap aur hum sabhi ke aangan mein
Shamaa jalti rahe toh behtar hai

(War is a problem in itself
What evil will war solve?
Today it will give death and destruction
Tomorrow it will lead to hunger and penury

That is why, oh dignified humans
It is better if we avoid going to war
Let all our courtyards, yours and mine
Be lit by joy instead)

Sahir's first anthology of poems, *Talkhiyaan*, addresses matters of social concern in a broad sense. Whether it is 'Sarzameen-e-Yaas' (The Land of My Failures), 'Kal Aur Aaj', 'Taj Mahal', 'Mere Geet', 'Mujhe Sochne Do', 'Subah-e-Navroz' (A New Dawn), 'Chakley' or 'Mere Geet Tumhaare Hain', the poems voice the anguish of the downtrodden without taking issue with a particular episode or occurrence. They are statements about the prevailing times instead of reactions to particular incidents. It is only when an event reached calamitous proportions that he reacts:

Jahaan-e-kuhna ke maflooz falsafadaano
Nizaam-e-nau ke taqaazey sawaal kartey hain

Yeh shahraahey isi waastey bani thee kya
Ki in pe desh ki janta sisak-sisak ke marey?
Zameen ne kya isi karan anaaj ugla thaa
Ki nasl-e-aadam-o-hawwa bilak bilak ke marey?[5]

(Oh paralysed viewers of the old world order
The stakeholders of the new order ask of you

---

5. From the poem 'Kahat-e-Bangal' (The Bengal Famine), published in *Talkhiyaan*.

Were these royal paths made so that
The citizens of the nation could die sobbing on them?
Had the soil borne grain so that
The descendents of Adam and Eve could die weeping on
  them?)

Sahir wrote 'Kahat-e-Bangal' in 1944 in response to the Bengal famine the preceding year. 'Aaj' (Today), written on the eve of India's independence, and 'Mafaahmat' (A Compromise), written in the context of the ensuing communal riots, are some of Sahir's other issue-based poems published in *Talkhiyaan*. However, such poems remain the exception rather than the norm in *Talkhiyaan*.

Sahir's next anthology, *Aao Ki Koi Khwaab Bunein*, published in 1971, is different. It consists of a number of poems like 'Parchhaaiyaan' and 'Aye Shareef Insaano' that were penned as a reaction to specific events that took place in the 1950s and 1960s.

'Khoon Phir Khoon Hai' (Blood Is Blood After All) is of this vintage. It was born as a reaction to the CIA-instigated assassination of Patrice Lumumba, the first legally elected prime minister of the Democratic Republic of the Congo and the hero of Congolese independence, in 1961.

> *Zulm phir zulm hai, badhta hai to mitt jaata hai*
> *Khoon phir khoon hai, tapkega toh jam jaayega . . .*
>
> *Tumney jis khoon ko maqtal mein dabaana chaaha*
> *Aaj woh kooncha-o-bazaar mein aa nikla hai*
> *Kahin shola, kahin naara, kahin pathhar bankar*
> *Khoon chalta hai toh rukta nahin sangeeno se*
> *Sar uthata hai toh dabta nahin aaeeno se*
>
> *Zulm ki baat hi kya, zulm ki aukaat hi kya*
> *Zulm bas zulm hai aagaaz se anjaam talak*
> *Khoon phir khoon hai, sau shakl badal sakta hai*
> *Aisi shakley ki mitao toh mitaaye na baney*

Aisey sholay, ki bujhao toh bujhaaye na baney
Aisey naarey ki dabao toh dabaaye na baney[6]

(Injustice is injustice, if it increases it must get wiped out
Blood is blood after all, if it spills it must clot . . .

The blood that you sought to repress by murder
The same blood has spilled out in the streets as well
As an ember, as a slogan, as a stone
When blood flows, no power can stop it
When rebels raise their head, no law can suppress them

What is injustice? What is its standing?
Injustice is simply injustice; from beginning to end
Blood is blood, capable of taking many shapes
Shapes that are indelible
Embers that are inextinguishable
Slogans that are irrepressible)

'The poem became very famous at that time. Although it was criticized for its virtually abusive language, particularly in the last verse – *Zulm ki baat hi kya, zulm ki aukaat hi kya, zulm bas zulm hai, aagaaz se anjaam talak* . . . – the fact is there was a great deal of anger in the world. The United Nations was also not willing to react. It was murder and everyone knew the CIA had engineered it. And Sahir gave it expression,' says Gauhar Raza.

Similarly, in 1969, on the occasion of Mirza Ghalib's hundredth death anniversary (15 February 1869), Sahir wrote 'Jashn-e-Ghalib'[7] (Celebrating Ghalib). He used the poem to expose the double standards of the political class who had gathered to commemorate Urdu's finest poet but were responsible for the demise of Urdu as a language:

---

6. From the poem 'Khoon Phir Khoon Hai', published in *Aao Ki Koi Khwaab Bunein*.
7. Published in *Aao Ki Koi Khwaab Bunein*.

Ravi Chopra/B.R. Films

Sahir (extreme left) with B.R. Chopra (standing). The two men were
on a similar wavelength, using Hindi cinema as a medium to air their
views on matters of social importance.

Ravi Chopra/B.R. Films

Celebrating the success of *Sadhana* (1958). From L to R: Vyjayanthimala (seated),
Manmohan Krishan (standing to Vyjayanthimala's left), Sahir at the mike and Yash
Chopra (extreme right in black).

Ruhan Kapoor

From L to R: Mahendra Kapoor, Yash Chopra, N. Datta and Sahir
Ludhianvi came together for some memorable songs in *Dhool Ka Phool*
(1959) and *Dharamputra* (1961).

S.M.M. Ausaja

Sahir (extreme left) and director Ramesh Saigal (extreme right)
at the recording of *Phir Subah Hogi* (1958).

Rajinder Kumar, B.R. Chopra, Mala Sinha and Yash Chopra are all attention as Sahir recites

At the premier of *Dharamputra*. Please note that Sahir is billed ahead of the composer in the marquee.

Manohar Iyer

From L to R: Sahir Ludhianvi, Yash Chopra and music director Ravi, creating magic with *Waqt* (1965).

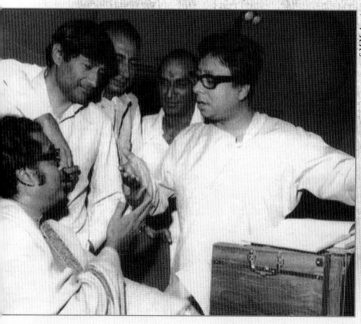

S.M.M. Ausaja

From L to R: Kishore Kumar, Dev Anand, Sahir, Yash Chopra and R.D. Burman at the recording for *Joshila* (1973).

From L to R: Music director Khayyam, producer Gulshan Rai, Sahir Ludhianvi and Lata Mangeskhar, possibly at a recording for *Trishul* (1978).

Manohar Iyer

Sahir Ludhianvi (second from left), Lata Mangeshkar and music director Ravi (extreme right). Sahir and Lata, allegedly, fell out sometime in the mid-to-late-1950s.

S.M.M. Ausaja

From L to R: Jan Nisar Akhtar, Sahir and a friend.

Trinetra Bajpai

From L to R: Sardar Jafri, Sahir, Khayyam, Ramesh Saigal. It was Sahir who
recommended Khayyam to Saigal for *Phir Subah Hogi*.

Mohd Rafi (holding the bouquet) and Madan Mohan with Sahir (partly hidden): they created one of the finest ghazals in Hindi cinema, '*Rang aur noor ki baarat*' in *Ghazal* (1964), which also had Sahir's immortal poem 'Taj Mahal' as a song.

Sahir Ludhianvi (extreme left) and music director Ravi (second from left). Outside of their association with the Chopras, Sahir and Ravi continued their good work in films like *Aaj Aur Kal* (1963), *Kaajal* (1965) and *Neel Kamal* (1968).

Manohar Iyer

At the funeral of close friend Jan Nisar Akhtar. The death of his mother and close friends like Jan Nisar Akhtar hastened his own demise.

Ajaib Chitrakar

Sahir back in Ludhiana for the golden jubilee celebrations of Government College, Ludhiana, in 1970 where he was even awarded a gold medal. Sahir is standing fourth from left, with Ajiab Chitrakar to his immediate right. On Sahir's left are noted Punjabi painter Harkishan Lall, Punjabi poet Shiv Kumar Batalvi, Jan Nisar Akhtar and Krishan Adeeb (extreme right). Keeping himself surrounded by friends was a part of Sahir's personality.

Jis ahad-e-siyaasat ne yeh zinda zabaan kuchli
Us ahad-e-siyaasat ko marhoomo ka gham kyun hai?
Ghalib jisey kehtey hain, Urdu hi ka shaayar thaa
Urdu par sitam dhaa kar, Ghalib pe karam kyun hai?

(The government that crushed this effervescent language
Why should that government grieve over the dead?
The man called Ghalib, was a poet of the Urdu language
Why should they be unfair to Urdu and benevolent towards
    Ghalib?)

Referring to 'Khoon Phir Khoon Hai' and 'Jashn-e-Ghalib', Gauhar Raza says that both poems were 'definitely meant to be issue-based . . . But because the lines were so profound, they transcend the occasions for which they were written. That is what Sahir is.'

A year later, in February 1970, he penned 'Gandhi Ho Ya Ghalib Ho'[8] (Be it Gandhi or Ghalib) on Mahatma Gandhi's hundredth birth anniversary (2 October 1869) and Ghalib's death centenary to lament the declining prominence of both men in society:

Khatam karo tahzeeb ki baat, band karo culture ka shor
Satya, ahinsa sab bakwaas, tum bhi kaatil hum bhi chor . . .

Gandhi ho ya Ghalib ho . . .
Khatam hua dono ka jashn
Aao, inhe ab kar de dafn

(Do away with talking about civility, stop screaming about
    culture
Truth and non-violence are irrelevant today, you are murderers
    and so are we . . .

Be it Gandhi or Ghalib . . .
The celebration of both individuals comes to an end
Come, let us bury them once and for all)

---

8. Ibid.

These issue-based poems once again underscore Sahir's sensitivity to oppression and his distaste for man's parochial ways. But what is even more remarkable about 'Parchhaaiyaan', 'Khoon Phir Khoon Hai' or 'Jashn-e-Ghalib' is that Sahir displayed a keen awareness of developments around him through these poems. He had by this time tasted unprecedented fame in the film industry, but instead of getting caught up in the claptraps of commercialism, he continued to use his art to highlight the various evils plaguing the world.

Yet, regardless of *Talkhiyaan*'s overwhelming success and his immensely perceptive poems in *Aao Ki Koi Khwaab Bunein*, Sahir and his poetry do not evoke the same interest as the works of Iqbal, Mir Taqi Mir and Mirza Ghalib among the Urdu intelligentsia in this country. Neither is Sahir taught in classrooms, nor is there a detailed critique of his film and non-film work in Urdu or English by any eminent scholar of Urdu.

'Perhaps, in his non-film poetry he was addressing the lowest common denominator. While keeping all aesthetics in mind, there was a desire that his poetry should be understood by as many as possible. And in that pursuit, sometimes, he didn't achieve the heights these other poets did. But he was an extremely popular poet, because he could be understood by people,' explains Javed Akhtar.

Raza Mir provides an equally plausible explanation:

> Despite the fact that several Urdu journals have devoted special issues to his work, Urdu critics like Intizar Husain have lauded him as a literary giant, and his songs continue to inspire many Urdu writers, one rarely sees a literary or hermeneutic analysis of Sahir's poems in English. Barring a fine and empathic, if critical, analysis by Carlo Coppola, most of Sahir's critics in English dismiss him as a pamphleteer, an ideologue or a propagandist. This treatment is not only Sahir's unfortunate lot. In the specialized world of Urdu criticism in English, there appears to be an implicit agreement that the works of PWA writers, while

they may be lauded as devices of organizing, are aesthetically inferior, and even harmful to Urdu poetry's classical traditions.

Why have these progressives been given such short shrift? I believe that this is not unique to Urdu literature. In fact, it is a highly common aspect in any literary criticism. It is not unusual for the canon in any field of literature to be wary of aesthetic experiments and to regard its outcome as aesthetic failure.[9]

Nevertheless, Raza Mir and his brother Ali Husain Mir remain convinced about Sahir's credentials as an avant-garde poet. They write:

Notwithstanding the short shrift he has received, Sahir's work does not allow the serious critic to wave it off, not simply because it is so popular, nor because it offers its own best defence through periodic references to its raison d'être, but because of the fact that Sahir pushed the boundaries of an explicitly political brand of poetry that served as an aesthetic experiment of the time.

The socialist literary theorist Nikolai Bukharin contended that 'poetic creation is one of the forms of ideological creation' and that poetry 'is one of the most powerful factors in social development as a whole' since 'the word itself is the product of social development and represents a definite condensing point in which a whole series of social factors find their expression'. Christopher Cauldwell, referring to the power of poetry as a unifying tool for the masses, writes that 'poetry is characteristically song, and song is characteristically something which, because of its rhythm, is sung in unison, and is capable of being the expression of a collective emotion', while George Thomson defines the poet as a prophet of the working class, only, 'at a higher level of sublimation'. Sahir was Bukharin's poet, Cauldwell's song-writer and Thomson's prophet.[10]

---

9. Mir Ali Raza, 'The Poetry of "No"', Outlookindia.com, 29 July 2004, http://www.outlookindia.com/article.aspx?224642
10. Raza Mir and Ali Husain Mir, *Anthems of Resistance*, IndiaInk, 2006, pp. 167–68.

13

A Man of Contradictions

Maana ke is jahaan ko gulzaar na kar sakey
Kaantey kuch kum hi kar gaye, guzrey jidhar se hum[1]

(I agree, I could not change this world entirely
But, hopefully, I made it a better place to live)

Undeniably, Sahir Ludhianvi was an outstanding poet, a great lyricist. The superlatives are easy to hand out. But beyond the plying of his art, he was in most other aspects of his life, remarkably human. In fact, the inherent paradoxes in his personality make it difficult to bracket him. He was a devoted friend, but was known to insult his friends on occasion as well. He alienated the best of composers in the industry, yet helped several other composers find success through their association with him. He was pretty vociferous in his criticism of religion, God and the merchants of faith, but at the same time, he composed some of the best devotional songs that one finds in Hindi cinema. Who then is the real Sahir Ludhianvi? Perhaps all of these. This is what makes him a difficult man to understand, but fascinating for that very reason.

---

1. A couplet by Sahir.

Sahir is largely believed to be an egoist who considered his own contribution to a song's success more than the music director's. Which probably explains his falling out with S.D. Burman among other music directors. But it would be unfair to simply paint him with that brush, without recognizing his contribution in enhancing the dignity of the lyricist. He used his clout as a poet and lyricist to establish a level footing between the composer and the songwriter. And in an industry where music directors lorded over lyricists, Sahir's stand often rubbed people the wrong way.

'He never bothered about money. It was always about his dignity, his terms and his position vis-à-vis the music director's,' recalled Yash Chopra.

It is this unrelenting battle for self-respect which did not allow Sahir to continue working with O.P. Nayyar following the success of *Naya Daur* (1957), or, for that matter, with the great music director, Naushad. Naqsh Lyallpuri comments:

> O.P. Nayyar had a habit of claiming the entire credit for the success of a film's soundtrack. He would try and relegate the lyricist to a secondary role. Sahir did not like this. He also did not approve of the fact that when music directors become successful, they ask for more money for themselves but are reluctant to pay the lyricist any better . . . And this is why, later on, he started insisting on being paid one rupee more than the music director . . . Naushad, too, wanted to work with Sahir. But Sahir was not very keen to work with him because he had heard of Naushad seeking a huge sum from the producers for his own work but, on the other hand, paying a pittance to the songwriter. Even when Shakeel Badayuni [Naushad's regular lyricist] made good money, it was owing to his association with Ravi and Hemant Kumar who paid him considerably better than Naushad.

Sahir even took this battle for equality for lyricists to the Government of India. As Yash Chopra narrated:

I think Mr Keskar was the minister of information and broadcasting then. Sahir asked him to mention the name of the playback singer and the music director while playing the song on All India Radio. Doesn't the songwriter have any contribution to the song? It was owing to his efforts that, thereafter, even the lyricist started getting mentioned on AIR. It was one of his biggest contributions.

*

Sahir was an atheist. From the very beginning, he reserved all his scorn for religion:

> *Aqaayid weham hain, mazhab khayaal-e-khaam hai saaki*
> *Azal se zehan-insaan basta-e-auhaam hai saaki*[2]

(Beliefs are false, religion an immature concept
From early on man has been brainwashed)

Having observed the communal riots of 1947 first-hand, he was particularly spiteful towards the custodians of religion as is clear from his songs 'Tu Hindu banega na Musalmaan banega' or 'Sansaar se bhaagey phirte ho'.

To quote Ali Husain Mir and Raza Mir, 'He not only challenged the very basis of religion but also despaired of a world where religious leaders were allowed to control the aspirations of the people and conjured up the image of an era where the sensibility of atheism would find a prominent place in society.'[3] They cite the following lines from Sahir's poem 'Tarah-e-Nau' (A New Foundation):

> *Bezaar hain kanisht-o-kalees se yeh jahaan*
> *Saudaagaraan-e-deen ki saudaagari ki khair*
> *Ilhaad kar raha hai murattab jahaan-e-nau*

---

2. From an aashaar (couplet) published in *Talkhiyaan*.
3. Raza Mir and Ali Husain Mir, *Anthems of Resistance*, IndiaInk, 2006, pp. 163–64.

Dair-o-haram ke heela-e-gaaratgari ki khair
Insaan ulat raha hai rukh-e-zeest se naqaab
Mazhab ke ehtemaam-e-fusoon parvari ki khair

(This world is tired of the temple and the mosque
Those who trade in religion, beware
Atheism is being propagated by the new world order
Those who sow the seeds of communal disharmony, beware
Man is unveiling the real face of life
Those who proliferate the magic of religion, beware)

Yet, this did not impede his songwriting skills when religious fervour was called for. Be it *'Aana hai toh aa raah mein'* (*Naya Daur*, 1957), *'Prabhu tero naam'* (*Hum Dono*, 1961) or *'Hey rom rom mein basne waale Ram'* (*Neel Kamal*, 1968), he often curbed his personal beliefs to praise the omnipotence of the Almighty. If anything, his own message in such songs was regarding the oneness of God.

Kaabey mein raho ya Kaashi mein, nisbat toh Usiki zaat se hai
Tum Ram kaho ke Rahim kaho, matlab toh Usiki baat se hai
Yeh masjid hai, woh butkhaana, chaahe yeh maano chaahe woh maano
Bhai maqsad toh hai dil ko samjhaana, chaahe yeh maano chaahe woh
   maano[4]

(You could live in Kaaba or in Kashi, both places relate to Him
You could call Him Ram or Rahim, the meaning remains the
   same
This is a masjid, that a temple, no matter what faith you follow
The only aspiration is to make hearts meet, no matter what faith
   you follow)

or

Teri hai zameen, Tera aasmaan, Tu bada meherbaan, Tu bakshish kar
Sabhi ka hai Tu, sabhi Tere, Khuda mere Tu bakshish kar[5]

---

4. From the song *'Kaabey mein raho ya Kaashi mein'* in *Dharamputra* (1961).
5. From the song *'Teri hai zameen, Tera aasmaan'* in *The Burning Train* (1980).

(The earth is Yours, as is the sky, You are most forgiving, show
   us Your mercy,
You belong to everybody, everybody looks to You, Oh Khuda,
   show us Your mercy)

Anwar explains her brother's attitude towards religion:

If I say that bhai jaan was actually a Sufi, people might dismiss it
for excessive sisterly love. But this is true and I say this with
confidence, that even though bhai jaan was not a strict
practitioner of religion and its rituals, he was a follower of all
the good things in every religion. And not only a follower, but,
to a certain extent, he would practise it as well. He remembered
several verses of the Quran by heart. It could be said that he had
a very sharp memory and that is why his remembering the verses
of the Quran should not surprise us. But not only did he remember
the verses, he would explain their meaning effortlessly as well.
If I put up any kind of sacred saying from the Quran on the wall,
he would never object to it . . .

   In the month of Ramzan, he would keep the room on the
ground floor open the entire month for the chowkidaar and
durbaan and would send iftaar and sehri with great discipline.
But he was against the formal obligations of religion.

   When the foundations of Parchhaiyaan [Sahir's house] were
being laid, maaji asked A.K. Nadiadwala, whom she considered
like her own son, to do the ceremonial breaking of the ground.
Sahir was most happy with this. But when maaji, according to
an old ritual, asked for goat's blood to be shed to mark this
auspicious beginning, Sahir was dead against it even though he
never disobeyed his mother's wishes. This does not mean that
bhai jaan was a vegetarian. He enjoyed eating goat's meat and
chicken, but he was against bloodshed in the name of religion for
such a cause.[6]

*

6. Saabir Dutt, *Fann Aur Shaksiyat*, Sahir Ludhianvi Number, Mahmood Ayoobi,
'Anwar Bibi Ke Bhai Jaan', pp. 45–46.

One of the criticisms levelled against Sahir Ludhianvi, as also a majority of the Progressive community who entered the world of Hindi cinema, was that he did not follow what he preached by way of his poetry. On the one hand, his poetry spoke of revolution and equality, of power to the masses, and cried foul of capitalism. Yet, on the other hand, he was comfortable in the entitlements capitalism had bestowed upon him. How else could he explain a chauffeur-driven car, his large house 'Parchhaiyaan' in Versova or those fine whiskies that he offered his friends and guests every time they dined with him?

'When they had no money, they were all card-carrying communists, but once they made their money they were worse than the worst capitalist,' observes yesteryear character actor Ram Mohan of the Progressive community while talking about Sahir Ludhianvi on the one occasion that I met him in his Juhu house in February 2010.

Mahendra Nath, brother of Krishan Chander and Sahir's friend, who too was a writer, disagrees. While he agrees that Progressive writers like Sahir had fallen in the eyes of the people because of their affluent lifestyles, he rebuts the argument. 'If all the Progressive writers moved out of their flats and stayed in huts instead, would that guarantee a revolution against the status quo in India?'[7]

*

But it is in his dealings with his friends that the contradictions in Sahir's personality emerged most vividly. Prakash Pandit, who met Sahir during the latter's stay in Delhi in 1949 and even stayed with him in the short time he spent in Delhi, came to know Sahir fairly intimately. In the introduction to his own compilation of

---

7. Ibid., Mahendra Nath, 'Sahir Ba Haisiyat Dost Aur Shaayar', p. 86.

Sahir's poetry, Prakash gives an interesting account of Sahir's enigmatic personality that manifested itself in daily life, highlighting the dichotomy in his relationship with his friends:

Sahir has just woken from his sleep (he would generally never wake up before 10–11 a.m.) and as always, has curled his tall frame in the shape of a jalebi, his long hair is unkempt and with his big red eyes, he stares at some distant object mesmerized. In this state of trance, he does not like any disturbance. Even his mother, whom he adores very much and who, after getting divorced from her zamindar husband, has only Sahir to support her, does not dare enter his room at this time. But then suddenly, Sahir gets restless, and shouts: 'Tea!'

And after this, for the entire day, and if he gets the opportunity, for the whole night as well, he talks non-stop. He cannot sit in one place for more than half an hour. The company of friends is like a blessing from the heavens for him. He offers them cigarette after cigarette. (Careful not to harm his own throat, he smokes his own cigarette in two separate halves, but very often ends up smoking both halves at one go.) He offers them [his friends] several rounds of tea (has more than a couple by himself). In this time, he entertains them not only with his own couplets and ghazals, but with the ghazals and couplets of other poets as well. He recites these with interesting anecdotes and suitable introductions. He remembers each and every incident from his life. He remembers the letters of his friends and articles from magazines word by word. He remembers every critique, favourable or unfavourable, written on his poetry till today. So much so, he remembers entire dialogues from the movies *Indrasabha* and *Shah Behram* which he saw as a child.

Then, at about 10, 11, 12 or 1 in the night, when his friends take his leave, promising to meet him the following day, and even if one brave heart decides to bear his company for longer, Sahir is consumed by an all-encompassing feeling of great loneliness. Suddenly, at this time, the dangerous seed of Bohemianism sprouts within him and he looks down on every individual in comparison to himself. At that time, the jovial, affable Sahir of the morning is a completely changed man. He recounts the conversations of the day (which he remembers word for word) time and again, using them to poke fun at those very friends whom he had praised in the morning. He passes all kind of insulting remarks to mock them and decides that he will never waste his time or money on such friends. But the very next day, when he sees the same friends, he seeks their company with great affection. He treats them to whisky instead of tea, feeds them to the extent of binging and, inexplicably, praises them for their qualities.

This ambiguity in his personality manifests itself in strange ways. He can get irritated, feel embarrassed or get frightened by the most trivial of issues. He is indecisive about everything. This indecisiveness extends not only towards the more serious issues in life, but even on the relatively mundane matter of which poem he should recite at a mushaira. Even in the matter of what to wear or what to eat, this indecisiveness plagues his behavior. He needs the help of friends even on such matters. Perhaps this is why he hasn't been able to get married until now. He does not approve of girls selected for him by others and there is no question of him finding someone by himself.

Because of such behavior on Sahir's part, which I often considered a façade, we would sometimes flare up at each other. I often felt that he was trying to make me an undeserving hero and I was not at all ready for this. Hence, I would lose no opportunity to make fun of him and put him down. While he would be preparing the grounds to prove the greatness of a new nazm of his, I would tell him the plot of a new story of mine, comparing myself with Chekov, Gorky or Guy de Maupassant. Pretending to be serious, I would recommend those clothes to him, which made him look funny. Many a time, I even made him have ice cream for breakfast. But slowly it dawned on me that he was more to be pitied than made fun of. He has not deliberately inculcated these habits, instead they have grown around him like weeds. Within the folds of these habits are the unfortunate circumstances in which he was raised and which along with other traits – both good and bad – became a part and parcel of his personality.[8]

Friends, as Prakash Pandit observes, meant everything to Sahir. Right from his childhood days, through his college years and then during his career in the Hindi film industry, he yearned for their company. Women came and went in his life, but the company of friends – whether Hameed Akhtar in Lahore or Jan Nisar Akhtar in Bombay – remained a part of his identity. He always looked to entertain them under the slightest pretext.

'We would always have to prepare food in large quantities. This is because bhai jaan never liked that if his friends stayed till meal time, they left without eating. Whatever had been cooked in the house, had to be sufficient for the guests as well. When we understood this, we took great care to ensure that there was always enough for everyone to eat. And when bhai jaan would come to know that food had been prepared for his friends as well, he would indeed be very happy,' remarks Anwar of her brother's generous disposition towards his friends.[9]

Such hospitality hardly went unnoticed among Sahir's friends. The renowned Urdu writer Wajida Tabassum recalls having an exchange with Sahir in this regard. Aware of the number of times she had eaten at Sahir's house, Wajida told him, '*Kasam se, aisa lagta hai ki ragon mein khoon ke bajaaye aapka namak daud raha hai.*' (I promise you, at times it appears that instead of blood the salt of your house runs through our veins.) But instead of taking the compliment graciously, Sahir appeared offended and asked Wajida with a fair

8. Prakash Pandit, *Sahir Ludhianvi (Life Sketch and Poetry)*, Rajpal and Sons, pp. 6–9, and English translation of this text at http://aligarians.com/2005/12/sahir-ludhianvi-by-parkash-pandit/
9. Saabir Dutt, *Fann Aur Shaksiyat*, Sahir Ludhianvi Number, Mahmood Ayoobi, 'Anwar Bibi Ke Bhai Jaan', p. 39.

degree of curtness, '*Arrey bhai koi insaan aaye, do ghadi baithey, baaton mein waqt nikalta hi chala jaaye, toh kya bhooka hi jaaney dein?*'(If someone comes to our house, sits for some time, indulges in some idle banter, should we let him go hungry?)[10]

But like Prakash Pandit points out, it didn't take much time for these congenial evenings with friends to degenerate into unpleasant gatherings if Sahir had too much to drink. As Ruhan Kapoor remarks, in later years, he became insufferable in this regard: 'He would get high very soon. And after drinks *aadmi shaitaan ho jaata hai* (man turns into a devil). His thoughts would come out uninhibited. People started avoiding him because he used to go out of control. He would start accusing and abusing anyone.'

Even Khushwant Singh writes of Sahir's drinking disapprovingly:

> I first met Sahir Ludhianvi at a small gathering of poets in the home of Dr Rafiq Zakaria and his wife Fatma. Zakaria was then a minister in the Maharashtra Government and lived in a spacious bungalow with a garden on Malabar Hill. The party was in honour of Firaq Gorakhpuri, who happened to be visiting Bombay. The guests included Akhtarul Imam, the novelist Krishan Chander, Sahir Ludhianvi and a few other lovers of Urdu poetry. The only misfit was Mota Chudasama, a Gujarati businessman who knew neither Urdu nor poetry. He was rich and a friend of the Zakarias. The party had just started with a few poets reading their compositions when Chudasama made some inane remark which upset Sahir. He exploded in bad temper: 'Who invited you here? If you know nothing, you should keep your mouth shut.' Or words to that effect. Chudasama walked out in a huff. The party was ruined.
>
> I learnt that Sahir was prone to losing his temper and behaving rudely. He was a heavy drinker. When he arrived at Zakaria's

10. Ibid., Wajida Tabassum, 'Aasman Chup Hai', p. 103.

home, he was already high. He expected to be served Scotch and soda. Instead he was served tea and pakodas. That may have triggered off the explosion.

Sahir's mother disapproved of her son's drinking habit as Singh observes:

> He invited me over to his bungalow by the sea in Juhu. I accompanied the Zakarias. I was on my guard lest I say something which might upset him. I spent most of the evening talking in Punjabi to his mother and a lady cousin or niece. I could sense his mother doted on him as he doted on his mother. More than once, she asked me: '*Puttar* (son), you tell him not to drink so much. He is ruining his health.' I didn't dare. I joined him for a couple of drinks, had my dinner and departed.[11]

It is not that Sahir drank to further a popular notion that linked Urdu poets to alcohol. He did not see any relation between shaayari and sharaab. When asked specifically by Naresh Kumar Shaad if there was any relation between the two, he said, 'Not at all. You don't need to be drunk to compose a sher. You can never write a good sher under the influence of alcohol.'

Not satisfied with the answer, Shaad asked Sahir pointedly, 'Then why do you drink?'

'I wear a shirt as well but wearing a shirt is not a qualification for a poet,' said Sahir with customary wit and frankness.

Softening a little, he went on to explain: 'I never used to drink . . . I took to it because of low blood pressure. I had to drink for about three to four years for medical reasons. It did me a world of good. Now I am used to it. Without drinking, I don't sleep well at night.'[12]

11. Khushwant Singh, 'Sahir's Tortured Soul', *The Tribune*, Saturday, 10 January 2004, http://www.tribuneindia.com/2004/20040110/windows/above.htm
12. Saabir Dutt, *Fann Aur Shaksiyat*, Sahir Ludhianvi Number, Naresh Kumar Shaad, 'Sahir Ke Saath Ek Shaam', p. 55.

Away from the influence of alcohol, though, Sahir was a magnanimous individual. 'He was helpful to his co-writers. He got so many people jobs. He took Anand Bakshi personally to meet film-maker L.V. Prasad. Anybody who wanted support, either professionally or financially, he was the first person to help,' said Yash Chopra.

There is the story of how he paid for the treatment of his friend from his days in Lahore, Ram Prakash Ashk, who was suffering from cancer. Ashk had helped Sahir cope with his monetary struggles during his stay in Lahore. Then, when Ashk came to Bombay to try his luck as a lyricist in films, he was diagnosed with the deadly disease. Sahir first had Ashk treated at the Tata Memorial Hospital in Bombay. When that did not work, he sent Ashk to America with a large sum of money to pay for his treatment. Ashk, however, succumbed to the disease.

Sahir's publisher, Amaranth Varma of Star Publications Pvt. Ltd, also benefited from Sahir's benevolence. Varma had launched the Star Pocket Book series in 1957 after Sahir had given him permission to publish his anthology of film songs *Gaata Jaaye Banjara* (The Gypsy Sings On). At that time, Varma could only afford a measly sum of one rupee per book as royalty to Sahir. Subsequently, when the time came, Varma sent a cheque of Rs 62.50 to Sahir as royalty for the number of copies that were sold of *Gaata Jaaye Banjara*.

In 1960, Varma went to Bombay to meet some writers for the purpose of publishing their works. He met Sahir, who introduced Varma not only to Krishan Chander but also to some other prominent writers like Rajinder Singh Bedi and Khwaja Ahmed Abbas. Varma remembered the positive impression Sahir created for his publishing house by presenting him in front of all the writers saying, '*Yeh royalty bhi dete hain.*' (He pays royalty as well.)[13]

---

13. This episode was narrated to me by Amarnath Varma when I met him at his Delhi office in May 2009.

Then there was Jan Nisar Akhtar, Progressive poet, film lyricist and Javed Akhtar's father. The two were considered inseparable. When Jan Nisar produced his only film *Bahu Begum* (1967), Sahir even wrote the songs for it, which included the memorable '*Hum intezaar karengey tera qayaamat tak*' (I shall wait for you until the day of judgement).

Theirs was a friendship based on great love and respect for each other, which did not preclude some good-natured banter. Sahir Ludhianvi had just received the Padma Shri in 1971. He told Jan Nisar Akhtar, '*Yaar Jan Nisar, ab sarkar ko tumhe bhi Padma Shri se nawaazna chahiye*' (Jan Nisar, the government should now honour you with the Padma Shri as well).

Perplexed by this sudden suggestion, Jan Nisar turned to Sahir and asked, '*Bhala aisa kyun?*' (Why do you say that?)

'*Ab yeh zillat mujh akele se bardaasht nahin hoti,*' said Sahir wryly. (I cannot bear this embarrassment alone.)[14]

Naqsh Lyallpuri recalls the friendship between the two:

> They were both involved in the Progressive Writers' Movement and their association extended on that front as well. Sahir had seen a lot of hardship in his life. Jan Nisar Akhtar, even then, was struggling and so, Sahir could relate to Jan Nisar's plight. Also, Jan Nisar was a very good poet. So, it should come as no surprise that the two got along really well.

Javed's assessment of the relationship between his father and Sahir, on the other hand, is more tongue-in-cheek:

> They were very, very close friends. For years they spent their evenings together, almost every day. I think they complemented each other well. Sahir was the talkative one. My father was, comparatively, a quiet person. That helped both of them. One could talk as much as he wanted to and the other could keep quiet as much as he wanted.

---

14. K.L. Narang Saqi, *Adeebon Ke Lateefey*, New Delhi, Halqa Arbab Zauq, 1992.

No wonder then that the death of his loved ones one after the other in quick succession hastened Sahir's own demise. His mother, with whom he shared an inexplicable bond, died in 1976. Jan Nisar Akhtar, too, died the same year while Krishan Chander, at whose house Sahir had stayed when he had come to Bombay, died a year later, in 1977.

Sarwar Shafi, Sahir's cousin, wrote of the impact her aunt's demise had on Sahir:

> We got to know of our aunt's demise in 1976 . . . After that, bhai jaan changed quite a bit. A happy demeanour gave way to sadness. He was troubled by his mother's absence. He did not meet too many people. He would often think that he'd been left alone in this world. He kept his mother's loss within him for four years. He stopped going for mushairas as well.[15]

Yash Chopra concurred with this assessment. 'After his mother's death, he went into a shell. He would say, "*Kuch mazaa nahin aa raha likhney ka.*" (I'm not enjoying writing any more.) His loneliness must have killed him.'

Hameed Akhtar, who came and stayed with Sahir in Bombay for a week in 1979, also saw a very different person from the Sahir he had last seen in 1948. He writes:

> He would never leave his house. At night, he would sleep in the bedroom, but in the morning would be found lying on the drawing room sofa. Initially, I gave it no thought. But there was more to it. His bedroom was in a far corner and Sahir was paranoid that if he had a heart attack in the night, who would hear him from the bedroom? That is why he would sleep in the drawing room which was connected to the kitchen . . . He would not go anywhere, but the driver had been ordered to report every day to work at 8 a.m., in uniform. Sahir feared that there

---

15. Saabir Dutt, *Fann Aur Shaksiyat*, Sahir Ludhianvi Number, Sarwar Shafi, 'Ammee Kehtee Thee', pp. 73–74.

might be a need to call the doctor . . . He had a kidney stone but this could not be operated upon because of the heart attack he had had. That is why he lived the final three or four years of his life not feeling too well, but also plagued by the anxiety of impending illness. One felt sorry for his plight. He would stare at the sky with his big eyes for hours together, as if looking for something that was lost. I was convinced, had he got married and had children, he would never have had to face such a plight.[16]

Finally, on 25 October 1980, at the age of fifty-nine, Sahir Ludhianvi suffered a massive heart attack while playing cards at the residence of his friend Dr R.P. Kapoor, and passed away.

---

16. Hameed Akhtar, *Ashnaiyaan Kya Kya*, pp. 104–05.

14

A Poet-Lyricist Like No Other

Ab ek raat agar kum jeeyein, toh kum hi sahi
Yahi bahut hai ki hum mashaaley jala ke jeeye[1]

(Even if I lived a night less, let it be so
At least I lit a spark while I lived)

The past few years have witnessed unprecedented popular upheaval against authoritarian and dictatorial regimes. From uprisings in Bahrain, Syria and Yemen to the ouster and subsequent trials of Libya's Muammar Muhammad al-Gaddafi, Egypt's Hosni Mubarak and Tunisia's Zine El Abidine Ben Ali, there has been a general awakening among the common man who is rising against government atrocities, human rights violations and corruption.

Meanwhile, Indians, largely isolated from developments in these countries, had misgivings with their own government. A group of people calling themselves representatives of 'civil society', led by

---

1. A couplet by Sahir in *Aao Ki Koi Khwaab Bunein*.

septuagenarian Anna Hazare, even demanded the formulation of a 'Lokpal Bill' which would bring to justice truant politicians and bureaucrats who misuse their office.

While the verdict is still out on the credentials and modus operandi of these self-appointed representatives of 'civil society', their noble intentions coupled with the sacrifices made by thousands in the Arab world to root out government excesses only lead us to the unequivocal truth propagated by Sahir in these lines from the title song in *Phir Subah Hogi*:

> *Haq maangney waalon ko jis din sooli na dikhayee jayegee*
> *Woh subah kabhi toh aayegi*
> *Woh subah hum hi se aayegi*

> (When those who demand their rights are not sent to the gallows
> That dawn shall come some day
> That dawn will come from us)

In their closing comments on Sahir, Raza Mir and Ali Husain Mir write:

> Sahir was a powerful poet of dissent, a conscience of society, an uncompromising critic of the Right and a strident persuader of the Left. He was a relentless opponent of reactionary cultural and social institutions. His verses were never lacking in virtuosity or depth. His poetry could be as fine-grained as Ghalib's and Mir's *ghazals*, as lyrical as Faiz's *nazms* and as inflected with philosophy as Hali's or Iqbal's *musaddas*[2] . . . We were fortunate to have had him in our midst.[3]

More importantly, there is a texture to Sahir's work that is eternal. His words go well beyond the film's situation. His songs in *Pyaasa, Naya Daur, Hum Dono, Chitralekha* and several other

---

2. A musaddas is a genre of Urdu poetry in which each unit consists of six lines.
3. Raza Mir and Ali Husain Mir, *Anthems of Resistance*, IndiaInk, 2006, p. 171.

films are reflective of this. They are not just songs specific to the context of the particular films, but are larger statements regarding life and humanity. That is why so many of his poems, 'Chakley', 'Yeh kiska lahu hai, kaun mara?' etc., lent themselves readily to film songs.

A perfect example of this timelessness in Sahir's poetry came to light on 4 March 2011 when Delhi's chief metropolitan magistrate Vinod Yadav went on to discharge Italian businessman Ottavio Quattrocchi from the two-decade-old Bofors pay-off case. The CMM said the country could not afford to spend hard-earned money on Quattrocchi's extradition, which had already cost Rs 250 crore. In summary of his verdict, the magistrate quoted Sahir Ludhianvi's song from *Gumraah* (1963), '*Chalo ik baar phir se*', saying, '*Woh afsaana jisey anjaam tak laana na ho mumkin / Usey ek khoobsurat modh dekar chhodna achchha.*'[4]

Equally laudable is Sahir's ability to give the film song an unmatched poetic quality. Even when he writes for a courtesan's character, like in *Mujhe Jeene Do*, he does so with great aesthetic finesse. Otherwise, it is hard to imagine a courtesan, pandering to a gathering of dacoits, using such refined language and beautiful imagery in her song:

> *Raat bhi hai kuch bheegi bheegi*
> *Chaand bhi hai kuch madham madham*
> *Tum aao toh aankhein kholey*
> *Soyee hui paayal ki chham chham . . .*
>
> *Taptey dil par yun girti hai*
> *Tere nazar se pyaar ki shabnam*
> *Jaltey huey jungle par jaisey*
> *Barkha barse ruk ruk tham tham*

---

4. http://news.outlookindia.com/item.aspx?713853.

(The night is coy and young
The moonlight, ethereal and beautiful
Your arrival spurs me
Into a state of excitement

This burning heart feels
The pleasant gaze of your love
Like a jungle consumed by fires
Is cooled by the arrival of rain)

'He proved one thing beyond any doubt: that film songs and good poetry are not contradictory. They are compatible and they can be complementary. To think that film songs cannot achieve a literary high is wrong. It is possible,' says Javed Akhtar of this aspect of Sahir's work.

Beyond that, he gave the film song an intellectual quotient. He would produce a philosophical train of thought even in a lighter moment. For example, *'Laga chunari mein daag'* from *Dil Hi Toh Hai* (1963) depicts an inane segment in the film's screenplay. Yet, Sahir's lyrics, supposedly inspired from the dohas of the great mystic poet Kabir, succinctly articulate an individual's lament of preoccupying himself with the material world ahead of more spiritual pursuits:

> *Laga chunari mein daag chhupaoon kaise?*
> *Ghar jaoon kaise? . . .*
>
> *Kori chunariya aatma mori, mail hai maayajaal*
> *Woh duniya more babul ka ghar, yeh duniya sasuraal*
> *Jaakey babul se nazrey milaoon kaise?*
> *Ghar jaoon kaise?*

(My conscience has been stained, how do I undo my sin?
How do I show my face when I return home? . . .

My conscience was unblemished, it is materialism that leads to
    sin
That world is where I belong, this world is alien to me

How do I return home and show my face?
How do I return home?)

Sahir Ludhianvi belonged to the golden era of the Hindi film song. His peers Majrooh Sultanpuri, Shailendra, Kaifi Azmi, Shakeel Badayuni and Rajinder Krishan – all contributed towards giving the film song its finest hour. Urdu poetry reached its zenith with the likes of Shakeel, Majrooh, Sahir and Kaifi plying their trade in the film industry.

Manohar Iyer observes of these lyricists' writing style:

> Each one had a style of his own. Whatever the style of the song, the language was rich and refined, which was consistent with the overall film, the situation, the character and the language/dialect spoken by them. The stars also made a difference – Dilip Kumar, the Hamlet of the Indian screen, was mostly seen as a doomed and dejected lover, crooning songs imbued with pathos and melancholy which were penned by Shakeel and Shailendra. Raj Kapoor played the eternal romantic tramp with a heart of gold and voiced either the common man's feelings written by Shailendra or serenaded his sweetheart with Hasrat Jaipuri's romantic lyrics. Dev Anand was portrayed as an amoral, ambitious, carefree, casual romantic hero singing frothy songs of Majrooh, Shailendra and Sahir. The lyrics helped establish the identity of all these stars.

Among these, Majrooh, Kaifi and Sahir were Progressive poets before they joined films. One would think that this shared background also reflected in their film work but this is not the case.

Majrooh was a brilliant songwriter. He retained his relevance for over fifty years from the time he wrote his first song 'Jab dil hi toot gaya' for Shah Jehan (1946) to songs like 'Pehla nasha' (Jo Jeeta Wohi Sikander, 1992) and 'Aaj main upar' (Khamoshi, 1996) in the 1990s. Yet, Majrooh and Sahir differed. Majrooh never introduced his political leanings into his film songs. He was a true geetkaar, who wrote strictly as per the demands of the film's script. According to Javed Akhtar:

> Majrooh was more lyrical than Sahir but, if I may say so, not as responsible as Sahir. He was an extremely talented writer. He was extremely prolific. He has written much more than Sahir. But he made compromises. Like in '*Sunn sunn sunn zaalima, pyaar humko tum se ho gaya*'[5] (Listen oh heartless one, I have fallen in love with you), when you are saying '*sunn*' you can't say '*tum*'. It should have been '*tujh*' or it could have been '*suno*'. But he felt that musically '*tujh*' will not sound good. He took liberties with grammar for the sake of better phonetics. Sahir never did such things.

Shakeel Badayuni was another great lyricist. With the title song of *Chaudhvin Ka Chaand* (1960) and '*Jab pyaar kiya toh darna kya*' (Why be afraid when you have dared to love – *Mughal-e-Azam*, 1960), he wrote two of the greatest love songs in Hindi cinema. He was an expert at conveying the many moods of romance.

Unfortunately, Shakeel, who largely remained confined to working with Naushad, did not go much beyond his romantic forte. Also as Gulzar says of Shakeel, 'He was extremely popular and wrote beautiful ghazals, but his language remained the same in all his films.' Gulzar extends this criticism of Majrooh as well by saying, 'So with Majrooh, who wrote "C-A-T-cat, *cat mane billi*"[6] to suit the language of the song, but used the same language, the same vocabulary with a heavy Urdu base most often.'[7]

Which is probably why Shakeel and Majrooh were never in the same league as Sahir.

---

5. From the movie *Aar Paar* (1954).
6. From the movie *Dilli Ka Thug* (1958).
7. Ganesh Anantharaman, *Bollywood Melodies*, 'The Songwriters', Penguin Books India, 2008, p. 132.

Kaifi Azmi is different from Shakeel and Majrooh and closer to
Sahir. Even Javed Akhtar believes that his father-in-law's lyrical
style was closest to Sahir's. 'Kaifi was also basically a poet, not a
songwriter. So was Sahir. They were poets who were writing
poetry for films. Kaifi's songs in *Kaagaz Ke Phool* could have been
Sahir's songs also. Or his (Kaifi's) songs in *Anupama*, in *Heer Ranjha*,'
says Javed.

But Javed points to an essential difference between the two:
'Sahir was much more sharp and focused. For example, consider
Kaifi's song in *Arth*, "Koyee ye kaise bataaye ke wo tanha kyun hai".
Sahir would never write these lines. He was much more sharp,
more focused, more real.'[8]

Unlike Sahir, though, it is not fair to judge Kaifi's legacy just as a
songwriter. Kaifi was much more than that. He wrote scripts and
dialogues for films as well. In *Heer Ranjha* (1970), he wrote the
dialogue of the entire film in verse, a first in Hindi Cinema. He also
wrote *Garam Hawa* (1973), which marked a high point of the New
Indian Cinema movement. From adapting a story that was originally
written by Ismat Chughtai, to writing its screenplay, dialogue and
lyrics, *Garam Hawa* is the perfect example of Kaifi's talent. His
talent had one more facet to it, one that he portrayed brilliantly in
Naseem (1995). Kaifi played a doting grandfather in the film set
against the backdrop of the 1992 Babri Masjid demolition.

The one lyricist who truly matches up to Sahir's quality is
Shailendra. The two came from totally different schools. Javed
explains, 'Shailendra was a real songwriter. Sahir's songs are like

---

8. 'Koyi ye kaise bataaye ke wo tanha kyun hai / Woh jo apna thaa, wahee aur kisi ka kyun
hai / Yahi duniya hai toh fir, aisee ye duniyaan kyun hai / Yahee hota hai toh, aakhir yahee
hota kyun hai? (How does anyone explain why they are troubled? / He who
belonged to me, why is he with someone else now / If this is the way the world
is, why is the world like this? / If this is how it happens, then why does it happen
this way?).

poems but Shailendra's songs are like lyrics. He was a lyricist in the real sense. Shailendra comes from the tradition of Kabir, Meera, Khusro. You get that kind of simplicity of these folk poets in Shailendra's lyrics.'

Gulzar elaborates:

> Shailendra found an effective way of merging his personal beliefs with his lyrics, without in any way sermonizing or propagating an ideology . . . But Shailendra did so without rejecting the film medium . . . 'Dil ka haal sune dilwaala' is a great example of this ability. So is 'Mera joota hai Japaani'.[9] Notice that the latter song was never a slogan. Only a simple man articulating a simple truth . . .

Sahir Ludhianvi merged his poetry and social conscience in all his songs, but he totally refused to learn the film medium, and wrote only what he wanted. He is the only poet whom the industry accepted as he is, with his language, his vocabulary and his imagery. Sahir is also the only poet whose songs became successful because of his lyrics, and not because of the tune or the singer, as was usually the case. In the history of Hindi cinema, this phenomenon of a lyricist succeeding entirely on his own terms happened only with Sahir.

I believe that in any song that becomes a hit, the primary factors are the rhythm and the tune. The words follow. In fact, the quality of the words depends on how much it matches the melody and the beat. That is why I consider the role of the lyricist as secondary to that of the composer. With Sahir, however, the songs succeeded on the merit of his words alone. The tune and the beat came only next. His words had a persona of their own. For instance, 'Pedon ki shaakhon pe soyi soyi chaandni aur thodi der mein thhak ke laut jaayegi' in the film Jaal. This language, this kind of expression did not exist in films till Sahir-saab came. He gave a new meaning to romanticism in films.[10]

---

9. Both songs from *Shri* 420 (1955).
10. Ganesh Anantharaman, *Bollywood Melodies*, 'The Songwriters', Penguin Books India, 2008, pp. 132–33.

The best way to understand the difference between Shailendra and Sahir is to see the contrasting characters they wrote for. Where Shailendra's songs for Raj Kapoor in *Shri 420* were about the loveable tramp from the lower sections of society, Sahir's lyrics for Vijay in *Pyaasa* was the voice of the intellectual. Shailendra's preferred medium, like in the songs of *Shri 420*, was *Khadi boli* or the Hindi language, while Sahir championed the cause of Urdu. Shailendra was inseparable from Raj Kapoor, Sahir from the Chopras. Shailendra sought recourse to films, after shunning the medium initially, only after he realized that this was the best way to make ends meet. Sahir, on the other hand, proactively sought a career in films. In this sense, the two were diametrically opposite.

A similar, but necessary, distinction must be made between Sahir and Kavi Pradeep. In some ways, Pradeep, who debuted in Hindi films with his songs for the movie *Kangan* (1939), could be seen as a precursor to Sahir. Ganesh Anantharaman writes of Pradeep, 'He, much before Sahir, used his pen with a sense of responsibility towards larger causes in society, within the constraints of commercial Hindi cinema.' He goes on to highlight Pradeep's lyrics in *'Ghar ghar mein Diwali hai, mere ghar mein andhera'* (Every house glows in the lights of Diwali, yet my home is filled with darkness) from the movie *Kismet* (1943):

> *Charon taraf laga hua meena bazaar hai*
> *Dhan ki jahan pe jeet garibon ki haar hai*
> *Insaniyat ke bhes mein phirta hain lutera*
> *Ji chahta sansar mein main aag laga doon*
> *Soye huye insaan ki qismat ko jaga doon*
> *Thokar se udaa doon main daya-o-dharam ka deraa*[11]

> (Every home is draped in prosperity
> Wherever wealth triumphs the poor suffer defeat

11. Ganesh Anantharaman, *Bollywood Melodies*, 'The Songwriters', Penguin Books India, 2008, pp. 104–05.

In the garb of humanity, man plunders at will
I am consumed by the desire to set the world ablaze
I wish to awake mankind's destiny
I want to reject this façade of magnanimity in the name of religion)

However, while the similarities with Sahir's work were apparent (*Yeh mehlo, yeh takhton, yeh taajon ki duniya*), Pradeep was fundamentally a staunch nationalist. He might have written the odd song to express his disappointment with mankind's increasingly depraved ways – '*Aaj ke insaan ko yeh kya ho gaya*'[12] (What has happened to man today?) – but these were exceptions rather than the rule. The only recurrent motif in his work was his commitment to the nation, the freedom struggle and a distinct pride in independent India. To this end, he penned some classics – '*Door hato aye duniyawaalo Hindustaan hamaara hai*'[13] (Stay away from us other nations of the world, India is ours), '*Hum layein hain toofaan se kashti nikaal ke*'[14] (We have brought back the boat having braved the tempest), '*Aao bachon tumhey dikhaen jhanki Hindustaan ki*'[15] (Come, children, let me show you a glimpse of India) – the sounds of which reverberate even today.

Sahir, having emerged as a poet in faraway Lahore in the early 1940s, could never have been influenced by Pradeep so far as the latter's socialistic lyrics were concerned. Sahir's own poems, a continuity of which were seen in his film lyrics, were largely an output of his own personal experiences. Most significantly, he didn't share Pradeep's enthusiasm for independent India. While he did write a few songs that were glowing expressions of patriotism (*Yeh desh hai veer jawaano ka*) or optimism regarding the nation state

---

12. *Amar Rahe Yeh Pyar* (1961).
13. *Kismet* (1943).
14. *Jagriti* (1954).
15. Ibid.

(*Jaagega insaan zamaana dekhega / Kal ka Hindustaan zamaana dekhega*), he was largely critical of it. His tirade against the nation was expressed all too frequently in songs like '*Jinhe naaz hai Hind par woh kahaan hain?*', '*Cheen-o-Arab humaara*' and '*Bacha le aye Maula, aye Ram!*'.

His poem 'Chhabbees Janvari'[16] (26th January), where he vented his ire in the most direct way possible on the leaders of the nation, is an example:

> *Daulat badhi toh mulk mein iflaas kyun badha?*
> *Khush-haali-e-awaam ke asbaab kya huye?* . . .
>
> *Mazhab ka rog aaj bhi kyun la-ilaaj hai?*
> *Woh nuskha-haaye-nadiro-naayaab kya huye?*
>
> *Har koocha shola-zaar hai, har shehar qatl-gaah*
> *Yakjahti-e-hayaat ke aadaab kya huye?* . . .
>
> *Mujrim hoon main agar, toh gunahgaar tum bhi ho*
> *Aye rehbaraaney-qaum, khataakaar tum bhi ho*
>
> (If wealth increased, why did poverty increase in the nation?
> What happened to the prosperity of the masses? . . .
>
> Why is there still no cure for communalism?
> What happened to those unique cures?
>
> Every road burns, every city is plagued by murder
> Where did the etiquette of togetherness disappear? . . .
>
> If I am culpable, so are you
> You, the leaders of this nation, are guilty as well)

It is this revolutionary tenor, a declared evangelism of the Progressive ideology and speaking up for the exploited that defines his work in films. From drawing attention to the plight of women,

---

16. Published in *Aao Ki Koi Khwaab Bunein*.

'Aurat ne janam diya mardon ko', to advocating communal harmony, 'Tu Hindu banega na Musalmaan banega' or stating his disgust for mankind's avaricious ways, 'Yeh duniya agar mil bhi jaaye toh kya hai?', Sahir constantly tugged at society's very conscience.

Above all, he wished for the formation of a classless society. Ganesh Anantharaman remarks, 'Sahir's poetry was unvarnished, hitting you straight with its cynicism. He never believed in sublimating his emotions or in pleasing the powers that be ... He may have been cynical of politics; but Sahir never lost faith in the collective power of people.'[17]

'Dhoom mache dhoom' (Festivities are in the air) from the film Kaala Patthar (1979) highlights this belief of Sahir's:

Pale na sog jahaan, sukhi ho log jahaan
Humko hai saath aisi duniya basaani
Seeno mein aag liye, hothon pe raag liye
Humko andheron mein hai shammey jalaani
Kaaley patthar ki kasam, jab talak dum mein hain dum
Hum yeh dekhengey rasme puraani, kar na paaye yahaan hukm-raani
Aaj se humne hai dil mein thaani, laayenge ek nayi rut suhaani

(Where no suffering exists, where people live happily
Together we have to build that world
With passion in our hearts, a song on our lips
We must illuminate the darkness
We promise, as long as we live
We shall see that the old order does not rule over us any longer
We promise today, we will usher in a better tomorrow)

According to Jan Nisar Akhtar:

There is no doubt that it is Sahir's accomplishment that he gave films such songs that are laced with political and social awareness.

---

17. Ganesh Anantharaman, Bollywood Melodies, 'The Songwriters', Penguin Books India, 2008, p. 114.

This was a big step, one which Sahir took with great bravery. Unlike most of our other poets, he did not fall prey to the big bad world of the film industry. Instead, riding on the strength of his pen, if on the one hand, he gave the film song the subtle charms of beauty and the pain of love, on the other, he gave it a social, material and economic consciousness as well. He did not cheat himself or his art; neither did he cheat the Progressive Writers' Movement or the people at large. He did what was expected of a socially aware poet and I congratulate him on this feat.[18]

In the introduction to his anthology of film songs, *Gaata Jaaye Banjara*, Sahir himself explains the hard-hitting, cerebral quality of his lyrics in films:

Films are the most effective medium of our age. If they are used to bring about constructive and positive change, people's thought processes and social progress can be influenced greatly and very rapidly. Unfortunately, not many from among us have bothered about this aspect of cinema because, like other things, even this is under the control of those who look at personal gain as more important than bringing about social improvement. This is why our film stories, film melodies and film lyrics are generally shallow. This is why literary circles consider film literature with distaste and hatred.

Because I have a relation with both films and literature, I find it necessary to point out a couple of things for the benefit of my literary friends. A film's songwriter does not have the freedom that a literary poet has. A songwriter has to always remain circumscribed by the film's plot. He has to choose his words and thoughts according to the description of each character in the film. This is similar to what a playwright has to do while representing a devotee, an atheist, a servant and master, a hero and villain, all kinds of characters in the same play. Similarly, it

---

18. Saabir Dutt, *Fann Aur Shaksiyat*, Sahir Ludhianvi Number, Jan Nisar Akhtar, 'Geeton Ka Rasiya', p. 398.

is important for a songwriter that he writes according to each character's behaviour and according to the plot, and presents all kinds of contrasting emotions with the same passion so that the contrasts in characters are brought out and the drama's impact benefits from such writing.

This is different from literary poetry and is difficult as well. That is why it is important for a critic that when he sits to critique a film's songs, he should not only consider which poet has written the songs, but for which character have the songs been written. He must also consider that film songs are written on already composed tunes. As a result, the poet in some places has to go against the established norms of literature and, instead of focusing on the right usage of words, has to pay greater attention to the lyrical quality of words.

While selecting words the lyricist also has to pay attention to the fact that people living in the far corners of the country, a majority of whom are illiterate and whose language is not Urdu or Hindi, are able to understand these words.

It is obvious that with all such preconditions, the output cannot be of the same level as literary poetry. Yet, this aspect of poetry cannot be ignored as it has its own significance. It has its own reach which is far greater than books, magazines, radio and theatre and through this we can have our views reach a greater amount of people in lesser time. I have always strived to bring songwriting as close to literary poetry and to use it to provide new political and social perspectives to people.

And so, if while going through this collection, you get a feeling that not only have your favourite songs been listed here but that your political leanings and interests have also been satisfied, I would think my efforts have not gone waste.[19]

Sahir Ludhianvi wrote on a whole gamut of issues. He was a savant who stood up for those who lived on the margins of society, stressed upon the need for communal harmony and remained opposed to

19. Ajaib Chitrakar, *Khaban Da Shaizada*, pp. 102–03.

war. At the same time, he championed the most frequently used theme in the Hindi film song, the love song, like few before or after him. Whether it was '*Jaane woh kaise log thay jinke pyaar ko pyaar mila*', '*Tum mujhe bhool bhi jao*', '*Aye meri zohrajabeen*', '*Neele gagan ke taley*', '*Abhi na jao chhod kar*', '*Yeh ishq ishq hai*' or the title song of *Kabhi Kabhie*, his understanding of romance, its associated moods and pitfalls, was at par with John Keats, Pablo Neruda or William Shakespeare.

Through his work, this poet from Ludhiana left us with much to think about, and to do so with a song on our lips.

Epilogue

Sometime in 1966–67, Sahir, his mother, his cousin and the writer Krishan Chander were travelling by car to Ludhiana. This in itself revealed a quirk about Sahir. He refused to travel anywhere by air. He only travelled by car, with a second car often following close behind, should the first break down.

But that is a story for another time.

Somewhere in the state of Madhya Pradesh, near Shivpuri, close to Gwalior, the car was stopped by dacoits. The leader of the pack, a notorious man by the name Daaku Maan Singh, took all five, including the driver, captive.

A few years before this incident, Sahir had worked on the songs of a dacoit-drama called *Mujhe Jeene Do*. Sunil Dutt played the protagonist, a dacoit (Thakur Jarnail Singh), who marries a courtesan Chameli Jaan (Waheeda Rehman). The two have a child. Chameli Jaan, anxious not to let her son follow in Jarnail Singh's footsteps, voices her concern through these lines written by Sahir:

> *Tere bachpan ko jawaani ki dua deti hoon*
> *Aur dua deke pareshaan si ho jaati hoon*
>
> *Mere munney, mere gulzaar ke nanhe paudhey*
> *Tujhko halaat ki aandhi se bachaane ke liye*
> *Aaj main pyaar ke aanchal mein chhupa leti hoon*
> *Kal yeh kamzor sahaara bhi na haasil hoga*
> *Kal tujhey kaanton bhari raah pe chalna hoga*
> *Zindagaani ki kadee dhoop mein jalna hoga*

(I pray your childhood leads to a better youth
And having given you my blessing, I worry

My child, the flower of my garden,
To save you from the tumultuous circumstances
Today I give you the comfort of my love
Tomorrow even this little shelter will not be available to you
Tomorrow your path will be beset by thorns
You will have to come to terms with the harshness of life)

The dacoits, as the story goes, had seen the film. The song was close to their hearts because it aptly mirrored their own struggles. On realizing that the man they held captive was the writer of this song, they let the lot of them go free.

Depending on where you read this episode or whom you hear it from, the details vary greatly. One version even suggested that the dacoits, on learning of Sahir's antecedents, regaled him all through the night with the choicest liquor in their possession. They even requested him to recite the song, which he did to their great delight.

Yash Chopra, nonetheless, confirmed having heard of this incident from Sahir himself. According to him, when the dacoits got to know who Sahir was, '*Unhoney izzat se jaaney diya* (They let them go respectfully).'

Even dacoits approved of him.

Timeline

8 March 1921: Abdul Hayee is born in Ludhiana, Punjab, to Chaudhri Fazl Mohammed and Sardar Begum.

1937: Adopts his *takhallus* and comes to be known as Sahir Ludhianvi subsequently.

1943: Leaves Government College, Ludhiana, and moves to Lahore.

1943-44: His first anthology of poems, *Talkhiyaan*, is published. Many believe this anthology to be as popular as the *Diwan-e-Ghalib*. While in Lahore he works as an editor at *Adab-e-Lateef*.

January 1946: Leaves Lahore to come to Bombay to write the songs for *Azaadi Ki Raah Par* (1948).

September 1947: Reaches Lahore in search of his mother, who has come there as part of a muhajir camp at the time of Partition.

June 1948: Flees Lahore and comes to Delhi where he works for a couple of Urdu publications, *Shah-raah* and *Preetladi*.

May 1949: Leaves for Bombay after spending almost a year in Delhi.

1951: Gains recognition for the songs of *Naujawaan*. Guru Dutt's film *Baazi* is released. Its songs become immensely successful, establishing Sahir as a lyricist.

1956: Writes his famous anti-war poem, 'Parchhaaiyaan'.

1957: *Pyaasa* is released after which S.D. Burman and he never work together again. In the same year, his first anthology of Hindi film songs is published under the Star Pocket Book series.

1963-64: Becomes the President of the Film Writers' Association (FWA) for the first time. He would serve as President of the FWA for two more terms, 1965-66 and 1967-70

1964: Wins his first Filmfare Award for Best Lyricist for '*Jo waada kiya woh nibhaana padega*' in *Taj Mahal* (1963).

22 November 1970: Is awarded a gold medal by Government College, Ludhiana, on the occasion of the latter's golden jubilee celebrations.

1971: His second anthology of poems, *Aao Ki Koi Khwaab Bunein*, is published from Delhi. In the same year he is awarded the Padma Shri by the Government of India.

1976: Sardar Begum, his mother, dies.

1977: Wins his second Filmfare Award for Best Lyricist for '*Kabhi kabhi mere dil mein*' in *Kabhi Kabhie* (1976).

25 October 1980: Dies of a heart attack at the age of fifty-nine while playing cards at his friend's residence.

List of Film Songs

Film Name	Year	Title	Singer(s)	Music Director(s)
Aazadi Ki Raah Pe	1948	Jaag Utha Hai Hindustan	Chorus	G.D. Kapoor
Aazadi Ki Raah Pe	1948	Bharat Janani Teri Jai Ho	B.S.Nanji, Gandhari & chorus	G.D. Kapoor
Aazadi Ki Raah Pe	1948	Mere Charkhe Mein Jeevan Ka Raag Sakhi	Kavita & chorus	G.D. Kapoor
Aazadi Ki Raah Pe	1948	Badal Rahi Hai Zindagi	B.S.Nanji & chorus	G.D. Kapoor
Baazi	1951	Aaj Ki Raat Piya	Geeta Dutt	S.D. Burman
Baazi	1951	Dekh Ke Akeli Mohe Barkha Sataaye (Tip Tip Tip)	Geeta Dutt & chorus	S.D. Burman
Baazi	1951	Mere Labon Pe Dekho	Kishore Kumar	S.D. Burman
Baazi	1951	Sharmaaye Kaahe Ghabraaye Kaahe	Shamshad Begum	S.D. Burman
Baazi	1951	Suno Gajar Kya Gaaye	Geeta Dutt & chorus	S.D. Burman
Baazi	1951	Tadbeer Se Bighadi Hui Taqdeer Bana Le	Geeta Dutt	S.D. Burman
Baazi	1951	Tum Bhi Na Bhoolo Balam	Geeta Dutt	S.D. Burman
Baazi	1951	Yeh Kaun Aaya	Geeta Dutt	S.D. Burman
Naujawan	1951	Dekho Aji Dekho Ji Kuchh Bhi Kar Lo	Lata Mangeshkar & Kishore Kumar	S.D. Burman

Film Name	Year	Title	Singer(s)	Music Director(s)
Naujawan	1951	Ek Aag Dehkata Raag	Manna Dey & chorus	S.D. Burman
Naujawan	1951	Hum Aur Tum Tum Aur Hum (O Piya Piya Piya)	Kishore Kumar & Shamshad Begum	S.D. Burman
Naujawan	1951	Jiya Jaaye Piya Aaja (Dil Ka Dard Na Jaane)	Lata Mangeshkar	S.D. Burman
Naujawan	1951	Mann Hua Baawra (Panghat Pe Dekho)	Mohd. Rafi, Geeta Dutt & chorus	S.D. Burman
Naujawan	1951	Thandi Hawaayein Lehra Ke	Lata Mangeshkar	S.D. Burman
Naujawan	1951	Zara Jhoom Le Jawaani Ka Zamaana	Mohd. Rafi, Geeta Dutt & chorus	S.D. Burman
Sazaa	1951	Tum Na Jaane Kis Jahaan Mein Kho Gaye	Lata Mangeshkar	S.D. Burman
Doraha	1952	Mohabbat Tarq Ki Maine Girebaan Si Liya Maine	Talat Mahmood	Anil Biswas
Jaal	1952	Chaandni Raatein Pyaar Ki Baatein (Yeh Raat Yeh)	Lata Mangeshkar & Hemant Kumar	S.D. Burman
Jaal	1952	Chaandni Raatein Pyaar Ki Baatein (Yeh Raat Yeh)	Hemant Kumar	S.D. Burman
Jaal	1952	Chori Chori Meri Gali Aana Hai Bura	Lata Mangeshkar & chorus	S.D. Burman
Jaal	1952	De Bhi Chuke Hum Dil	Kishore Kumar & Geeta Dutt	S.D. Burman

Film Name	Year	Title	Singer(s)	Music Director(s)
Jaal	1952	Kaisi Yeh Jaagi Agan	Lata Mangeshkar & chorus	S.D. Burman
Jaal	1952	Pighla Hai Sona Door Gagan Par	Lata Mangeshkar	S.D. Burman
Jaal	1952	Soch Samajh Kar Dil Ko Lagaana	Geeta Dutt	S.D. Burman
Jaal	1952	Zor Laga Ke Haiyya	Geeta Dutt & chorus	S.D. Burman
Lal Kunwar	1952	Aayi Hoon Main Raja Tere Dwar Sawaali	Suraiya & chorus	S.D. Burman
Lal Kunwar	1952	Aawaz Deta Hai Solah Ka Din	Asha Bhonsle	S.D. Burman
Lal Kunwar	1952	Bach Ke Humse Bhala Kahan Jaaoge	Asha Bhonsle, Geeta Dutt & chorus	S.D. Burman
Lal Kunwar	1952	Chal Ae Dil Raah Mein Koi Sahaara	?	S.D. Burman
Lal Kunwar	1952	Dil Ka Bhed Jaan Lo Ho Sake Toh	Asha Bhonsle	S.D. Burman
Lal Kunwar	1952	Nighaahein Kyon Milaayi Thi Gar Yoon Chhod Jaana Tha	Suraiya	S.D. Burman
Lal Kunwar	1952	Preet Sataaye Teri Yaad Na Jaaye Teri	Suraiya	S.D. Burman
Lal Kunwar	1952	Raja Jani Laga Mohe Nainwa Ka Baan Re	Shamshad Begum	S.D. Burman
Lal Kunwar	1952	Tum Jo Mile Aarzoo Ko Dil Ki Raah Mil Gayi	Suraiya	S.D. Burman
Lal Kunwar	1952	Woh Nighaah Jab Bhi Uthi Ghir Ke Badli Chhaa Gayi	?	S.D. Burman

Film Name	Year	Title	Singer(s)	Music Director(s)
Lal Kunwar	1952	Yeh Din Nahin Aah Bharne Ke Din	?	S.D. Burman
Alif Laila	1953	Bahaar Aayi Khili Kaliyaan	Lata Mangeshkar	Shyam Sundar
Alif Laila	1953	Dilon Ke Shikaar Ko Kataar Leke Aayi Hoon	Asha Bhonsle	Shyam Sundar
Alif Laila	1953	Khamosh Kyon Ho	Mohd. Rafi & Lata Mangeshkar	Shyam Sundar
Alif Laila	1953	Kya Raat Suhaani Hai	Mohd. Rafi, Lata Mangeshkar & chorus	Shyam Sundar
Alif Laila	1953	Mere Naghmon Mein	Talat Mahmood	Shyam Sundar
Alif Laila	1953	Raatein Pyaar Ki Beet Jaayengi	Asha Bhonsle & chorus	Shyam Sundar
Alif Laila	1953	Tujhko Bhulaana Mere Bas Mein Nahin	Lata Mangeshkar	Shyam Sundar
Alif Laila	1953	Yeh Bebasi Yeh Mera Haal-e-Jaar Dekh Toh Le	Talat Mahmood	Shyam Sundar
Armaan	1953	Bharam Teri Wafaaon Ka	Talat Mahmood	S.D. Burman
Armaan	1953	Chaahe Kitna Mujhe Tum Bulaao Ji (duet)	Asha Bhonsle & Talat Mahmood	S.D. Burman
Armaan	1953	Chaahe Kitna Mujhe Tum Bulaao Ji (solo)	Asha Bhonsle	S.D. Burman
Armaan	1953	Jaadubhari Yeh Fizaayein	Geeta Dutt	S.D. Burman
Armaan	1953	Jab Duniya Badli Hai Phir Kyon Na	Asha Bhonsle	S.D. Burman
Armaan	1953	Main Pankh Laga Ke	Asha Bhonsle	S.D. Burman

261

Film Name	Year	Title	Singer(s)	Music Director(s)
Armaan	1953	Yeh Hansi Yeh Khushi	Geeta Dutt	S.D. Burman
Armaan	1953	Krodh Kapat Ke Andhiyaare Mein	Manna Dey & chorus	S.D. Burman
Baabla	1953	Humrey Munder Bole Kaaga Sakhi Ri	Rajkumari	S.D. Burman
Baabla	1953	Jag Mein Aaye Koi	Talat Mahmood	S.D. Burman
Baabla	1953	Lehron Ke Rele Sang Naiyya Meri Khele	Pt. Hridaynath Mangeshkar	S.D. Burman
Baabla	1953	Raat Ke Raahi Thak Mat Jaana (female)	Lata Mangeshkar	S.D. Burman
Baabla	1953	Raat Ke Raahi Thak Mat Jaana (male)	Manna Dey & chorus	S.D. Burman
Baabla	1953	Raat Khushi Ki Aayi	Lata Mangeshkar	S.D. Burman
Humsafar	1953	Haseen Chaandni Bheegi Bheegi Hawaein	Geeta Dutt	Ali Akbar Khan
Humsafar	1953	Kisi Ne Nazar Se Nazar Jab Mila Di	Asha Bhonsle & Talat Mahmood	Ali Akbar Khan
Humsafar	1953	Koi Door Bajaaye Bansuri	Lata Mangeshkar	Ali Akbar Khan
Humsafar	1953	Mat Karo Kisi Se Pyaar Zamaana Naazuk Hai	Geeta Dutt	Ali Akbar Khan
Humsafar	1953	O Ji Aankhon Waalon Dekho Dekho	Geeta Dutt & chorus	Ali Akbar Khan
Humsafar	1953	Prabhuji Tori Leela Aparmpaar Re	Kishore Kumar & chorus	Ali Akbar Khan
Humsafar	1953	Tumhein Dulhan Mili Humein Bhabhi Mili	Kishore Kumar & chorus	Ali Akbar Khan
Humsafar	1953	Aaj Sabko Naya Ek Khazana Mila	?	Ali Akbar Khan

262

Film Name	Year	Title	Singer(s)	Music Director(s)
Jeevan Jyoti	1953	Balma Ne Mann Har Leenha	Asha Bhonsle	S.D. Burman
Jeevan Jyoti	1953	Chaandni Ki Paalki Mein Baith Kar	Asha Bhonsle	S.D. Burman
Jeevan Jyoti	1953	Chhayi Kaari Badariya	Lata Mangeshkar	S.D. Burman
Jeevan Jyoti	1953	Darshan Pyaase Nain Hamaare (snippet)	Asha Bhonsle & chorus	S.D. Burman
Jeevan Jyoti	1953	Lag Gayi Akhiyan Tum Se Mori	Mohd. Rafi & Geeta Dutt	S.D. Burman
Jeevan Jyoti	1953	Saari Khushiyan Saath Aayin Aap Jab Aaye	Shamshad Begum	S.D. Burman
Jeevan Jyoti	1953	So Ja Re Meri Aakhiyon Ke Taare	Lata Mangeshkar	S.D. Burman
Shahenshah	1953	Aayi Bahaarein Le Ke Raatein Pyaar Ki	Asha Bhonsle & chorus	S.D. Burman
Shahenshah	1953	Chaahat Ka Khazana Hai Tere Liye	Lata Mangeshkar	S.D. Burman
Shahenshah	1953	Gham Kyon Ho Jeene Waalon Ko Jeete Jee	Lata Mangeshkar	S.D. Burman
Shahenshah	1953	Jhaam Thaam Le Sochte Hi Sochte Na Beete Saari Raat	Shamshad Begum	S.D. Burman
Shahenshah	1953	Khaak Hua Dil Jalte Jalte	Lata Mangeshkar	S.D. Burman
Shahenshah	1953	Koi Raag Chhed Dabi Aag Chhed	Asha Bhonsle	S.D. Burman
Shahenshah	1953	Le Le Dil Ko Le Le Kismat Ke Hain Yeh Mele	Geeta Dutt	S.D. Burman
Shahenshah	1953	Naazon Ke Pale Kaanton Pe Chale	Talat Mahmood	S.D. Burman

Film Name	Year	Title	Singer(s)	Music Director(s)
Shahenshah	1953	Shaahi Ki Zanjeerein Todte Chalo	Manna Dey & chorus	S.D. Burman
Sholey	1953	Nighaahein Mila Aur Ek Jaam Le Le	Hemant Kumar & Geeta Dutt	Dhani Ram
Angaarey	1954	Hey Raj-Dulaari Bitiya Ri	Lata Mangeshkar & chorus	S.D. Burman
Angaarey	1954	Doob Gaye Aakash Mein	Talat Mahmood	S.D. Burman
Angaarey	1954	Gori Ke Nainon Mein Nindiya Bhari	Kishore Kumar & Shamshad Begum	S.D. Burman
Angaarey	1954	Pyaar Bhare Dhadkanon Ke Haar Leke	Lata Mangeshkar	S.D. Burman
Angaarey	1954	Pyaar Bulaaye Tohe Kab Se	Asha Bhonsle & chorus	S.D. Burman
Angaarey	1954	Roop Ki Rani Aayi Pyaar Ki Daulat Laayi	Shamshad Begum	S.D. Burman
Angaarey	1954	Tere Saath Chal Rahe Hain	Lata Mangeshkar & Talat Mahmood	S.D. Burman
Angaarey	1954	Ummeed Ki Jholi Mein Kyon Bhar Diye Angaarey	Lata Mangeshkar	S.D. Burman
Angaarey	1954	Unhein Kho Kar Dukh Dil Ki Dua Se Aur Kya Maangun	Lata Mangeshkar	S.D. Burman
Angaarey	1954	Uss Basti Ko Jaane Waale	Lata Mangeshkar	S.D. Burman
Radha Krishna	1954	Dheeth Langar Natkhat Harjai Tohe Laaj	Lata Mangeshkar	S.D. Burman
Radha Krishna	1954	Tum Bansi Ho Main Taan Hum Tum Do Nahin	Lata Mangeshkar & Geeta Dutt	S.D. Burman

Film Name	Year	Title	Singer(s)	Music Director(s)
Saavdhan	1954	Aaj Kisi Ke Haathon Ne	Asha Bhonsle	Vasant Ramchandra
Saavdhan	1954	Chalo Hato Jaao	Asha Bhonsle	Vasant Ramchandra
Saavdhan	1954	Jhanan Jhanan Baaje Mori Jhaanjhan	Asha Bhonsle	Vasant Ramchandra
Saavdhan	1954	Mohabbat Ki Nazar Jab Meharbaan Maloom Hoti Hai	Asha Bhonsle	Vasant Ramchandra
Saavdhan	1954	Nazar Se Dil Mein Samaane Waale	Asha Bhonsle	Vasant Ramchandra
Saavdhan	1954	Piye Jaa Piye Jaa (Aap Aaye Hain Nasihat)	Khan Mastana, Balbir & chorus	Vasant Ramchandra
Saavdhan	1954	Raat Muskuraati Hai Dhadkane Jagaati Hai	Asha Bhonsle & Geeta Dutt	Vasant Ramchandra
Taxi Driver	1954	Ae Meri Zindagi	Lata Mangeshkar	S.D. Burman
Taxi Driver	1954	Chaahe Koi Khush Ho Ya Gaaliyan Hazaar De	Kishore Kumar, Johnny Walker & chorus	S.D. Burman
Taxi Driver	1954	Dekho Maane Nahin Roothi Haseena	Asha Bhonsle & Jagmohan Bakshi	S.D. Burman
Taxi Driver	1954	Dil Jale Toh Jale	Lata Mangeshkar	S.D. Burman
Taxi Driver	1954	Dil Se Mila Ke Dil	Lata Mangeshkar	S.D. Burman
Taxi Driver	1954	Jaayein Toh Jaayein Kahan (female)	Lata Mangeshkar	S.D. Burman
Taxi Driver	1954	Jaayein Toh Jaayein Kahan (male)	Talat Mahmood	S.D. Burman
Taxi Driver	1954	Jeene Do Aur Jiyo	Asha Bhonsle	S.D. Burman

Film Name	Year	Title	Singer(s)	Music Director(s)
Chingaari	1955	Jiyunga Jab Talak	Talat Mahmood	Manohar
Devdas	1955	Aan Milo Aan Milo Shyam Saanwre	Geeta Dutt & Manna Dey	S.D. Burman
Devdas	1955	Ab Aage Teri Marzi	Lata Mangeshkar	S.D. Burman
Devdas	1955	Jisse Tu Qabool Kar Le	Lata Mangeshkar	S.D. Burman
Devdas	1955	Kisko Khabar Thi	Talat Mahmood	S.D. Burman
Devdas	1955	Manzil Ki Chaah Mein	Mohd. Rafi & chorus	S.D. Burman
Devdas	1955	Mitwa Lagi Re	Talat Mahmood	S.D. Burman
Devdas	1955	O Alble Panchhi	Asha Bhonsle & Usha Mangeshkar	S.D. Burman
Devdas	1955	O Jaane Waale Ruk Jaa	Lata Mangeshkar	S.D. Burman
Devdas	1955	Saajan Ki Ho Gayi Gori	Geeta Dutt & Manna Dey	S.D. Burman
Devdas	1955	Woh Na Aayenge Palat Kar	Mubarak Begum	S.D. Burman
House No. 44	1955	Aag Lagi Bangle Mein (Tum Chalo Hamaare Saath)	Asha Bhonsle	S.D. Burman
House No. 44	1955	Chup Hai Dharti Chup Hain Chaand Sitaare	Hemant Kumar	S.D. Burman
House No. 44	1955	Dekh Idhar O Jaadugar	Asha Bhonsle	S.D. Burman
House No. 44	1955	Dum Hai Baaki Toh Gham Nahin	Asha Bhonsle	S.D. Burman
House No. 44	1955	Khaaye Jaa Khaaye Ja Khaana Khaaye Ja (snippet)	Asha Bhonsle	S.D. Burman
House No. 44	1955	Oonche Sur Mein Gaaye Jaa	Kishore Kumar	S.D. Burman

Film Name	Year	Title	Singer(s)	Music Director(s)
House No. 44	1955	Peechhe Peechhe Aa Kar	Lata Mangeshkar & Hemant Kumar	S.D. Burman
House No. 44	1955	Phaili Hui Hain Sapnon Ki Baahein	Lata Mangeshkar	S.D. Burman
House No. 44	1955	Teri Duniya Mein Jeene Se Toh Behtar Hai	Hemant Kumar	S.D. Burman
Joru Ka Bhai	1955	Surmayi Raat Hai Subah Ka Intezaar Kaun Kare	Lata Mangeshkar	Jaidev
Joru Ka Bhai	1955	Teri Zulfon Se Pyaar Kaun Kare	Talat Mahmood	Jaidev
Marine Drive	1955	Ab Woh Karam Karein Ke Sitam	Mohd. Rafi	N. Dutta
Marine Drive	1955	Apne Khyalon Ko Samjha Dijiye	Lata Mangeshkar	N. Dutta
Marine Drive	1955	Bata Ae Aasmaan Waale	Mohd. Rafi & chorus	N. Dutta
Marine Drive	1955	Dil Bhi Mit Jaaye (Raatein Jaga Ke)	Asha Bhonsle	N. Dutta
Marine Drive	1955	Mohabbat Yoon Bhi Hoti Hai	Mohd. Rafi, Asha Bhonsle & chorus	N. Dutta
Marine Drive	1955	Raat Sunsaan Hai	Asha Bhonsle	N. Dutta
Milaap	1955	Bachna Zara Yeh Zamaana Hai Bura	Mohd. Rafi, Geeta Dutt & chorus	N. Dutta
Milaap	1955	Chaahe Bhi Jo Dil	Geeta Dutt	N. Dutta
Milaap	1955	Dard Ka Saaz Bhi Hai	Lata Mangeshkar	N. Dutta
Milaap	1955	Humse Bhi Kar Lo Meethi Meethi Do Baatein	Geeta Dutt	N. Dutta

Film Name	Year	Title	Singer(s)	Music Director(s)
Milaap	1955	Jaate Ho Toh Jaao Jaaoge Kahan	Geeta Dutt	N. Dutta
Milaap	1955	Piya Khul Ke Na Nain Milaaye (two parts)	Asha Bhonsle	N. Dutta
Milaap	1955	Yeh Bahaaron Ka Samaa (female)	Lata Mangeshkar	N. Dutta
Milaap	1955	Yeh Bahaaron Ka Samaa (male)	Hemant Kumar	N. Dutta
Munimji	1955	Aankh Khulte Hi Tum Chhup Gaye Kahan	Lata Mangeshkar	S.D. Burman
Munimji	1955	Dil Ki Umangein Hain Jawaan	Geeta Dutt & Hemant Kumar	S.D. Burman
Munimji	1955	Ek Nazar Bas Ek Nazar Jaan-e-Tamanna	Lata Mangeshkar	S.D. Burman
Munimji	1955	Jeevan Ke Safar Mein Raahi (female)	Lata Mangeshkar	S.D. Burman
Munimji	1955	Jeevan Ke Safar Mein Raahi (male)	Kishore Kumar	S.D. Burman
Munimji	1955	Saajan Bin Neend Na Aaye	Lata Mangeshkar	S.D. Burman
Munimji	1955	Zindagi Hai Zinda	Geeta Dutt & chorus	S.D. Burman
Railway Platform	1955	Andher Nagri Chowpat Raja	Mohd. Rafi, Asha Bhonsle, Batish & Manmohan Krishan	Madan Mohan
Railway Platform	1955	Basti Basti Parbat Parbat (two parts)	Mohd. Rafi	Madan Mohan
Railway Platform	1955	Bhajo Ram Bhajo Ram	Asha Bhonsle, S.D.Batish & chorus	Madan Mohan
Railway Platform	1955	Chaand Madham Hai Aasmaan Chup Hai	Lata Mangeshkar	Madan Mohan

Film Name	Year	Title	Singer(s)	Music Director(s)
Railway Platform	1955	Dekh Tere Bhagwan Ki Haalat Kya Ho Gayi	Mohd. Rafi, S.D.Batish, Manmohan Krishan & chorus	Madan Mohan
Railway Platform	1955	Jiya Kho Gaya Tera Ho Gaya	Lata Mangeshkar	Madan Mohan
Railway Platform	1955	Sakhi Ri Tori Doliyan Uthaayenge Kahaar	Lata Mangeshkar	Madan Mohan
Society	1955	Dil Ka Taraana	Geeta Dutt	S.D. Burman
Society	1955	Dil Nahin Toh Na Sahi	Asha Bhonsle & chorus	S.D. Burman
Society	1955	Kahan Ho Tum	Lata Mangeshkar	S.D. Burman
Society	1955	Lehron Mein Jhoolun	Asha Bhonsle	S.D. Burman
Society	1955	Nighaah Ko Tere Jalwe Ki Aas Rehti Hai	Mohd. Rafi & Balbir	S.D. Burman
Society	1955	Reham Kabhi Toh Farmaao	Mohd. Rafi & Geeta Dutt	S.D. Burman
Society	1955	Samajh Gaye Hum Toh	Geeta Dutt	S.D. Burman
Society	1955	Sharmeeli Nighaahein Kehti Hain	Asha Bhonsle & chorus	S.D. Burman
Chandrakaanta	1956	Ji Chaahta Hai Aaj Kahin Door Jaayiye	Mohd. Rafi & Asha Bhonsle	N. Dutta
Chandrakaanta	1956	Kismat Agar Hai Saath Tumhaare	Asha Bhonsle	N. Dutta
Chandrakaanta	1956	Main Nahin Maanunga Maati Ke Putle	Mohd. Rafi	N. Dutta
Chandrakaanta	1956	Maine Chaand Aur Sitaaron Ki Tamanna Ki Thi	Mohd. Rafi	N. Dutta
Chandrakaanta	1956	Mast Ho Kar Zara Jhoom Le	Asha Bhonsle & chorus	N. Dutta

Film Name	Year	Title	Singer(s)	Music Director(s)
Chandrakaanta	1956	Mujhko Laga Hai Saal Solvaan	Shamshad Begum	N. Dutta
Chandrakaanta	1956	Swami Tere Darshan Ko Aayi Brijbala	Geeta Dutt & chorus	N. Dutta
Chandrakaanta	1956	Zindagi Tang Hai	Mohd. Rafi & Asha Bhonsle	N. Dutta
Funtoosh	1956	Aankh Jhuka Kar Baithne Waale (Bandar Jaisi Surat)	Kishore Kumar	S.D. Burman
Funtoosh	1956	Ae Johnny Jeene Mein Kya Hai	Asha Bhonsle	S.D. Burman
Funtoosh	1956	Ae Meri Topi Palat Ke Aa	Kishore Kumar	S.D. Burman
Funtoosh	1956	Dene Waala Jab Bhi Deta	Kishore Kumar & chorus	S.D. Burman
Funtoosh	1956	Dukhi Mann Mere Sun Mera Kehna	Kishore Kumar	S.D. Burman
Funtoosh	1956	Humne Kisi Pe Dore Daalne Hain	Asha Bhonsle & Kishore Kumar	S.D. Burman
Funtoosh	1956	Phul Gendwa Na Maaro	Asha Bhonsle	S.D. Burman
Funtoosh	1956	Pyaar Ne Kitne Sapne Dekhe	Asha Bhonsle	S.D. Burman
Funtoosh	1956	Woh Dekhein Toh Unki Inaayat	Asha Bhonsle & Kishore Kumar	S.D. Burman
Bade Sarkaar	1957	Aha Ha Jawaani Jhoomti Hai	Asha Bhonsle	O.P. Nayyar
Bade Sarkaar	1957	Bol Mera Kya Kasoor	Asha Bhonsle	O.P. Nayyar
Bade Sarkaar	1957	Jab Hum Tum Dono Raazi	Asha Bhonsle	O.P. Nayyar
Bade Sarkaar	1957	Jahan Jahan Khayaal Jaata Hai	Mohd. Rafi & Geeta Dutt	O.P. Nayyar
Naya Daur	1957	Aana Hai Toh Aa Raah Mein	Mohd. Rafi	O.P. Nayyar
Naya Daur	1957	Dil Leke Daga Denge	Mohd. Rafi	O.P. Nayyar
Naya Daur	1957	Ek Deewana Aate Aate	Asha Bhonsle	O.P. Nayyar

270

Film Name	Year	Title	Singer(s)	Music Director(s)
Naya Daur	1957	Maang Ke Saath Tumhaara	Mohd. Rafi & Asha Bhonsle	O.P. Nayyar
Naya Daur	1957	Main Bambai Ka Babu	Mohd. Rafi	O.P. Nayyar
Naya Daur	1957	Reshmi Salwaar Kurta Jaali Da	Asha Bhonsle & Shamshad Begum	O.P. Nayyar
Naya Daur	1957	Saathi Haath Badhaana	Mohd. Rafi, Asha Bhonsle & chorus	O.P. Nayyar
Naya Daur	1957	Udein Jab Jab Zulfein Teri	Mohd. Rafi & Asha Bhonsle	O.P. Nayyar
Naya Daur	1957	Yeh Desh Hai Veer Jawaanon Ka	Mohd. Rafi, S. Balbir & chorus	O.P. Nayyar
Pyaasa	1957	Aaj Sajan Mohe Ang Laga Lo	Geeta Dutt	S.D. Burman
Pyaasa	1957	Gham Iss Qadar Badhe (verse)	Mohd. Rafi	S.D. Burman
Pyaasa	1957	Ho Laakh Museebat Raste Mein	Mohd. Rafi & Geeta Dutt	S.D. Burman
Pyaasa	1957	Hum Aapki Aankhon Mein	Mohd. Rafi & Geeta Dutt	S.D. Burman
Pyaasa	1957	Jaane Kya Tu Ne Kahi	Geeta Dutt	S.D. Burman
Pyaasa	1957	Jaane Woh Kaise Log Thay Jinke	Hemant Kumar	S.D. Burman
Pyaasa	1957	Jinhe Naaz Hai Hind Par Woh Kahan	Mohd. Rafi	S.D. Burman
Pyaasa	1957	Rut Phiri Par Din Hamaare (not included in the movie)	Geeta Dutt	S.D. Burman
Pyaasa	1957	Sar Jo Tera Chakraaye Ya Dil Dooba Jaaye	Mohd. Rafi	S.D. Burman
Pyaasa	1957	Tang Aa Chuke Hain Kashm-e-Kash-e-Zindagi Se Hum	Mohd. Rafi	S.D. Burman
Pyaasa	1957	Yeh Duniya Agar Mil Bhi Jaaye (Yeh Mahalon)	Mohd. Rafi	S.D. Burman

271

Film Name	Year	Title	Singer(s)	Music Director(s)
Pyaasa	1957	Yeh Hanste Hue Phool Yeh Mehka Hua Gulshan (verse)	Mohd. Rafi	S.D. Burman
Tumsa Nahin Dekha	1957	Yoon Toh Humne Laakh Haseen Dekhe Hain	Mohd. Rafi	O.P. Nayyar
12 O'Clock	1958	Dekh Idhar Ae Haseena	Mohd. Rafi & Geeta Dutt	O.P. Nayyar
12 O'Clock	1958	Saiyan Teri Aankhon Mein	Shamshad Begum	O.P. Nayyar
Light House	1958	Aa Aa Aa Chhori Aa	Mohd. Rafi & Geeta Dutt	N. Dutta
Light House	1958	Kal Ki Baatein Kal Pe Chhodo	Mohd. Rafi & Suman Kalyanpur	N. Dutta
Light House	1958	Kis Jagah Jaayein Kis Ko Dikhlaayein	Asha Bhonsle	N. Dutta
Light House	1958	Mastt Pawan Mastt Gagan	Asha Bhonsle & chorus	N. Dutta
Light House	1958	Nainon Se Naina Laage Woh Kya Kahenge Aage	Asha Bhonsle	N. Dutta
Light House	1958	Tang Aa Chuke Hain Kashm-e-Kash-e-Zindagi Se Hum	Asha Bhonsle	N. Dutta
Light House	1958	Tu Kaala Main Gori	Mohd. Rafi, Asha Bhonsle & chorus	N. Dutta
Phir Subah Hogi	1958	Aasmaan Pe Hai Khuda	Mukesh	Khayyam
Phir Subah Hogi	1958	Chin-o-Arab Hamaara	Mukesh	Khayyam
Phir Subah Hogi	1958	Do Boondein Saawan Ki	Asha Bhonsle	Khayyam
Phir Subah Hogi	1958	Jis Pyaar Mein Yeh Haal Ho	Mohd. Rafi & Mukesh	Khayyam

272

Film Name	Year	Title	Singer(s)	Music Director(s)
Phir Subah Hogi	1958	Phir Na Kijiye Meri Gustaakh Nighaahi Ka Gila	Asha Bhonsle & Mukesh	Khayyam
Phir Subah Hogi	1958	Sabki Khair Ho Baba	Mohd. Rafi, Chaandbala & chorus	Khayyam
Phir Subah Hogi	1958	Woh Subah Kabhi Toh Aayegi (three parts)	Mukesh	Khayyam
Phir Subah Hogi	1958	Woh Subah Kabhi Toh Aayegi (duet)	Asha Bhonsle & Mukesh	Khayyam
Sadhana	1958	Aaj Kyon Humse Parda Hai	Mohd. Rafi & S Balbir	N. Dutta
Sadhana	1958	Aise Waise Thikaanon Pe Jaana Bura Hai	Lata Mangeshkar	N. Dutta
Sadhana	1958	Aurat Ne Janam Diya Mardon Ko	Lata Mangeshkar	N. Dutta
Sadhana	1958	Kahoji Tum Kya Kya Khareedoge	Lata Mangeshkar	N. Dutta
Sadhana	1958	Sambhal Ae Dil	Mohd. Rafi & Asha Bhonsle	N. Dutta
Sadhana	1958	Tora Manwa Kyon Ghabraaye Re	Geeta Dutt	N. Dutta
Sone Ki Chidiya	1958	Chhuk Chhuk Rail Chali	Asha Bhonsle & chorus	O.P. Nayyar
Sone Ki Chidiya	1958	Pyaar Par Bas Toh Nahin Hai (duet)	Asha Bhonsle & Talat Mahmood	O.P. Nayyar
Sone Ki Chidiya	1958	Pyaar Par Bas Toh Nahin Hai (solo)	Asha Bhonsle	O.P. Nayyar
Sone Ki Chidiya	1958	Raat Bhar Ka Hai Mehmaan Andhera (duet)	Mohd. Rafi & Asha Bhonsle	O.P. Nayyar
Sone Ki Chidiya	1958	Raat Bhar Ka Hai Mehmaan Andhera (solo)	Mohd. Rafi	O.P. Nayyar

273

Film Name	Year	Title	Singer(s)	Music Director(s)
Sone Ki Chidiya	1958	Sach Bata Tu Mujhpe Fida	Asha Bhonsle & Talat Mahmood	O.P. Nayyar
Sone Ki Chidiya	1958	Saiyan Jabse Ladi Hain Akhiyan	Asha Bhonsle	O.P. Nayyar
Bhai Behen	1959	Beta Darr Mat Aahein Bhar Mat	Mohd. Rafi	N. Dutta
Bhai Behen	1959	In Ujale Mehlon Ke Tale	Asha Bhonsle	N. Dutta
Bhai Behen	1959	Jaate Jaate Ishaaron Se Maar Gayi Re	Mohd. Rafi & Geeta Dutt	N. Dutta
Bhai Behen	1959	Mere Dil Mat Ro Jo Haal Hua Kisi Ka Na Ho	Lata Mangeshkar	N. Dutta
Bhai Behen	1959	Mere Nadeem Mere Humsafar Udaas Na Ho	Sudha Malhotra	N. Dutta
Bhai Behen	1959	O Bachchon Sun Lo Baat	Asha Bhonsle & chorus	N. Dutta
Bhai Behen	1959	O Chhokri Tu Hai Rass Bhare Phalon Ki Tokri	Mohd. Rafi & Suman Kalyanpur	N. Dutta
Bhai Behan	1959	Uth Jaayenge Jahan Se	Sudha Malhotra	N. Dutta
Chaar Dil Chaar Raahein	1959	Intezaar Aur Abhi Aur Abhi	Lata Mangeshkar	Anil Biswas
Chaar Dil Chaar Raahein	1959	Kachchi Hai Umariya Kori Hai Chunariya	Meena Kapoor & chorus	Anil Biswas
Chaar Dil Chaar Raahein	1959	Koi Maane Na Maane Magar Jaan-e-Mann	Lata Mangeshkar	Anil Biswas
Chaar Dil Chaar Raahein	1959	Nahin Kiya Toh Karke Dekh	Mukesh	Anil Biswas
Chaar Dil Chaar Raahein	1959	Sathi Re ~ Qadam Qadam Se Dil Se Dil Mila	Mukesh, Manna Dey, Mahendra Kapoor, Meena K & chorus	Anil Biswas

Film Name	Year	Title	Singer(s)	Music Director(s)
Chaar Dil Chaar Raahein	1959	Stella O Stella Tera Johnny Tha Ab Tak Akela	Mahendra Kapoor & Meena Kapoor	Anil Biswas
Dhool Ka Phool	1959	Arrey Apni Khatir Jeena Hai	Mahendra Kapoor, Sudha Malhotra & chorus	N. Dutta
Dhool Ka Phool	1959	Daaman Mein Daag Laga Baithe	Mohd. Rafi	N. Dutta
Dhool Ka Phool	1959	Jhukti Ghata Gaati Hawa	Asha Bhonsle & Mahendra Kapoor	N. Dutta
Dhool Ka Phool	1959	Jo Tum Muskuraa Do (Dhadakne Lage Dil Ke Taaron)	Asha Bhonsle & Mahendra Kapoor	N. Dutta
Dhool Ka Phool	1959	Kaase Kahun Mann Ki Baat	Sudha Malhotra	N. Dutta
Dhool Ka Phool	1959	Kuchh Der Har Ek Cheez Ko (snippet)	Mahendra Kapoor	N. Dutta
Dhool Ka Phool	1959	Tere Pyaar Ka Aasra Chaahta Hoon	Lata Mangeshkar & Mahendra Kapoor	N. Dutta
Dhool Ka Phool	1959	Tu Hindu Banega Na Musalmaan Banega	Mohd. Rafi	N. Dutta
Dhool Ka Phool	1959	Tu Mere Pyaar Ka Phool Hai	Lata Mangeshkar	N. Dutta
Didi	1959	Bachchon Tum Taqdeer Ho	Mohd. Rafi & Asha Bhonsle	N. Dutta
Didi	1959	Humne Suna Tha Ek Hai Bharat	Mohd. Rafi, Asha Bhonsle & Sudha Malhotra	N. Dutta
Didi	1959	Mama Ji Ke Raaket Par	Asha Bhonsle & chorus	N. Dutta
Didi	1959	Mere Bhaiya Ko Sandesha Pahunchaana	Lata Mangeshkar	N. Dutta
Didi	1959	Pyaar Hi Darkaar Hai Mujhe	Asha Bhonsle	N. Dutta

Film Name	Year	Title	Singer(s)	Music Director(s)
Didi	1959	Tum Mujhe Bhool Bhi Jaao	Mukesh & Sudha Malhotra	Sudha Malhotra
Lal Nishaan	1959	Yeh Husn Yeh Ada (Surat Toh Dekhiye)	Mohd. Rafi, Sudha Malhotra & chorus	Nirmal Kumar
Naach Ghar	1959	Ae Dil Zubaan Na Khol	Lata Mangeshkar	N. Dutta
Naach Ghar	1959	Dil Tujhko Diya Tha Dildaar Maan Ke	Lata Mangeshkar	N. Dutta
Naach Ghar	1959	Door Se Yoon Na Tarsaao	Lata Mangeshkar	N. Dutta
Naach Ghar	1959	Dukh Jo Diye Hain Duniya Ne	Mohd. Rafi & Lata Mangeshkar	N. Dutta
Naach Ghar	1959	Jaan-e-Mann Chilman Utha Kar Dekh Le	Mohd. Rafi & Asha Bhonsle	N. Dutta
Naach Ghar	1959	Main Banjaara Door Ka (Allah Ke Naam Pe Maula)	Mohd. Rafi	N. Dutta
Naach Ghar	1959	Main Hoon Mr. John	Mohd. Rafi & Geeta Dutt	N. Dutta
Naach Ghar	1959	Meri Sun Toh O Pardesi	Mohd. Rafi & Lata Mangeshkar	N. Dutta
Naach Ghar	1959	Tere Sheharon Se Raja Humein Bann Hi Bhale	Mohd. Rafi & Lata Mangeshkar	N. Dutta
Naach Ghar	1959	Tumhein Kaise Kahun	Mohd. Rafi & Lata Mangeshkar	N. Dutta
Baabar	1960	Haseenon Ke Jalwe	Mohd. Rafi, Sudha M, Manna Dey, Asha Bhonsle & chorus	Roshan
Baabar	1960	Pyaam-e-Ishq-o-Mohabbat Humein Pasand Nahin	Sudha Malhotra	Roshan

276

Film Name	Year	Title	Singer(s)	Music Director(s)
Baabar	1960	Salaam-e-Hasrat Qabool Kar Lo	Sudha Malhotra	Roshan
Baabar	1960	Tum Ek Baar Mohabbat Ka Imtehaan Toh Lo	Mohd. Rafi	Roshan
Baabar	1960	Tum Maa Ho Tum Aisa Na Karo	Sudha Malhotra	Roshan
Barsaat Ki Raat	1960	Garjat Barsat Saawan Aayo Re	Suman Kalyanpur & Kamal Barot	Roshan
Barsaat Ki Raat	1960	Ji Chaahta Hai Choom Loon	Asha Bhonsle, Sudha Malhotra, Balbir, Bande Hasan & chorus	Roshan
Barsaat Ki Raat	1960	Kya Gham Jo Andheri Hain Raatein (snippet)	Mohd. Rafi	Roshan
Barsaat Ki Raat	1960	Maine Shayad Tumhein Pehle Bhi	Mohd. Rafi	Roshan
Barsaat Ki Raat	1960	Mayoos Toh Hoon Waade Se Tere	Mohd. Rafi	Roshan
Barsaat Ki Raat	1960	Mujhe Mil Gaya Bahaana Teri Deed Ka	Lata Mangeshkar	Roshan
Barsaat Ki Raat	1960	Na Toh Caravan Ki Talaash Hai	Mohd. Rafi, Manna Dey, Batish, Sudha Malhotra, Asha Bhonsle & chorus	Roshan
Barsaat Ki Raat	1960	Nighaah-e-Naaz Ke Maaron Ka	Asha Bhonsle, Sudha Malhotra, Shankar-Shambhu & chorus	Roshan
Barsaat Ki Raat	1960	Zindagi Bhar Nahin Bhoolegi	Mohd. Rafi & Lata Mangeshkar	Roshan
Girl Friend	1960	Aaj Mujhe Kuchh Kehna Hai	Kishore Kumar & Sudha Malhotra	Hemant Kumar
Girl Friend	1960	Aaj Rona Pada Toh Samjhe	Kishore Kumar	Hemant Kumar
Girl Friend	1960	Boom Boom Boom Karega	Asha Bhonsle & Kishore Kumar	Hemant Kumar

Film Name	Year	Title	Singer(s)	Music Director(s)
Girl Friend	1960	Jhuk Jhuk Bhoori Maa Ko Pranam Karo	Kishore Kumar	Hemant Kumar
Girl Friend	1960	Kehte Hain Ise Paisa	Lata Mangeshkar, Hemant Kumar, Ranu Mukherjee & chorus	Hemant Kumar
Girl Friend	1960	Na Dhela Lagta Hai	Kishore Kumar & Daisy Irani	Hemant Kumar
Girl Friend	1960	O Madam Come Come	Kishore Kumar	Hemant Kumar
Hum Hindustani	1960	Hum Jab Chalein Toh	Mohd. Rafi & chorus	Usha Khanna
Masoom	1960	Yeh Haath Hi Apni Daulat Hain	Sudha Malhotra	Robin Banerjee
Dharamputra	1961	Aaj Ki Raat Muraadon Ki Raat	Mahendra Kapoor	N. Dutta
Dharamputra	1961	Bhool Sakta Hai Bhala Kaun Yeh Pyaari Aankhein	Mahendra Kapoor	N. Dutta
Dharamputra	1961	Chaahe Yeh Maano Chaahe Woh	Mahendra Kapoor, Balbir & chorus	N. Dutta
Dharamputra	1961	Jai Janani Jai Bharat Maata	Mahendra Kapoor & chorus	N. Dutta
Dharamputra	1961	Main Jab Bhi Akeli Hoti Hoon	Asha Bhonsle	N. Dutta
Dharamputra	1961	Mere Dilbar Mujh Par Khafa Na Ho	Mohd. Rafi & chorus	N. Dutta
Dharamputra	1961	Naina Kyon Bhar Aaye	Asha Bhonsle	N. Dutta
Dharamputra	1961	Yeh Kiska Lahu Hai Kaun Mara	Mahendra Kapoor	N. Dutta
Hum Dono	1961	Abhi Na Jaao Chhod Ke	Mohd. Rafi & Asha Bhonsle	Jaidev
Hum Dono	1961	Allah Tero Naam Ishwar Tero Naam	Lata Mangeshkar & chorus	Jaidev
Hum Dono	1961	Jahan Mein Aisa Kaun Hai	Asha Bhonsle	Jaidev
Hum Dono	1961	Kabhi Khud Pe Kabhi Halaat Pe Rona Aaya	Mohd. Rafi	Jaidev

Film Name	Year	Title	Singer(s)	Music Director(s)
Hum Dono	1961	Main Zindagi Ka Saath Nibhaata Chala Gaya	Mohd. Rafi	Jaidev
Hum Dono	1961	Prabhu Tero Naam Jo Dhyaaye	Lata Mangeshkar	Jaidev
Dilli Ka Dada	1962	Aji Hum Dilli Ke Daade Hain	Mahendra Kapoor & Mukesh	N. Dutta
Dilli Ka Dada	1962	Humne Bhi Mohabbat Ki Thi Magar	Asha Bhonsle & Mahendra Kapoor	N. Dutta
Dilli Ka Dada	1962	O Zara Suno Ji	Mohd. Rafi	N. Dutta
Dilli Ka Dada	1962	Rimjhim Rimjhim Saawan Barse	Asha Bhonsle & Manna Dey	N. Dutta
Kala Samandar	1962	Mohabbat Karo Toh Karo	Mohd. Rafi,	N. Dutta
		Chhup Chuppake	Asha Bhonsle & chorus	
Aaj Aur Kal	1963	Itni Haseen Itni Jawaan Raat Kya Karein	Mohd. Rafi	Ravi
Aaj Aur Kal	1963	Kehte Hain Jisko Ishq	Shamshad Begum & Usha Mangeshkar	Ravi
Aaj Aur Kal	1963	Maut Kitni Bhi Sangdil Ho Magar	Asha Bhonsle	Ravi
Aaj Aur Kal	1963	Mohe Chhedo Na Kaanha Bajariya Mein	Asha Bhonsle	Ravi
Aaj Aur Kal	1963	Mujhe Gale Se Laga Lo (duet)	Mohd. Rafi & Asha Bhonsle	Ravi
Aaj Aur Kal	1963	Mujhe Gale Se Laga Lo (solo)	Asha Bhonsle	Ravi
Aaj Aur Kal	1963	Raja Sahab Ghar Nahin	Asha Bhonsle & Mahendra Kapoor	Ravi
Aaj Aur Kal	1963	Takht Na Hoga Taj Na Hoga	Mohd. Rafi, Geeta Dutt, Manna Dey & chorus	Ravi

Film Name	Year	Title	Singer(s)	Music Director(s)
Aaj Aur Kal	1963	Yeh Waadiyaan Yeh Fizaayein	Mohd. Rafi	Ravi
Bahurani	1963	Balma Anadi Mann Bhaaye	Lata Mangeshkar	C. Ramchandra
Bahurani	1963	Bane Aisa Samaaj	Lata Mangeshkar, Asha Bhonsle, Manna Dey & chorus	C. Ramchandra
Bahurani	1963	Eetal Ke Ghal Mein Teetal	Hemant Kumar	C. Ramchandra
Bahurani	1963	Kaam Krodh Aur Lobh Ka Maara	Mahendra Kapoor	C. Ramchandra
Bahurani	1963	Main Jaagun Saari Rain	Lata Mangeshkar	C. Ramchandra
Bahurani	1963	Umr Hui Tumse Mile	Lata Mangeshkar & Hemant Kumar	C. Ramchandra
Bahurani	1963	Yeh Husn Mera Yeh Ishq Tera	Asha Bhonsle & chorus	C. Ramchandra
Dil Hi Toh Hai	1963	Aap Abhi Ishq Ki Tehzeeb Se	Suman Kalyanpur	Roshan
Dil Hi Toh Hai	1963	Bhoole Se Mohabbat Kar Baitha	Mukesh	Roshan
Dil Hi Toh Hai	1963	Chura Le Na Tumko Yeh Mausam Suhaana	Suman Kalyanpur & Mukesh	Roshan
Dil Hi Toh Hai	1963	Dil Jo Bhi Kahega	Mukesh	Roshan
Dil Hi Toh Hai	1963	Gusse Mein Jo Nikhra Hai	Mukesh	Roshan
Dil Hi Toh Hai	1963	Laaga Chunri Mein Daag	Manna Dey	Roshan
Dil Hi Toh Hai	1963	Nighaahein Milaane Ko Jee Chaahta Hai	Asha Bhonsle & chorus	Roshan
Dil Hi Toh Hai	1963	Parda Uthe Salaam Ho Jaaye	Asha Bhonsle, Manna Dey & chorus	Roshan

Film Name	Year	Title	Singer(s)	Music Director(s)
Dil Hi Toh Hai	1963	Tum Agar Mujhko Na Chaaho Toh Koi Baat Nahin	Mukesh	Roshan
Dil Hi Toh Hai	1963	Tumhaari Mastt Nazar	Lata Mangeshkar & Mukesh	Roshan
Dil Hi Toh Hai	1963	Yoon Hi Dil Ne Chaaha Tha	Suman Kalyanpur	Roshan
Gumraah	1963	Aap Aaye Toh Khayaal-e-Dil-e-Nashaad Aaya	Mahendra Kapoor	Ravi
Gumraah	1963	Chalo Ik Baar Phir Se Ajnabi Ban Jaayein Hum Dono	Mahendra Kapoor	Ravi
Gumraah	1963	Ek Pardesi Door Se Aaya	Asha Bhonsle	Ravi
Gumraah	1963	Ek Thi Ladki Meri Saheli	Asha Bhonsle	Ravi
Gumraah	1963	In Hawaaon Mein In Fizaaon Mein (two parts)	Asha Bhonsle & Mahendra Kapoor	Ravi
Gumraah	1963	Murga Murgi Bole Kukadukoo	Asha Bhonsle & Usha Mangeshkar	Ravi
Gumraah	1963	Yeh Hawa Yeh Fizaan Udaas Jaise Mera Dil	Mahendra Kapoor	Ravi
Mujhe Jeene Do	1963	Ab Koi Gulshan Na Ujade	Mohd. Rafi & chorus	Jaidev
Mujhe Jeene Do	1963	Maang Mein Bhar Le	Asha Bhonsle & chorus	Jaidev
Mujhe Jeene Do	1963	Mohe Na Yoon Ghoor Ke Dekho	Lata Mangeshkar & chorus	Jaidev
Mujhe Jeene Do	1963	Raat Bhi Hai Kuchh Bheegi Bheegi	Lata Mangeshkar & chorus	Jaidev
Mujhe Jeene Do	1963	Tere Bachpan Ko Jawaani Ki	Lata Mangeshkar	Jaidev
Pyaar Ka Bandhan	1963	Bojh Utha Le Saathi	Mohd. Rafi & chorus	Ravi

281

Film Name	Year	Title	Singer(s)	Music Director(s)
Pyaar Ka Bandhan	1963	Ek Pyaar Ke Bandhan Ki Khatir (two parts)	Asha Bhonsle	Ravi
Pyaar Ka Bandhan	1963	Ghoda Pishauri Mera Taanga Lahori Mera	Mohd. Rafi	Ravi
Pyaar Ka Bandhan	1963	Zara Bach Ke O Baliye	Asha Bhonsle, Mahendra Kapoor & chorus	Ravi
Taj Mahal	1963	Chaandi Ka Badan Sone Ki Nazar	Mohd. Rafi, Asha Bhonsle, Manna Dey, Mahendra Kapoor & chorus	Roshan
Taj Mahal	1963	Husn Se Hai Duniya Haseen	Asha Bhonsle & chorus	Roshan
Taj Mahal	1963	Jo Baat Tujh Mein Hai Teri Tasveer Mein Nahin	Mohd. Rafi	Roshan
Taj Mahal	1963	Jo Waada Kiya Woh Nibhaana Padega (three parts)	Mohd. Rafi & Lata Mangeshkar	Roshan
Taj Mahal	1963	Jurm-e-Ulfat Pe Humein Log Sazaa Dete Hain	Lata Mangeshkar	Roshan
Taj Mahal	1963	Jurm-e-Ulfat Pe Humein (Mushaira)	Lata Mangeshkar, Minoo Purshottam, Asha Bhonsle & Suman Kalyanpur	Roshan
Taj Mahal	1963	Khuda-e-Bartar Teri Zameen Par	Lata Mangeshkar	Roshan
Taj Mahal	1963	Na Na Na Re Haath Na Lagaana	Suman Kalyanpur & Minoo Purshottam	Roshan

Film Name	Year	Title	Singer(s)	Music Director(s)
Taj Mahal	1963	Paon Chhoo Lene Do	Mohd. Rafi	Roshan
Chaandi Ki Deewar	1964	Ashqon Mein Jo Paaya Hai	Talat Mahmood	N. Dutta
Chaandi Ki Deewar	1964	Barso Ram Dhadaake Se Budiya Marr Gayi Phaake Se	Mahendra Kapoor & chorus	N. Dutta
Chaandi Ki Deewar	1964	Jo Kehne Se Tum Sharmaati Ho	Mohd. Rafi & Asha Bhonsle	N. Dutta
Chaandi Ki Deewar	1964	Ka Se Kul Duniya Hamaari (two parts)	Asha Bhonsle & chorus	N. Dutta
Chaandi Ki Deewar	1964	Kahin Qaraar Na Ho Kahin Khushi Na Mile	Mohd. Rafi	N. Dutta
Chaandi Ki Deewar	1964	Laage Tohse Naina	Talat Mahmood & Asha Bhonsle	N. Dutta
Chaandi Ki Deewar	1964	Mohe La De Chunariya Laal	Suman Kalyanpur & Geeta Dutt	N. Dutta
Chaandi Ki Deewar	1964	Yeh Duniya Do-Rangi Hai	Mohd. Rafi	N. Dutta
Chitralekha	1964	Ae Ri Jaane Na Doongi	Lata Mangeshkar	Roshan
Chitralekha	1964	Chhaa Gaye Baadal	Mohd. Rafi & Asha Bhonsle	Roshan
Chitralekha	1964	Kaahe Tarsaaye Jiyera	Asha Bhonsle & Usha Mangeshkar	Roshan
Chitralekha	1964	Maara Gaya Brahmchaari	Manna Dey	Roshan
Chitralekha	1964	Mann Re Tu Kaahe Na Dheer Dhare	Mohd. Rafi	Roshan
Chitralekha	1964	Sakhi Ri Mera Mann	Lata Mangeshkar	Roshan
Chitralekha	1964	Sansaar Se Bhaage Phirte Ho	Lata Mangeshkar	Roshan
Dooj Ka Chaand	1964	Chaand Takta Hai Idhar	Mohd. Rafi & Suman Kalyanpur	Roshan
Dooj Ka Chaand	1964	Jhaankti Hai Meri Aankhon Se Kaza	Suman Kalyanpur & Shyama Hemadi	Roshan

Film Name	Year	Title	Singer(s)	Music Director(s)
Dooj Ka Chaand	1964	Lo Apna Jahaan Duniya Waalon	Asa Singh Mastana	Roshan
Dooj Ka Chaand	1964	Mehfil Se Uth Jaane Waalon	Mohd. Rafi	Roshan
Dooj Ka Chaand	1964	Mujhe Tujhse Ishq Nahin (snippet)	Mohd. Rafi	Roshan
Dooj Ka Chaand	1964	Pade Barkha Phuhaar	Lata Mangeshkar	Roshan
Dooj Ka Chaand	1964	Phul Gendwa Na Maaro	Manna Dey	Roshan
Dooj Ka Chaand	1964	Sajan Salona Maang Lo	Lata Mangeshkar & Asha Bhonsle	Roshan
Dooj Ka Chaand	1964	Sun Ae Mah-Jabeen Mujhe Tujhse Ishq Nahin	Mohd. Rafi	Roshan
Ghazal	1964	Ada Qaatil Nazar Barq-e-Bala	Asha Bhonsle	Madan Mohan
Ghazal	1964	Dil Khush Hai Aaj Unse Mulaqaat Ho Gayi	Mohd. Rafi	Madan Mohan
Ghazal	1964	Ishq Ki Garmi-e-Jazbaat Kise Pesh Karun	Mohd. Rafi	Madan Mohan
Ghazal	1964	Meri Mehboob Kahin Aur Mila Kar Mujhe	Mohd. Rafi	Madan Mohan
Ghazal	1964	Mujhe Yeh Phool Na De	Mohd. Rafi & Suman Kalyanpur	Madan Mohan
Ghazal	1964	Naghma-o-Sher Ki Saugaat Kise Pesh Karun	Lata Mangeshkar	Madan Mohan
Ghazal	1964	Rang Aur Noor Ki Baraat Kise Pesh Karun	Mohd. Rafi	Madan Mohan

Film Name	Year	Title	Singer(s)	Music Director(s)
Ghazal	1964	Unse Nazarein Mili Aur Hijaab Aa Gaya	Lata Mangeshkar, Minoo Purshottam & chorus	Madan Mohan
Shagoon	1964	Bujha Diye Hain Khud Apne Haathon	Suman Kalyanpur	Khayyam
Shagoon	1964	Gori Sasural Chali	Jagjit Kaur & chorus	Khayyam
Shagoon	1964	Itne Kareeb Aake Bhi	Talat Mahmood & Mubarak Begum	Khayyam
Shagoon	1964	Parbaton Ke Pedon Par	Mohd. Rafi & Suman Kalyanpur	Khayyam
Shagoon	1964	Tum Apna Ranj-o-Gham	Jagjit Kaur	Khayyam
Shagoon	1964	Tum Chali Jaaogi Parchhaaiyan Reh Jaayengi	Mohd. Rafi	Khayyam
Shagoon	1964	Yeh Raat Bahut Rangeen Sahi (different in the movie)	Mohd. Rafi	Khayyam
Shagoon	1964	Zindagi Zulm Sahi	Suman Kalyanpur	Khayyam
Bahu Beti	1965	Aaj Hai Karwa Chauth Sakhi Ri	Asha Bhonsle	Ravi
Bahu Beti	1965	Bharat Maa Ki Aankh Ke Taaron	Asha Bhonsle	Ravi
Bahu Beti	1965	Jiyo Toh Aise Jiyo	Mohd. Rafi	Ravi
Bahu Beti	1965	Meri Jaan Na Sata Tu	Mohd. Rafi	Ravi
Bahu Beti	1965	Meri Maang Ke Rang Mein Tu Ne	Asha Bhonsle	Ravi
Bahu Beti	1965	Rangeen Fizaan Hai	Asha Bhonsle & Mahendra Kapoor	Ravi

Film Name	Year	Title	Singer(s)	Music Director(s)
Bahu Beti	1965	Sab Mein Shaamil Ho Magar Sabse Juda Lagti Ho	Mohd. Rafi	Ravi
Kaajal	1965	Aapke Paas Jo Aayega	Mahendra Kapoor	Ravi
Kaajal	1965	Agar Mujhe Na Mili Tum Toh Main Yeh Samjhunga	Asha Bhonsle & Mahendra Kapoor	Ravi
Kaajal	1965	Chham Chham Ghunghru Bole	Asha Bhonsle	Ravi
Kaajal	1965	Chhoo Lene Do Nazuk Honthon Ko	Mohd. Rafi	Ravi
Kaajal	1965	Iss Husn Mujjasim Ki Kahin Neend Na Toote	Mohd. Rafi	Ravi
Kaajal	1965	Kisi Ka Husn Rahe	Mohd. Rafi	Ravi
Kaajal	1965	Mehfil Mein Teri Yoon Hi	Mohd. Rafi & Asha Bhonsle	Ravi
Kaajal	1965	Mere Bhaiya Mere Chanda Mere Anmol Ratan	Asha Bhonsle	Ravi
Kaajal	1965	Muddat Ki Tamanna Ka Sila	Mahendra Kapoor	Ravi
Kaajal	1965	Samjhi Thi Keh Yeh Ghar Mera Hai	Asha Bhonsle	Ravi
Kaajal	1965	Tora Mann Darpan Kehlaaye (two parts)	Asha Bhonsle	Ravi
Kaajal	1965	Yeh Zulf Agar Khul Ke Bikhar Jaaye	Mohd. Rafi	Ravi
Kaajal	1965	Zara Si Aur Pila De (Jai Bam Bhola) - Album Version)	Mohd. Rafi & Asha Bhonsle	Ravi

Film Name	Year	Title	Singer(s)	Music Director(s)
Kaajal	1965	Zara Si Aur Pila De (Hum Hain Bhola) - Film Version)	Mohd. Rafi	Ravi
Waqt	1965	Aage Bhi Jaane Na Tu	Asha Bhonsle	Ravi
Waqt	1965	Ae Meri Zohra-Jabeen	Manna Dey	Ravi
Waqt	1965	Chehre Pe Khushi Chhaa Jaati Hai	Asha Bhonsle	Ravi
Waqt	1965	Din Hain Bahaar Ke	Asha Bhonsle & Mahendra Kapoor	Ravi
Waqt	1965	Hum Jab Simat Ke Aapke	Asha Bhonsle & Mahendra Kapoor	Ravi
Waqt	1965	Kaun Aaya Ke Nighaahon Mein	Asha Bhonsle	Ravi
Waqt	1965	Maine Dekha Hai	Asha Bhonsle & Mahendra Kapoor	Ravi
Waqt	1965	Waqt Se Din Aur Raat	Mohd. Rafi	Ravi
Bahu Begum	1967	Aise Mein Tujhko Dhoondh Ke Laaun Kahan Se	Mohd. Rafi, Manna Dey & chorus	Roshan
Bahu Begum	1967	Duniya Kare Sawaal Toh Hum Kya Jawab Dein	Lata Mangeshkar	Roshan
Bahu Begum	1967	Hum Intezaar Karenge (duet)	Mohd. Rafi & Asha Bhonsle	Roshan
Bahu Begum	1967	Hum Intezaar Karenge (solo)	Mohd. Rafi	Roshan
Bahu Begum	1967	Log Kehte Hain Ke Tumse Kinaara	Mohd. Rafi	Roshan
Bahu Begum	1967	Nikle The Kahan Jaane Ke Liye	Asha Bhonsle	Roshan
Bahu Begum	1967	Pad Gaye Jhoole	Lata Mangeshkar, Asha Bhonsle & chorus	Roshan

Film Name	Year	Title	Singer(s)	Music Director(s)
Bahu Begum	1967	Sirf Apne Khayalon Ki Parchhaaiyan Hain	Asha Bhonsle	Roshan
Bahu Begum	1967	Vaaqif Hoon Khoob Ishq Ke	Mohd. Rafi, Manna Dey & chorus	Roshan
Humraaz	1967	Kisi Patthar Ki Murat Se	Mahendra Kapoor	Ravi
Humraaz	1967	Na Munh Chhupa Ke Jiyo	Mahendra Kapoor	Ravi
Humraaz	1967	Neele Gagan Ke Tale	Mahendra Kapoor	Ravi
Humraaz	1967	Tu Husn Hai Main Ishq Hoon	Asha Bhonsle & Mahendra Kapoor	Ravi
Humraaz	1967	Tum Agar Saath Dene Ka Waada Karo	Mahendra Kapoor & chorus	Ravi
Aankhein	1968	Gairon Pe Karam Apnon Pe Sitam	Lata Mangeshkar	Ravi
Aankhein	1968	Lut Jaa Lut Jaa Yeh Hi Din Hain	Asha Bhonsle, Kamal Barot & Usha Mangeshkar	Ravi
Aankhein	1968	Meri Sun Le Arj Banwaari	Lata Mangeshkar	Ravi
Aankhein	1968	Milti Hai Zindagi Mein	Lata Mangeshkar	Ravi
Aankhein	1968	Tujhko Rakhe Ram Tujhko Allah Rakhe	Asha Bhonsle, Manna Dey & Mehmood	Ravi
Aankhein	1968	Uss Mulk Ki Sarhad Ko Koi Chhoo Nahin Sakta	Mohd. Rafi	Ravi
Do Kaliyan	1968	Bachche Mann Ke Sachche	Lata Mangeshkar	Ravi
Do Kaliyan	1968	Chitnandan Aage Naachungi	Asha Bhonsle	Ravi
Do Kaliyan	1968	Murga Murgi Pyaar Se Dekhein	Lata Mangeshkar	Ravi

288

Film Name	Year	Title	Singer(s)	Music Director(s)
Do Kaliyan	1968	Muslim Ko Taslim Arz Hain, Hindo Ko Pranaam	Manna Dey	Ravi
Do Kaliyan	1968	Sajna O Sajna Aise Mein Jee Na Jala	Asha Bhonsle	Ravi
Do Kaliyan	1968	Tumhaari Nazar Kyon Khafa Ho Gayi	Mohd. Rafi & Lata Mangeshkar	Ravi
Do Kaliyan	1968	Tumhaari Nazar Kyon Khafa Ho Gayi (sad)	Mohd. Rafi & Lata Mangeshkar	Ravi
Do Kaliyan	1968	Yeh Samaa Yeh Rut Yeh Nazaare	Mohd. Rafi & Lata Mangeshkar	Ravi
Izzat	1968	Baant Ke Khaao Iss Duniya Mein (Keh Gaye Father Ibrahim)	Manna Dey	Laxmikant Pyarelal
Izzat	1968	Jaagi Badan Mein Jwaala	Lata Mangeshkar & chorus	Laxmikant Pyarelal
Izzat	1968	Kya Miliye Aise Logon Se Jinki Fitrat Chhupi Rahe	Mohd. Rafi	Laxmikant Pyarelal
Izzat	1968	Pyaar Ke Bukhaar Ko Utaar Mere Manwa	Manna Dey	Laxmikant Pyarelal
Izzat	1968	Ruk Jaa Zara Kidhar Ko Chala	Lata Mangeshkar	Laxmikant Pyarelal
Izzat	1968	Sar Par Lamba Top Leke Aayega	Mohd. Rafi & Asha Bhonsle	Laxmikant Pyarelal
Izzat	1968	Yeh Dil Tum Bin Kahin Lagta Nahin	Mohd. Rafi & Lata Mangeshkar	Laxmikant Pyarelal
Neel Kamal	1968	Aaja Tujhko Pukaare Mera Pyaar (two parts)	Mohd. Rafi	Ravi
Neel Kamal	1968	Babul Ki Duaayein Leti Jaa (two parts)	Mohd. Rafi	Ravi

Film Name	Year	Title	Singer(s)	Music Director(s)
Neel Kamal	1968	Hey Rom Rom Mein Basne Waale Ram	Asha Bhonsle	Ravi
Neel Kamal	1968	Khaali Dabba Khaali Botal	Manna Dey & Mehmood	Ravi
Neel Kamal	1968	Mujhe Toh Roop Iska Vichkaar Lagta	Asha Bhonsle & chorus	Ravi
Neel Kamal	1968	Sharma Ke Yoon Na Dekh Ada Ke Makaam Se	Mohd. Rafi	Ravi
Neel Kamal	1968	Woh Zindagi Jo Thi Ab Tak	Asha Bhonsle	Ravi
Vaasna	1968	Aaj Iss Darja Pila Do	Mohd. Rafi	Chitragupta
Vaasna	1968	Itni Naazuk Na Bano	Mohd. Rafi	Chitragupta
Vaasna	1968	Jeene Waale Jhoom Ke Jee Mastaana Ho Ke Jee	Lata Mangeshkar	Chitragupta
Vaasna	1968	Main Sadke Jaaun	Lata Mangeshkar	Chitragupta
Vaasna	1968	Mulk Mein Bachchon Ki Gar Sarkaar Ho	Lata Mangeshkar, Asha Bhonsle & chorus	Chitragupta
Vaasna	1968	Yeh Parbaton Ke Daayere	Mohd. Rafi & Lata Mangeshkar	Chitragupta
Aadmi Aur Insaan	1969	Bacha Le Ae Maula Ae Ram (Bina Sifarish Mile Naukari)	Mohd. Rafi	Ravi
Aadmi Aur Insaan	1969	Ijaazat Ho Toh Poochhein Aap Hi Se	Asha Bhonsle & Mahendra Kapoor	Ravi
Aadmi Aur Insaan	1969	Itni Jaldi Na Karo	Asha Bhonsle	Ravi
Aadmi Aur Insaan	1969	Jaagega Insaan Zamaana Dekhega	Mahendra Kapoor & chorus	Ravi
Aadmi Aur Insaan	1969	O Neele Parbaton Ki Dhaara	Asha Bhonsle & Mahendra Kapoor	Ravi

Film Name	Year	Title	Singer(s)	Music Director(s)
Aadmi Aur Insaan	1969	Yaara Dildaara Mera Dil Karta	Mahendra Kapoor, Balbir, Joginder Singh & chorus	Ravi
Aadmi Aur Insaan	1969	Yaara Dildaara Mera Dil Karta (sad)	Mahendra Kapoor	Ravi
Aadmi Aur Insaan	1969	Zindagi Itefaaq Hai (duet)	Asha Bhonsle & Mahendra Kapoor	Ravi
Aadmi Aur Insaan	1969	Zindagi Itefaaq Hai (solo)	Asha Bhonsle	Ravi
Aadmi Aur Insaan	1969	Zindagi Ke Rang Kayi Re	Asha Bhonsle	Ravi
Nanha Farishta	1969	Arrey Chanda Kaahe Ka Tera Mama	Manna Dey, Mahendra Kapoor & Manhar Udhas	Kalyanji Anandji
Nanha Farishta	1969	O Re O Sharaabi Tujhmein Ek Kharaabi	Asha Bhonsle	Kalyanji Anandji
Nanha Farishta	1969	Bachche Mein Hai Bhagwan	Mohd. Rafi, Manna Dey & Kishore Kumar	Kalyanji Anandji
Nanha Farishta	1969	O Natkhat Nanhi Laadli	Lata Mangeshkar	Kalyanji Anandji
Paisa Ya Pyaar	1969	Ber Le Lo Ber Mewa Gareebon Ka	Asha Bhonsle	Ravi
Paisa Ya Pyaar	1969	Insaanon Ne Paise Ke Liye	Hemant Kumar	Ravi
Paisa Ya Pyaar	1969	Jaane Kyon Baar Baar	Asha Bhonsle	Ravi
Paisa Ya Pyaar	1969	Mil Le Mil Le Mujhe Chhoo Nahin	Mohd. Rafi & Asha Bhonsle	Ravi
Paisa Ya Pyaar	1969	Tu Bhi Number Ek Main Bhi Number Ek	Asha Bhonsle & Kishore Kumar	Ravi
Mann Ki Aankhein	1970	Arri Maa Gauri Maa	Asha Bhonsle & chorus	Laxmikant Pyarelal
Mann Ki Aankhein	1970	Bahut Der Tum Ne Sataaya Hai Mujhko	Asha Bhonsle	Laxmikant Pyarelal

291

Film Name	Year	Title	Singer(s)	Music Director(s)
Mann Ki Aankhein	1970	Chala Bhi Aa Aaja Rasiya	Mohd. Rafi & Lata Mangeshkar	Laxmikant Pyarelal
Mann Ki Aankhein	1970	Dil Kahe Ruk Ja Re Ruk Ja	Mohd. Rafi	Laxmikant Pyarelal
Mann Ki Aankhein	1970	Kya Tum Wohi Ho	Mohd. Rafi & Suman Kalyanpur	Laxmikant Pyarelal
Mann Ki Aankhein	1970	Meri Jaan Dil Garmaati	Lata Mangeshkar, Manna Dey & chorus	Laxmikant Pyarelal
Naya Raasta	1970	Apne Andar Zara Jhaank Mere Watan	Mohd. Rafi	N. Dutta
Naya Raasta	1970	Chunar Mori Kori	Mohd. Rafi, Asha Bhonsle & chorus	N. Dutta
Naya Raasta	1970	Ishwar Allah Tere Naam Sabko Sanmati De Bhagwan	Mohd. Rafi & chorus	N. Dutta
Naya Raasta	1970	Jaan Gayi Main Toh Jaan Gayi	Asha Bhonsle	N. Dutta
Naya Raasta	1970	Maine Pi Sharaab Tumne Kya Piya	Mohd. Rafi	N. Dutta
Naya Raasta	1970	Mere Saiyan Padun Paiyan	Asha Bhonsle	N. Dutta
Naya Raasta	1970	Ponchh Kar Ashq Apni Aankhon Se	Mohd. Rafi	N. Dutta
Naya Raasta	1970	Zulfon Ke Mehkate Saaye Hain	Asha Bhonsle	N. Dutta
Samaaj Ko Badal Daalo	1970	Ab Akele Hi Chalna Padega (two parts)	Manna Dey	Ravi
Samaaj Ko Badal Daalo	1970	Amma Ik Roti De Baba Ik Roti De	Lata Mangeshkar & Usha Mangeshkar	Ravi
Samaaj Ko Badal Daalo	1970	Bhookh Pyaas Aur Zulm Ki Duniya	Mohd. Rafi	Ravi
Samaaj Ko Badal Daalo	1970	Dharti Maa Ka Maan Hamaara	Mohd. Rafi, Manna Dey & chorus	Ravi

Film Name	Year	Title	Singer(s)	Music Director(s)
Samaaj Ko Badal Daalo	1970	Paayal Chham Chham Bole Sakhi	Asha Bhonsle & Usha Mangeshkar	Ravi
Samaaj Ko Badal Daalo	1970	Samaaj Ko Badal Daalo	Mohd. Rafi	Ravi
Samaaj Ko Badal Daalo	1970	Taaron Ki Chhaon Mein (two parts)	Mohd. Rafi & Lata Mangeshkar	Ravi
Samaaj Ko Badal Daalo	1970	Tum Apni Saheli Ko Itna Bata Do	Mohd. Rafi & Asha Bhonsle	Ravi
Samaaj Ko Badal Daalo	1970	Yeh Mausam Yeh Khuli Hawa	Mohd. Rafi, Asha Bhonsle & chorus	Ravi
Ganga Tera Pani Amrit	1971	Ganga Tera Pani Amrit (three parts - film versions)	Mohd. Rafi & chorus	Ravi
Ganga Tera Pani Amrit	1971	Ganga Tera Pani Amrit (album version)	Mohd. Rafi & chorus	Ravi
Ganga Tera Pani Amrit	1971	Humein Yaari Se Garaz	Mahendra Kapoor & Manna Dey	Ravi
Ganga Tera Pani Amrit	1971	Iss Dharti Iss Khule Gagan Ka Kya Kehna	Mohd. Rafi & Asha Bhonsle	Ravi
Ganga Tera Pani Amrit	1971	O Ladke Makhan Se	Asha Bhonsle	Ravi
Sansaar	1971	Bas Ab Tarsaana Chhodo	Asha Bhonsle & Kishore Kumar	Chitragupta
Sansaar	1971	Haathon Mein Kitaab Baalon Mein Gulaab	Kishore Kumar	Chitragupta
Sansaar	1971	Maa Tu Aansoo Ponchh Le Apne	Usha Mangeshkar	Chitragupta
Sansaar	1971	Mere Babu Khilone Le Jaa	Asha Bhonsle	Chitragupta
Sansaar	1971	Mile Jitni Sharaab Main Toh Peeta Hoon	Kishore Kumar	Chitragupta
Sansaar	1971	Raja Jani Na Maaro Nainwa Ke Teer Re	Krishna Kalle	Chitragupta

Film Name	Year	Title	Singer(s)	Music Director(s)
Sansaar	1971	Yeh Duniya Teri Na Meri	Kishore Kumar	Chitragupta
Bhai Ho To Aisa	1972	Aaja Meri Jawaani Ko	Lata Mangeshkar	Sonik Omi
Bhai Ho To Aisa	1972	Ae Phuljhadi, Ae Gulchhadi	Mohd. Rafi	Sonik Omi
Bhai Ho To Aisa	1972	Bol Meri Gudiya	Lata Mangeshkar & Kishore Kumar	Sonik Omi
Bhai Ho To Aisa	1972	Chor Chor Humne Fasaaya	Lata Mangeshkar	Sonik Omi
Bhai Ho To Aisa	1972	Sun Le Naag Raja	Asha Bhonsle	Sonik Omi
Dastaan	1972	Ek Toh Yeh Bairi Saawan	Asha Bhonsle	Laxmikant Pyarelal
Dastaan	1972	Jaisa Karam Kare Hai Koi (snippet)	Hemant Kumar	Laxmikant Pyarelal
Dastaan	1972	Koi Aaya Lachak Uthi Kaaya	Asha Bhonsle	Laxmikant Pyarelal
Dastaan	1972	Na Tu Zameen Ke Liye Hai Na Aasmaan Ke Liye	Mohd. Rafi	Laxmikant Pyarelal
Dastaan	1972	O Maria My Sweetheart	Mahendra Kapoor, Asha Bhonsle & chorus	Laxmikant Pyarelal
Dastaan	1972	O Mela Jagwaala Saathi Mere (part i)	Mahendra Kapoor	Laxmikant Pyarelal
Dastaan	1972	O Mela Jagwaala Saathi Mere (part ii)	Mahendra Kapoor	Laxmikant Pyarelal
Aa Gale Lag Jaa	1973	Ae Mere Bete Sun Mera Kehna (part i)	Kishore Kumar	R.D. Burman
Aa Gale Lag Jaa	1973	Tera Mujhse Hai Pehle Ka Naata Koi (part i)	Kishore Kumar	R.D. Burman

Film Name	Year	Title	Singer(s)	Music Director(s)
Aa Gale Lag Jaa	1973	Tera Mujhse Hai Pehle Ka Naata Koi (part ii)	Kishore Kumar & Sushma Shreshtha	R.D. Burman
Aa Gale Lag Jaa	1973	Waada Karo Nahin Chhodogi	Lata Mangeshkar & Kishore Kumar	R.D. Burman
Aa Gale Lag Jaa	1973	Na Koi Dil Mein Samaaya	Kishore Kumar	R.D. Burman
Daag	1973	Ab Chaahe Maa Roothe Ke Baba	Lata Mangeshkar & Kishore Kumar	Laxmikant Pyarelal
Daag	1973	Hawa Chale Kaise Na Tu Jaane	Lata Mangeshkar	Laxmikant Pyarelal
Daag	1973	Hum Aur Tum Tum Aur Hum	Lata Mangeshkar & Kishore Kumar	Laxmikant Pyarelal
Daag	1973	Jab Bhi Jee Chaahe Nayi Duniya Basa Lete Hain Log	Lata Mangeshkar	Laxmikant Pyarelal
Daag	1973	Mere Dil Mein Aaj Kya Hai	Kishore Kumar	Laxmikant Pyarelal
Daag	1973	Ni Main Yaar Manaana Ni	Lata Mangeshkar & Minoo Purshottam	Laxmikant Pyarelal
Dhundh	1973	Jo Yahan Tha Woh Wahan Kyon Kar Hua	Asha Bhonsle & Usha Mangeshkar	Ravi
Dhundh	1973	Jobana Se Chunariya (written by Ravi - credit to Sahir)	Asha Bhonsle & Manna Dey	Ravi
Dhundh	1973	Sansaar Ki Har Shai Ka Itna Hi Fasaana Hai (pt. i)	Mahendra Kapoor	Ravi

Film Name	Year	Title	Singer(s)	Music Director(s)
Dhundh	1973	Sansaar Ki Har Shai Ka Itna Hi Fasaana Hai (pt. ii)	Mahendra Kapoor	Ravi
Dhundh	1973	Uljhan Suljhe Na Rasta Soojhe Na	Asha Bhonsle	Ravi
Joshila	1973	Dil Mein Jo Baatein Hain	Asha Bhonsle & Kishore Kumar	R.D. Burman
Joshila	1973	Jo Baat Ishaaron Mein Kahi	Lata Mangeshkar	R.D. Burman
Joshila	1973	Kaanp Rahi Main	Asha Bhonsle	R.D. Burman
Joshila	1973	Kiska Rasta Dekhe Ae Dil Ae Saudai	Kishore Kumar	R.D. Burman
Joshila	1973	Kuchh Bhi Kar Lo Ek Din Tumko	Lata Mangeshkar & Kishore Kumar	R.D. Burman
Joshila	1973	Mehfil Mein Chhupaane Pade Jazbaat	Lata Mangeshkar	R.D. Burman
Joshila	1973	Sharma Na Yoon Ghabra Na Yoon	Asha Bhonsle & Dev Anand	R.D. Burman
Joshila	1973	Sona Rupa Laayo Re	Asha Bhonsle	R.D. Burman
Mehmaan	1973	Chhod Arrey Ja Mujhe Na Pakad	Mohd. Rafi & Asha Bhonsle	Ravi
Mehmaan	1973	Khule Gagan Ke Neeche	Minoo Purshottam	Ravi
Mehmaan	1973	Meri Chaahat Rahegi Hamesha Jawaan	Mohd. Rafi	Ravi
Mehmaan	1973	Ram Rahim Krishna Karim	Mahendra Kapoor, Deedar S. Pardesi & Minoo Pushottam	Ravi
Mehmaan	1973	Tu Darr Mat Darr Mat Yaara	Asha Bhonsle	Ravi
Mehmaan	1973	Uff Yeh Jawaani Yeh Ada	Mohd. Rafi	Ravi
36 Ghante	1974	Chup Ho Aaj Kaho Kya Hai Baat	Kishore Kumar	Sapan Chakravarty
36 Ghante	1974	Jaane Aaj Kya Hua	Asha Bhonsle & Kishore Kumar	Sapan Chakravarty

Film Name	Year	Title	Singer(s)	Music Director(s)
36 Ghante	1974	Teen Lok Pe Raj Tihaara (Rakhiyo Nazar Shri Ram Re)	Asha Bhonsle & Mahendra Kapoor	Sapan Chakravarty
36 Ghante	1974	Yahan Bandhu Aate Ko Hai Jaana	Mukesh	Sapan Chakravarty
Deewaar	1975	Deewaron Ka Jungle Jiska Aabadi Hai Naam	Manna Dey	R.D. Burman
Deewaar	1975	Idhar Ka Maal Udhar (unreleased)	Bhupinder Singh & chorus	R.D. Burman
Deewaar	1975	Keh Doon Tumhein Ya Chup Rahun	Asha Bhonsle & Kishore Kumar	R.D. Burman
Deewaar	1975	Koi Marr Jaaye Kisi Pe Yeh Kahan Dekha Hai	Asha Bhonsle & chorus	R.D. Burman
Deewar	1975	Maine Tujhe Maanga Tujhe Paaya Hai	Asha Bhonsle & Kishore Kumar	R.D. Burman
Ek Mahal Ho Sapnon Ka	1975	Dekha Hai Zindagi Ko Kuchh Itna Kareeb Se	Kishore Kumar	Ravi
Ek Mahal Ho Sapnon Ka	1975	Dil Mein Kisi Ke Pyaar Ka Jalta Hua Diya (female)	Lata Mangeshkar	Ravi
Ek Mahal Ho Sapnon Ka	1975	Dil Mein Kisi Ke Pyaar Ka Jalta Hua Diya (male)	Kishore Kumar	Ravi
Ek Mahal Ho Sapnon Ka	1975	Ek Mahal Ho Sapnon Ka	Mohd. Rafi & Lata Mangeshkar	Ravi
Ek Mahal Ho Sapnon Ka	1975	Gulon Ka Rang Ho Tum	Lata Mangeshkar	Ravi
Ek Mahal Ho Sapnon Ka	1975	Humse Poochho Ke Haqeeqat Kya Hai (snippet)	Kishore Kumar	Ravi

Film Name	Year	Title	Singer(s)	Music Director(s)
Ek Mahal Ho Sapnon Ka	1975	Paisa - Dushman Mohabbat Ka Paisa	Kishore Kumar	Ravi
Ek Mahal Ho Sapnon Ka	1975	Zindagi Guzaarne Ko Saathi Ek Chahiye	Mohd. Rafi	Ravi
Zameer	1975	Aanka Baanka Tali Talaaka	Kishore Kumar, Manna Dey & chorus	Sapan Chakravarty
Zameer	1975	Ab Yahan Koi Nahin Aayega	Kishore Kumar	Sapan Chakravarty
Zameer	1975	Bade Dinon Mein Khushi Ka Din Aaya (two parts)	Mahendra Kapoor	Sapan Chakravarty
Zameer	1975	Phoolon Ke Dhere Hain	Kishore Kumar	Sapan Chakravarty
Zameer	1975	Tum Bhi Chalo Hum Bhi Chale (duet)	Asha Bhonsle & Kishore Kumar	Sapan Chakravarty
Zameer	1975	Tum Bhi Chalo Hum Bhi Chale (solo)	Kishore Kumar	Sapan Chakravarty
Zameer	1975	Zindagi Hansne Gaane Ke Liye Hai	Kishore Kumar & chorus	Sapan Chakravarty
Kabhi Kabhie	1976	Kabhi Kabhi Mere Dil Mein Khayal Aata Hai	Amitabh Bachchan	
Kabhi Kabhie	1976	Kabhi Kabhi Mere Dil Mein Khayal Aata Hai	Lata Mangeshkar & Mukesh	Khayyam
Kabhi Kabhie	1976	Kabhi Kabhi Mere Dil Mein Khayal Aata Hai	Mukesh	Khayyam
Kabhi Kabhie	1976	Main Har Ek Pal Ka Shayar Hoon	Mukesh	Khayyam
Kabhi Kabhie	1976	Main Pal Do Pal Ka Shayar Hoon	Mukesh	Khayyam

Film Name	Year	Title	Singer(s)	Music Director(s)
Kabhi Kabhie	1976	Mere Ghar Aayi Ek Nanhi Pari	Lata Mangeshkar	Khayyam
Kabhi Kabhie	1976	Pyaar Kar Liya To Kya	Kishore Kumar	Khayyam
Kabhi Kabhie	1976	Surkh Jode Ki	Lata Mangeshkar	Khayyam
Kabhi Kabhie	1976	Tera Haath Haath Mein Ho Agar	Amitabh Bachchan	Khayyam
Kabhi Kabhie	1976	Tera Phoolon Jaisa Rang	Lata Mangeshkar & Kishore Kumar	Khayyam
Kabhi Kabhie	1976	Tere Chehre Se Nazar Nahin Hat-ti	Lata Mangeshkar & Kishore Kumar	Khayyam
Kabhi Kabhie	1976	Woh Mere Beech Nahin Aaye	Amitabh Bachchan	Madan Mohan
Laila Majnu	1976	Ab Agar Humse Khudai Bhi Khafa Ho Jaaye	Mohd. Rafi & Lata Mangeshkar	Madan Mohan
Laila Majnu	1976	Barbaad-e-Mohabbat Ki Dua Saath Liye Jaa	Mohd. Rafi	Madan Mohan
Laila Majnu	1976	Hoke Mayoos Tere Dar Se Sawaali Na Gaya	Mohd. Rafi, Aziz Nazan, Shankar Shambbhu, Ambar Kumar & chorus	Madan Mohan
Laila Majnu	1976	Husn Haazir Hai Mohabbat Ki Sazaa Paane Ko	Lata Mangeshkar	Madan Mohan
Laila Majnu	1976	Iss Reshmi Pazeib Ki Jhankaar Ke Sadke	Mohd. Rafi & Lata Mangeshkar	Madan Mohan

Film Name	Year	Title	Singer(s)	Music Director(s)
Laila Majnu	1976	Laila Majnu Do Badan Ik Jaan The (part i)	Rajkumar Rizvi, Anuradha Paudwal & Preeti Sagar	Jaidev
Laila Majnu	1976	Laila Majnu Do Badan Ik Jaan The (part ii)	Rajkumar Rizvi & Preeti Sagar	Jaidev
Laila Majnu	1976	Likhkar Tera Naam Zameen Par	Mohd. Rafi & Lata Mangeshkar	Madan Mohan
Laila Majnu	1976	Main Tere Dar Pe Aaya Hoon	Mohd. Rafi	Madan Mohan
Laila Majnu	1976	Yeh Deewane Ki Zidd Hai	Mohd. Rafi	Jaidev
Shankar Shambhu	1976	Bheege Hue Jalwon Par	Mohd. Rafi & Asha Bhonsle	Kalyanji Anandji
Shankar Shambhu	1976	Gar Nibhaane Ki Himmat Na Thi	Asha Bhonsle	Kalyanji Anandji
Shankar Shambhu	1976	Hum Lootne Aaaye Hain	Aziz Nazan, Jani Babu Qawwal & chorus	Kalyanji Anandji
Shankar Shambhu	1976	Mera Dil Chura Kar Na Aankhein Chura	Suman Kalyanpur	Kalyanji Anandji
Shankar Shambhu	1976	Yeh Duniya Hai Naqli Chehron Ka Mela	Mahendra Kapoor, Kishore Kumar & Sulakshana Pandit	Kalyanji Anandji
Amaanat	1977	Bhus Bhar Diya Meri Chaahat Mein	Manna Dey	Ravi
Amaanat	1977	Bujhe Bujhe Rang Hain Nazaaron Ke	Asha Bhonsle	Ravi
Amaanat	1977	Cycle Pe Haseenon Ki Toli	Mohd. Rafi,	Ravi
Amaanat	1977	Door Reh Ka Na Karo Baat	Manna Dey & Asha Bhonsle Mohd. Rafi	Ravi

Film Name	Year	Title	Singer(s)	Music Director(s)
Amaanat	1977	Har Ek Dil Mein Koi Armaan Hai Amaanat	Mohd. Rafi	Ravi
Amaanat	1977	Matlab Nikal Gaya Toh	Mohd. Rafi	Ravi
Amaanat	1977	Teri Jawaani Tapta Maheena	Mohd. Rafi	Ravi
Jagriti	1977	Ae Mere Nanhe Gulfam	Asha Bhonsle	Laxmikant Pyarelal
Jagriti	1977	Hum Hain Teri Santaan Yeh Pran Teri Den Hai	Suman Kalyanpur	Laxmikant Pyarelal
Jagriti	1977	Main Hero Gaaunga Ek Gaana	Asha Bhonsle & Minoo Purshottam	Laxmikant Pyarelal
Jagriti	1977	Meharbaan Kaise Kaise	Asha Bhonsle	Laxmikant Pyarelal
Nawaab Sahib	1978	Ab Se Pehle Toh Yeh Dil Ki Haalat Na Thi	Usha Mangeshkar	C.Arjun
Nawaab Sahib	1978	Ek Khawaab-e-Tamanna Bhoole Thay	Asha Bhonsle	C.Arjun
Nawaab Sahib	1978	Hum Mein Hai Kya Ke Humein Koi Haseena Chaahe	Mohd. Rafi	C.Arjun
Nawaab Sahib	1978	Ladke Ki Aaj Main Mubarakbaadi	Johnny Whisky & eunuchs	C.Arjun
Nawaab Sahib	1978	Uss Jaan-e-Do Aalam Ka Jalwa	Mohd. Rafi, Manna Dey & chorus	C.Arjun
Trishul	1978	Aapki Mehki Hui Zulf Ko	Yesudas & Lata Mangeshkar	Khayyam
Trishul	1978	Gapuji Gapuji Gam Gam	Lata Mangeshkar & Nitin Mukesh	Khayyam
Trishul	1978	Jaa Ri Behna Jaa Tu Apne Ghar Jaa	Kishore Kumar, Yesudas & Pamela Chopra	Khayyam

Film Name	Year	Title	Singer(s)	Music Director(s)
Trishul	1978	Jaan-e-Mann Tum Kamaal Karti Ho	Lata Mangeshkar & Kishore Kumar	Khayyam
Trishul	1978	Kabhi Kasmein Na Todein (Jo Ho Yaar Apna)	Lata Mangeshkar & Kishore Kumar	Khayyam
Trishul	1978	Mohabbat Bade Kaam Ki Cheez Hai	Lata Mangeshkar, Kishore Kumar & Yesudas	Khayyam
Trishul	1978	Tu Mere Saath Rahega Munne (two parts)	Lata Mangeshkar	Khayyam
Hum Tere Aashiq Hain	1979	Chain Nahin (Zara Hans Kar Karle Baat)	Asha Bhonsle & Mahendra Kapoor	Ravindra Jain
Hum Tere Aashiq Hain	1979	Hindi Hinglish Ki Pothi (Nainwa Ki Bhasha)	Asha Bhonsle	Ravindra Jain
Hum Tere Aashiq Hain	1979	Maanvata Ki Jeet Hui	Kishore Kumar	Ravindra Jain
Hum Tere Aashiq Hain	1979	Maar Liya Maidaan	Asha Bhonsle & Kishore Kumar	Ravindra Jain
Hum Tere Aashiq Hain	1979	Mushkil Hai Ab Raaz Chhupana	Asha Bhonsle & Mahendra Kapoor	Ravindra Jain
Hum Tere Aashiq Hain	1979	Ta Dhin Naacho Re Masti Mein Aake	Asha Bhonsle & chorus	Ravindra Jain
Kala Patthar	1979	Baahon Mein Teri Masti Ke	Mohd. Rafi & Lata Mangeshkar	Rajesh Roshan
Kala Patthar	1979	Dhoom Mache Dhoom	Mohd. Rafi, Mahendra Kapoor	Rajesh Roshan
Kala Patthar	1979	Ik Raasta Hai Zindagi	Lata Mangeshkar & S.K.Mohan Lata Mangeshkar & Kishore Kumar	Rajesh Roshan

Film Name	Year	Title	Singer(s)	Music Director(s)
Kala Patthar	1979	Jaggiya Jaggiya Jaggiya (part i)	Mahendra Kapoor & Pamela Chopra	Rajesh Roshan
Kala Patthar	1979	Jaggiya Jaggiya Jaggiya (part ii)	Mahendra Kapoor	Rajesh Roshan
Kala Patthar	1979	Meri Dooron Se Aayi Baraat	Lata Mangeshkar & chorus	Rajesh Roshan
Kala Patthar	1979	Mujhe Pyaar Ka Tohfa De Ke	Mohd. Rafi & Usha Mangeshkar	Rajesh Roshan
Chambal Ki Kasam	1980	Baaje Shehnai Ri Banno Tore Angana	Jagjit Kaur	Khayyam
Chambal Ki Kasam	1980	Chanda Re Mere	Lata Mangeshkar	Khayyam
Chambal Ki Kasam	1980	Jaan-e-Mann Jo Teri Mansha (Kaun Hai Mujrim)	Mahendra Kapoor & Manna Dey	Khayyam
Chambal Ki Kasam	1980	Kuchh Aur Behak Jaaun	Lata Mangeshkar	Khayyam
Chambal Ki Kasam	1980	Marta Hai Koi Toh	Lata Mangeshkar	Khayyam
Chambal Ki Kasam	1980	Parmeshwar Rakhwala	Lata Mangeshkar	Khayyam
Chambal Ki Kasam	1980	Sher Ka Husn Ho	Mohd. Rafi	Khayyam
Chambal Ki Kasam	1980	Simti Hui Yeh Ghadiyaan	Mohd. Rafi & Lata Mangeshkar	Khayyam
Chehre Pe Chehra	1980	Aa Aaj Hain Har Khushi Raat Mein	Dilraj Kaur & chorus	N. Dutta
Chehre Pe Chehra	1980	Aaj Socha Hai Khayalon Mein Bula Kar	Mohd. Rafi & Sulakshana Pandit	N. Dutta
Chehre Pe Chehra	1980	Jaam Le Jaam	Asha Bhonsle	N. Dutta
Chehre Pe Chehra	1980	Jhuke Rahein Tamaam Sar (Yeh Raat Nek Raat Hai)	Manna Dey & chorus	N. Dutta
Chehre Pe Chehra	1980	Main Hoon Pari Adaaon Bhari	Asha Bhonsle & chorus	N. Dutta
Chehre Pe Chehra	1980	Tumse Kehna Hai	Sulakshana Pandit	N. Dutta

Film Name	Year	Title	Singer(s)	Music Director(s)
Insaaf Ka Tarazu	1980	Hai Jo Yehi Pyaar Ka Trailor	Asha Bhonsle, Mahendra Kapoor & Hemlata	Ravindra Jain
Insaaf Ka Tarazu	1980	Hazaar Khwaab Haqeeqat Ka Roop	Asha Bhonsle & Mahendra Kapoor	Ravindra Jain
Insaaf Ka Tarazu	1980	Insaaf Ka Tarazu Jo Haath Mein	Mahendra Kapoor	Ravindra Jain
Insaaf Ka Tarazu	1980	Log Aurat Ko Faqat Jism Samajh Lete Hain	Asha Bhonsle	Ravindra Jain
The Burning Train	1980	Jab Tak Ambar Par Taare Hon	Asha Bhonsle & Kishore Kumar	R.D. Burman
The Burning Train	1980	Kisi Ke Waade Pe Kyon Aitbaar Humne Kiya	Asha Bhonsle	R.D. Burman
The Burning Train	1980	Meri Nazar Hai Tujhpe	Asha Bhonsle	R.D. Burman
The Burning Train	1980	Pal Do Pal Ka Saath Hamaara	Mohd. Rafi, Asha Bhonsle & chorus	R.D. Burman
The Burning Train	1980	Pehli Nazar Mein	Mohd. Rafi, Asha Bhonsle Usha Mangeshkar & Kishore Kumar	R.D. Burman
The Burning Train	1980	Teri Hai Zameen Tera Aasmaan	Sushma Shreshtha, Padmini Kolhapure & chorus	R.D. Burman
Dhanwan	1981	Balle Balle Ni Reshmi Dupatte Waaliye	Lata Mangeshkar, Mahnedra Kapoor & Amit Kumar	Hridaynath Mangeshkar
Dhanwan	1981	Idhar Aa Aa Bhi Jaa	Kishore Kumar	Hridaynath Mangeshkar

Film Name	Year	Title	Singer(s)	Music Director(s)
Dhanwan	1981	Kuchh Log Mohabbat Ko	Lata Mangeshkar	Hridaynath Mangeshkar
Dhanwan	1981	Maaro Bhar Bhar Kar Pichkaari	Lata Mangeshkar, Kishore Kumar & chorus	Hridaynath Mangeshkar
Dhanwan	1981	Yeh Aankhein Dekh Kar Hum	Lata Mangeshkar & Suresh Wadkar	Hridaynath Mangeshkar
Deedar-e-Yaar	1982	Chal Chal Lifaafe (Co-lyricist - Kaifi Azmi)	Kishore Kumar	Laxmikant Pyarelal
Deedar-e-Yaar	1982	Eid Ka Din Hai (Co-lyricist - Kaifi Azmi)	Mohd. Rafi, Asha Bhonsle & chorus	Laxmikant Pyarelal
Deedar-e-Yaar	1982	Mere Dildaar Ka Baankpan	Mohd. Rafi & Kishore Kumar	Laxmikant Pyarelal
Deedar-e-Yaar	1982	Tumko Dekha Toh Samajh Mein Aaya	Lata Mangeshkar	Laxmikant Pyarelal
Jiyo Aur Jeene Do	1982	Seeta Ke Liye Likha Hai	Mohd. Rafi	Laxmikant Pyarelal
Jiyo Aur Jeene Do	1982	Sirf Dekho Humein Chhoone Ki Tamanna Na Karo	Asha Bhonsle	Laxmikant Pyarelal
Lakshmi	1982	Halaat Se Ladna Mushkil Tha	Asha Bhonsle	Usha Khanna
Lakshmi	1982	Seeta Bhi Jahan Sukh Pa Na Saki	Mahendra Kapoor	Usha Khanna
Sachche Moti (Raju)	1962/67	Ae Mere Meharbaan Ab Na Le Imtehaan	Mahendra Kapoor & Suman Kalyanpur	N. Dutta
Sachche Moti (Raju)	1962/67	Arrey O Deewane Khushi Ke Zamaane	Geeta Dutt	N. Dutta
Sachche Moti (Raju)	1962/67	Chaahe Dekhe Ghoor Ke	Mohd. Rafi & Asha Bhonsle	N. Dutta

305

Film Name	Year	Title	Singer(s)	Music Director(s)
Sachche Moti (Raju)	1962/67	Garz Ho Toh Nakhre Dikhaati Hai Biwi	Mohd. Rafi	N. Dutta
Sachche Moti (Raju)	1962/67	Mere Munne Re Seedhi Raah Pe Chalna	Geeta Dutt	N. Dutta
Sachche Moti (Raju)	1962/67	Sachche Ka Hai Bolbala	Asha Bhonsle & Sudha Malhotra	N. Dutta
Chingaari	1989	Har Waqt Tere Husn Ka Hota Hai	Mahendra Kapoor	Ravi
Chingaari	1989	Main Kaun Hoon Main Kya Hoon	Asha Bhonsle & Mahendra Kapoor	Ravi
Chingaari	1989	Meri Baari Re Kaahe Ko Bhoole Banwaari	Asha Bhonsle & Usha Mangeshkar	Ravi
Chingaari	1989	Pighli Aag Se Saagar Bhar Le	Asha Bhonsle	Ravi
Chingaari	1989	Teri Karam Kahaani Teri Aatma Bhi Jaane	Manna Dey	Ravi
Chingaari	1989	Tu Bol Na Bol Bas Reh Mere Kol	Asha Bhonsle & Mahendra Kapoor	Ravi
Chingaari	1989	Woh Dekh Ude Kaag (Ae Yaar Mujhe Thaam)	Asha Bhonsle & David	Ravi

Notes:

1. This filmography is courtesy Anupama Sharma but has been verified by cross-checking Har Mandir Singh 'Humraaz's *Hindi Film Geet Kosh*, Volumes 2, 3 and 4 and with Manohar Iyer's records.
2. Films like *Tumsa Nahin Dekha* (1957), for which Sahir has written only one song, only that particular song has been included in this list.
3. Unreleased films like *Kaafir* and Sahir's work as lyricist in other regional films do not form part of this filmography.
4. The author has attempted to provide an exact list of Sahir's work in Hindi cinema through this filmography. Any error in this list, however, is seriously regretted.

Select Bibliography

Ajaib Chitrakar, *Sahir: Khaaban Da Shaizada* (Punjabi), Punjabi University Patiala, 1988

Amrita Pritam, *Raseedi Tikkat* (Autobiography in Hindi), Kitaabghar Prakashan, 2008

Azhar Javed, *Nakaamey Mohabbat* (Urdu), Takhleeqkar Publishers, 2007

Dinesh Raheja and Jitendara Kothari, *The Hundred Luminaries of Hindi Cinema*, India Book House Publishers, 1996

Ganesh Anantharaman, *Bollywood Melodies: A History of the Hindi Film Song*, Penguin Books India, 2008

Hameed Akhtar, *Ashnaiyaan Kya Kya* (Urdu), Jang Publishers Lahore, 2003

Khwaja Ahmad Abbas, *I Am Not an Island: An Experiment in Autobiography*, ImprintOne, 2010

Manek Premchand, *Yesterday's Melodies Today's Memories*, Jharna Books, 2004

M.K. Raghavendra, *Seduced by the Familiar: Narration and Meaning in Indian Popular Cinema*, Oxford University Press, 2008

Nasreen Munni Kabir, *Guru Dutt: A Life in Cinema*, Oxford University Press, 2005

———, *Talking Songs: Javed Akhtar in Conversation with Nasreen Munni Kabir*, Oxford University Press, 2005

———, *Talking Films: Conversations on Hindi Cinema with Javed Akhtar*, Oxford University Press, 2012

Prakash Pandit, *Sahir Ludhianvi: Life Sketch and Poetry* (Hindi), Rajpal and Sons, 2007

Rachel Dwyer, *Yash Chopra: Fifty Years in Indian Cinema*, Roli Books: The Lotus Collection, 2002

Raza Mir and Ali Husain Mir, *Anthems of Resistance*, IndiaInk, 2006

Saabir Dutt, *Fann Aur Shaksiyat*, Sahir Ludhianvi Number (Urdu), Sahir Publishing House, 1985

Sajjad Zaheer, *The Light: A History of the Movement for Progressive Literature in the Indo-Pak Subcontinent*, A Translation of Roshnai, Translated from Urdu by Amina Azfar, Oxford University Press, 2006

Sathya Saran, *Ten Years with Guru Dutt: Abrar Alvi's Journey*, Penguin Viking, 2008

Sahir Rachnawaali – Talkhiyaan, Gaata Jaaye Banjara, Aao Ki Koi Khwaab Bunein (Hindi), Hindi Book Centre, 2007

Shaukat Kaifi, *Kaifi & I: A Memoir*, Edited and translated by Nasreen Rehman, Zubaan, 2010

Syed Zeyaur Rahman Prof. Dr, *Sahir Ludhianvi: Hayaat Aur Shaayari* (Urdu), Educational Publishing House, 2009

Uma Trilok, *Amrita-Imroz: A Love Story*, Penguin Books India, 2006

Vinay Lal, *Deewaar: The Footpath, the City and the Angry Young Man*, HarperCollins Publishers India, 2011

Index of Poems and Film Songs

Index

Acknowledgements

My sincere thanks to Dev Anand, Yash Chopra, Ravi Sharma, Khayyam, Salim Khan, Javed Akhtar, Sudha Malhotra, Ravi Chopra, Farooq Sheikh, Ramesh Talwar, Ram Mohan, Ruhan Kapoor, Naqsh Lyallpuri, Omi of Sonik-Omi, Arun Dutt, Sanjeev Kohli, Ajaib Chitrakar, Hameed Akhtar, Salma Siddiqui, R.K. Munir, Imroz, Trinetra Bajpai, Ali Peter John, Jalees Sherwani, Dr Uma Trilok, Gauhar Raza, Najma Zaheer Baquer, Seema Baquer, Amarnath Varma, K. Vijayakrishnan, Prof. Bhupinder Parihar, Professor A.K. Maleri, Ali Hussain Mir, Sathya Saran, Pramila Le Hunte, Anupama Sharma, Nasreen Munni Kabir, Siddharth Kak, Mudar Patherya, Gulan Kripalani, Naveen Pandita, Kausar Munir, Mariam Munir, Pushan Kripalani, Nishant Nayak, Aslam Rizvi, Jyoti Neggi, Jai Arjun Singh, Rahul Bhattacharya, Shruti Debi, Dr Anwar Zaheer Ansari, Anees Amrohvi of Takhleeqkar Publishers, Dr Khursheed Alam, Professor Kalra, Vidya Krishnan, Prachi Pinglay-Plumber, Kirandeep Kaur, Ashwini Deshmukh, Zarar Paloba, Raju bhai of Sarvodaya DVD library, Shuka Jain, Iti Khurana and all the other members of the HarperCollins staff involved with this book.

I would also like to express my genuine gratitude to the following people:

To my close friend Aniruddh Kaushal, who willingly agreed to accompany me to his native Ludhiana and helped me take my first steps in this endeavor with confidence. To Rehana Munir, who contributed to this book in various ways – from suggesting its title, to critiquing the first draft and her constant interest and words of encouragement for my work. To Dr Kewal Dheer, who unconditionally lent me his support from the first time I met him in Ludhiana and played the biggest part in helping me trace the early part of Sahir's life. To Sayyed Mumtaz for her remarkable discipline and dedication in helping me translate all the Urdu literature available on Sahir. To Manohar Iyer, whom I have incessantly troubled ever since I first met him in December 2009 and who has been the most outstanding source of information for much of Sahir's work and the history of the Hindi film song. To Ajitha G.S. for showing genuine interest in my manuscript and being ever so patient with me subsequently. To Abhilasha Ojha for setting aside everything else that she was doing and giving me the most objective, unbiased and constructive feedback on my first draft. To Shantanu Ray Chaudhuri, whose knowledge, editing skills and temperament are worth emulating. To Aabhas Sharma, my dear friend, great sounding board and true confidante. To Vidya for so many, many things. I can never thank you enough.

Finally, this book is the culmination of a journey, which I had undertaken beginning May 2009. Since then, there have been several people whose reassurances and wishes kept me from losing my way. Truly, in the words of the late Majrooh Sultanpuri:

Main akela hi chala thaa jaanib-e-manzil magar,
Log saath aate gaye aur kaarvaan banta gaya

(I set out alone in search of my destination
But people kept joining me along the way and turned it into a
   procession)